Lecture Notes in Computer Scien

Commenced Publication in 1973
Founding and Former Series Editors:
Gerhard Goos, Juris Hartmanis, and Jan van Leeuwen

Oleg Sokolsky   Serdar Taşıran (Eds.)

Runtime
Verification

7th International Workshop, RV 2007
Vancover, Canada, March 13, 2007
Revised Selected Papers

 Springer

Volume Editors

Oleg Sokolsky
University of Pennsylvania
Department of Computer and Information Science
3330 Walnut Street, Philadelphia, PA, USA
E-mail: sokolsky@cis.upenn.edu

Serdar Taşıran
Koç University
College of Engineering
Rumeli Feneri Yolu, Sariyer, 34450, Istanbul, Turkey
E-mail: stasiran@ku.edu.tr

Library of Congress Control Number: 2007941510

CR Subject Classification (1998): D.2, D.3, F.3, K.6

LNCS Sublibrary: SL 2 – Programming and Software Engineering

ISSN   0302-9743
ISBN-10   3-540-77394-0 Springer Berlin Heidelberg New York
ISBN-13   978-3-540-77394-8 Springer Berlin Heidelberg New York

Springer is a part of Springer Science+Business Media

springer.com

© Springer-Verlag Berlin Heidelberg 2007
Printed in Germany

Typesetting: Camera-ready by author, data conversion by Scientific Publishing Services, Chennai, India
Printed on acid-free paper   SPIN: 12208111   06/3180   5 4 3 2 1 0

Preface

Runtime verification is a recent direction in formal methods research, which is complementary to such well-established formal verification methods as model checking. Research in runtime verification deals with formal languages suitable for expressing system properties that are checkable at run time; algorithms for checking of formal properties over an execution trace; low-overhead means of extracting information from the running system that is sufficient for checking of the property. Applications of runtime verification technology include post-deployment monitoring of system correctness and performance; construction of formally specified test oracles; collection of statistics about system behavior, among others.

The Workshop on Runtime Verification was started in 2001 and has been held annually since then. The workshop was co-located with the Conference on Computer-Aided Verification (CAV) in 2001–2003 and 2005–2006; and with the European Joint Conferences on Theory and Practice of Software (ETAPS) in 2004. In 2007, the workshop was held on March 13, 2007 in Vancouver, British Columbia, Canada, co-located to the Conference on Aspect-Oriented Software Development (AOSD) in order to explore the emerging connections between the two communities.

RV 2007 attracted contributions from the core area of runtime verification, as well as related research areas such as testing, static and dynamic analysis of programs, and aspect-oriented programming. The Program Committee selected 16 out of 29 submissions. Each submitted paper was reviewed by at least three Program Committee members. Submitted papers were supplemented by an invited talk given by Cindy Eisner (IBM Research Haifa). This volume contains expanded versions of the presentations made at the workshop. The expanded versions were again reviewed by the Program Committee.

September 2007

Oleg Sokolsky
Serdar Tasiran

Conference Organization

Program Committee

Mehmet Aksit, University of Twente, The Netherlands
Howard Barringer, University of Manchester, UK
Saddek Bensalem, VERIMAG Laboratory, France
Eric Bodden, McGill Univeristy, Canada
Bernd Finkbeiner, Saarland University, Germany
Cormac Flanagan, University of California, Santa Cruz, USA
Vijay Garg, University of Texas, Austin, USA
Klaus Havelund, NASA Jet Propulsion Laboratory/Columbus Technologies, USA
Gerard Holzmann, NASA Jet Propulsion Laboratory, USA
Moonzoo Kim, KAIST, Korea
Martin Leucker, Technical University of Munich, Germany
Oege de Moor, Oxford University, UK
Klaus Ostermann, Darmstadt University of Technology, Germany
Shaz Qadeer, Microsoft Research
Grigore Rosu, University of Illinois, Urbana-Champaign, USA
Henny Sipma, Stanford University, USA
Oleg Sokolsky (Co-chair), University of Pennsylvania, USA
Scott Stoller, State University of New York, Stony Brook, USA
Mario Südholt, Ecole des Mines de Nantes-INRIA, France
Serdar Tasiran (Co-chair), Koc University, Turkey

Steering Committee

Klaus Havelund, NASA Jet Propulsion Laboratory, USA
Gerard Holzmann, NASA Jet Propulsion Laboratory, USA
Insup Lee, University of Pennsylvania, USA
Grigore Rosu, University of Illinois, Urbana-Champaign, USA

External Reviewers

Andreas Bauer
Selma Ikiz
David Rydeheard
Christian Schallhart

Table of Contents

PSL for Runtime Verification: Theory and Practice

Cindy Eisner

IBM Haifa Research Laboratory
eisner@il.ibm.com

Abstract. PSL is a property specification language recently standardized as IEEE 1850™-2005 PSL. It includes as its *temporal layer* a linear temporal logic that enhances LTL with regular expressions and other useful features. PSL and its precursor, Sugar, have been used by the IBM Haifa Research Laboratory for formal verification of hardware since 1993, and for informal (dynamic, simulation runtime) verification of hardware since 1997. More recently both Sugar and PSL have been used for formal, dynamic, and runtime verification of software. In this paper I will introduce PSL and briefly touch on theoretical and practical issues in the use of PSL for dynamic and runtime verification.

1 Introduction

PSL stands for Property Specification Language. Its temporal layer is a linear temporal logic that enhances LTL [19] with regular expressions and other useful features. PSL originated as the branching temporal logic Sugar at the IBM Haifa Research Laboratory, and in October 2005 was standardized as IEEE 1850-2005 (PSL).

PSL has four layers: the Boolean, the modeling, the temporal, and the verification layers. The *Boolean layer* is used to define Boolean expressions. For instance, a & b is a Boolean expression (in the Verilog flavor) indicating the conjunction of a and b. The Boolean layer comes in five flavors, corresponding to the hardware description languages VHDL, Verilog, SystemVerilog and SystemC and to GDL, the language of IBM's RuleBase model checker. Although other flavors are not yet an official part of the language, it is very easy to define new ones. See, for instance, [7], which describes a C flavor of PSL.

The flavor affects the syntax of the *modeling layer* as well, which is used to describe the environment of the design under test. For instance, constraints on the inputs would be described in the modeling layer. The modeling layer can also be used to describe auxiliary signals (in software: variables) that are not part of the design, but are used as part of the verification. For example, the modeling layer statement assign a = b & c; lets the signal name a be used in place of the Boolean expression b & c.

The *temporal layer* is the heart of the language, and consists of an LTL-based temporal logic incorporating regular expressions. A formula over this temporal

O. Sokolsky and S. Tasiran (Eds.): RV 2007, LNCS 4839, pp. 1–8, 2007.

logic is called a PSL *property*. For example, `always(req -> eventually! ack)` is a PSL property saying that whenever `req` is asserted, `ack` should be asserted sometime in the future, and `always {req ; ack ; grant} |=> {busy[*] ; done}` is a PSL property that says that whenever `req` is asserted followed by `ack` and then by `grant`, `busy` should be asserted and stay so until `done` occurs. The temporal layer also allows an elementary form of quantification, so that the property `forall i in {0:7}: always ((req & tag==i) -> eventually! (ack & tag==i))` says that whenever `req` is asserted, eventually an associated `ack` will occur, where the association is indicated by a matching value of `tag`. Other features include a clock operator that can be used to change the default view of time, and the `abort` operator, described in Section 3 below.

The *verification layer* contains directives that tell the verification tool what to do with a PSL property: e.g., should it be asserted (checked), or should it be assumed, or perhaps used as the basis for coverage measurement? The verification layer also provides a way to group sets of directives into a `vunit`, or verification unit, which can be referred to by name in the verification tool.

PSL is good for hardware verification, and various tools for both formal and dynamic hardware verification using PSL are available from companies such as IBM, Cadence, Mentor graphics, etc. PSL is also good for software verification, and PSL or its precursor, Sugar, has been used internally at IBM for software model checking [4][10][11], as well as within a `C++` based simulation environment [9]. More recently, it has also been used externally for runtime verification of software [7].

Intuitively, dynamic and runtime verification have a linear view of time. In the remainder of this paper, I will explain why the move from branching time Sugar to linear time PSL, a big deal in theory, was not a problem in practice and required no modification to our runtime simulation checker generator FoCs (nor to our model checker RuleBase). I will present the truncated semantics that were developed to support non-maximal finite paths as seen in dynamic and runtime verification, and show how they are related to the support of resets in a reactive system, and finally I will discuss the FoCs approach to the issue of how time "ticks" in software.

2   Masking Branching vs. Linear Time

In branching time logics such as CTL [8] and PSL's precursor, Sugar, time is *branching*. That is, the semantics are given with respect to a state in the model, and every possible future of that state is considered. In linear time logics such as LTL [19] and PSL, time is *linear*. That is, the semantics are given with respect to set of ordered states (a path) in the model, and thus every state has a single successor. In theory, this is a very big deal. The complexity of branching time model checking is better than that of linear time model checking [21], the expressive power of the two is incomparable [17], and of course, only linear time makes sense for dynamic and runtime verification.

In practice, however, the issue is not such an important one. The overlap between linear and branching time is a large one, and the vast majority of properties used in practice belong to the overlap. Furthermore, there is a simple syntactic test that can be used to confirm that a syntactically similar CTL/LTL formula pair is equivalent [17]. As an example, the test confirms that the CTL formula $AG(p \rightarrow AXq)$ is equivalent to the LTL formula $G(p \rightarrow Xq)$. The test does not work for every equivalent pair; for example, it does not confirm that the CTL formula $AG(\neg p \rightarrow AX \neg q)$ is equivalent to the LTL formula $G((Xq) \rightarrow p)$, even though the pair are equivalent. However, it works in enough cases to make it practically useful: for instance, the *simple subset* of PSL [5][12] obeys the test.

For this reason, the move from the original CTL-based semantics of Sugar to the current, LTL-based semantics of PSL was not a major issue in practice, neither for IBM's model checker RuleBase [20] nor for its dynamic verification tool FoCs [1]. In both cases, the move is masked by the *Sugar compiler*. For RuleBase, it checks whether a (linear) PSL formula passes the syntactic test of [17] and if so, uses the established (branching) algorithms. For FoCs, the tool has always used a syntactic test similar to that of [17] to weed out branching formulas that cannot be checked dynamically, and the same test weeds out linear formulas for which the dynamic checking is not trivial.

3   Finite Paths and the Truncated Semantics

In the sequel, I will use PSL syntax corresponding to the basic LTL operators, as follows: `always` is equivalent to the LTL operator G, and the PSL operators `eventually!`, `until`, `until!`, `next` and `next!` correspond to the LTL operators F, W, U, X and $X!$, respectively.

Traditionally, LTL semantics over finite paths [18] are defined for maximal paths in the model. That is, if we evaluate a formula over a finite path under traditional LTL finite semantics, it is because the last state of the path has no successor in the model. For a long time, finite paths on non-maximal paths were treated in an ad-hoc manner – see [6], for instance. In [14], we considered in detail the problem of reasoning with temporal logic on non-maximal paths.

A *truncated path* is a finite, not necessarily maximal path. Truncated paths are seen by incomplete formal methods, such as bounded model checking, and also by dynamic and runtime verification (at any point before the program ends we have seen a partial, non-maximal path). In the *truncated semantics*, there are three *views* of a finite path. The *weak* view takes a lenient view of truncated paths – a property holds even if there is doubt about the status of the property on the full path. The *strong* view is a strict view of truncated paths – a property does not hold if there is doubt about the status of the property on the full path. The *neutral* view of a truncated path is simply the traditional semantics for a maximal path.

For example, on a finite path such that p holds at every state on the path, the property `always p` might or might not hold on the full path: if it turns out that the truncated path continues with a p at every state, our property will hold on the full path, but if there is even one future state with no p, it will not hold. Thus, the property holds in the weak view, and does not hold in the strong view. It holds in the neutral view, because `always p` holds on our path if we consider it to be maximal.

As another example, consider a finite path such that q holds at no state on the path. The property `eventually! q` might or might not hold on the full path: if there is a future q, the property holds, otherwise it does not. Thus, `eventually! q` holds in the weak view, and does not hold in the strong view. It does not hold in the neutral view, because `eventually! q` does not hold on such a path if we consider it to be maximal. If q does hold for some state on the path, then the property holds in the neutral view, and there is no doubt that it will hold as well on any continuation of the path. Thus, on such a path the property holds in the weak, neutral and strong views.

Consider now a finite path on which p holds at states 2, 4 and 20, and q holds at state 15. As with our previous examples, the property `always (p -> eventually! q)` might or might not hold on the full path, depending on how the truncated path continues. Thus the property holds in the weak view and does not hold in the strong view. It does not hold in the neutral view, because `always (p -> eventually! q)` does not hold on our path if we consider it to be maximal – the p that holds at state 20 is missing a q. Even if there were such a future q, for instance if p held at states 2, 4 and 20 and q held at states 15 and 25 – then there still would be doubt about whether the property holds on the full path, because there might be a future p that does not see an appropriate q. Thus, our property would still hold in the weak view and not hold in the strong view. However, it does hold in the neutral view on our new path, because the neutral semantics do not worry about possible futures – they consider the path to be maximal.

The weak view can be understood as a weakening of all operators (assuming negation-normal form) [13], and the strong view can be understood as a strengthening of all operators (under the same assumption). Thus, it is easy to see that `eventually!` φ holds weakly on any path for any φ (including *false*): `eventually!` φ is equivalent to `true until!` φ. Weakening this gives `true until` φ, which holds on any path for any φ. Similarly, we can show that `always` φ does not hold strongly on any path for any φ (including *true*), because `always` φ is equivalent to φ `until false`. Strengthening that gives φ `until! false`, which holds on no path for no φ.

In practice, very few formulas hold strongly on any path, because most formulas begin with the `always` operator. Thus, the weak view of truncated paths is most useful in practice. However, the strong view is dual to the weak, and giving it up would result in a logic not closed under negation.

On an infinite path, the weak, neutral and strong views coincide [14]. Nevertheless, the truncated semantics can be useful in the context of infinite paths, because an infinite path may contain finite, non-maximal segments. They can be useful in the context of finite maximal paths for the same reason. For instance, a hardware reset or a software event such as "clear form", "start over", or "new query" may partition a path into two parts: a finite, truncated part until the reset or software event, and a possibly infinite, possibly maximal part (depending on whether or not the original path was maximal) afterwards. The PSL abort operator truncates a path and moves to the weak view. Thus, the property always (φ abort reset) partitions the path into segments at every occurrence of reset (discarding the states on which reset occurs). The property φ must hold neutrally on the final segment, and weakly on the remaining segments (each of which was followed in the original path by a state on which reset held).

The point of the abort operator can be best appreciated by comparing it to the until operator. Both of the following properties:

$$(\text{always } (p - > \text{ eventually! } q)) \text{ abort reset} \tag{1}$$

$$(p - > \text{ eventually! } q) \text{ until reset} \tag{2}$$

need (p -> eventually! q) to hold up until reset holds. However, they differ with respect to what happens at that point. Consider a path π of length 20 such that p holds at states 2 and 10, q holds at state 4, and reset holds at state 15. Property 1 holds on such a path, because the abort operator truncates the path at the occurrence of reset and takes us to the weak view. Since the sub-property (always (p -> eventually! q)) holds weakly on the truncated path, Property 1 holds on the original path. However, Property 2 does not hold on path π, because sub-property (p -> eventually! q) does not hold at state 10.

The behavior of the abort operator is very easy to describe in an informal manner, but very difficult to formalize. Our first try, the *abort semantics* [14], defined simply

$w \models \varphi$ abort $b \iff$
      either $w \models \varphi$ or
      there exist $j < |w|$ and word w' such that $w^j \models b$ and $w^{0..j-1}w' \models \varphi$

This looks intuitive, but turns out not to be what we wanted. Consider the property (eventually! false) abort b on a path where b occurs at some point. We want the property to hold on such a path, because we want eventually! false to hold in the weak view on a finite path. To see this, recall that eventually! false is equivalent to true until! false. If we weaken the until! operator we get true until false which holds on any path. However, looking back to the proposed semantics, there is no w' we can choose that will give us what we want. Others [3] were more successful, but ended up with a semantics that required intricate manipulations of two contexts within the semantics of the existing LTL operators.

We have since presented two simple and elegant formulations. The original truncated semantics, presented in [14], directly defines semantics for each of the three views (weak, neutral and strong). The result is a semantics that is equivalent to the *reset semantics* of [3], but whose presentation is much cleaner and easier to grasp. The ⊤, ⊥ approach to the truncated semantics, presented in [15], takes another tack, and folds the three views into an equivalent but more compact representation. It does so by adding two new letters, ⊤ and ⊥, to the alphabet, such that everything holds on ⊤, including `false`, and nothing holds on ⊥, including `true`. With these two new letters, the original formulation of the semantics presented above works because we can choose a w' consisting entirely of the letter ⊤. While the ⊤, ⊥ approach uses a slightly more cryptic formulation than the original truncated semantics, we have found it useful in characterizing the relation between the weak and strong views, as described in [13].

4   The FoCs Approach to the Ticking of Time

PSL does not dictate how time ticks. The formal semantics (see for instance Appendix B of [12]) is based on a sequence of states, but how those states are derived from the hardware or software under verification is not defined. This is good news for software, because it means that the formal semantics can be used as is. However, it does not provide any practical answers.

FoCs is a tool that takes PSL properties and translates them into monitors that allow the use of PSL in event-based software. Originally, FoCs was designed for hardware simulations [1], but it can work with other event-based software as well. In the FoCs approach, the responsibility for time belongs to the application. If the user has embedded a PSL property in C (or other) code, FoCs will translate the property into a state machine embedded in the code at the location where the property originally appeared. Then, time is considered to have ticked when the state machine is reached at runtime. The FoCs approach is a *generic* solution for any language, but of course it is not a *general* solution for any application, in the case that some other definition of the ticking of time is desired.

Acknowledgements

PSL was and continues to be the work of many people. I would particularly like to acknowledge my IBM colleagues Ilan Beer, Shoham Ben-David, Dana Fisman and Avner Landver for their early work on Sugar, and Dana Fisman, Avigail Orni, Dmitry Pidan and Sitvanit Ruah for more recent work on PSL.

The members of the Accellera FVTC (Formal Verification Technical Committee) and the IEEE P1850 PSL Working Group are too numerous to mention by name – a complete list can be found in the respective standards [2] [16] – but I would particularly like to thank Harry Foster and Erich Marschner, chairman and co-chairman of the FVTC and chairman and secretary of the IEEE P1850 Working Group, for leading the process that led to standardization.

The work described in Section 3 was joint work with Dana Fisman, John Havlicek, Yoad Lustig, Anthony McIsaac, Johan Mårtensson and David Van Campenhout (in various combinations).

Thank you to Dmitry Pidan for his explanation of the FoCs approach to the ticking of time.

References

1. Abarbanel, Y., Beer, I., Gluhovsky, L., Keidar, S., Wolfsthal, Y.: FoCs - automatic generation of simulation checkers from formal specifications. In: Emerson, E.A., Sistla, A.P. (eds.) CAV 2000. LNCS, vol. 1855, Springer, Heidelberg (2000)
2. Accellera property specification language reference manual, http://www.eda.org/vfv/docs/psl_lrm-1.1.pdf
3. Armoni, R., Bustan, D., Kupferman, O., Vardi, M.Y.: Aborts vs resets in linear temporal logic. In: Garavel, H., Hatcliff, J. (eds.) ETAPS 2003 and TACAS 2003. LNCS, vol. 2619, Springer, Heidelberg (2003)
4. Barner, S., Glazberg, Z., Rabinovitz, I.: Wolf - bug hunter for concurrent software using formal methods. In: CAV, pp. 153–157 (2005)
5. Ben-David, S., Fisman, D., Ruah, S.: The safety simple subset. In: Ur, S., Bin, E., Wolfsthal, Y. (eds.) First International Haifa Verification Conference. LNCS, vol. 3875, pp. 14–29. Springer, Heidelberg (2005)
6. Biere, A., Cimatti, A., Clarke, E., Zhu, Y.: Symbolic model checking without BDDs. In: Cleaveland, W.R. (ed.) ETAPS 1999 and TACAS 1999. LNCS, vol. 1579, Springer, Heidelberg (1999)
7. Cheung, P.H., Forin, A.: A C-language binding for PSL. In: Technical Report MSR-TR-2006-131, Microsoft Research (2006)
8. Clarke, E., Emerson, E.: Design and synthesis of synchronization skeletons using branching time temporal logic. In: Kozen, D. (ed.) Logics of Programs. LNCS, vol. 131, pp. 52–71. Springer, Heidelberg (1982)
9. Dahan, A., Geist, D., Gluhovsky, L., Pidan, D., Shapir, G., Wolfsthal, Y., Benalycherif, L., Kamdem, R., Lahbib, Y.: Combining system level modeling with assertion based verification. In: ISQED, pp. 310–315 (2005)
10. Eisner, C.: Model checking the garbage collection mechanism of SMV. In: Stoller, S.D., Visser, W. (eds.) Electronic Notes in Theoretical Computer Science, vol. 55, Elsevier, Amsterdam (2001)
11. Eisner, C.: Formal verification of software source code through semi-automatic modeling. Software and Systems Modeling 4(1), 14–31 (2005)
12. Eisner, C., Fisman, D.: A Practical Introduction to PSL. Springer, Heidelberg (2006)
13. Eisner, C., Fisman, D., Havlicek, J.: A topological characterization of weakness. In: Proc. 24th Annual ACM Symposium on Principles of Distributed Com puting (PODC), pp. 1–8 (2005)
14. Eisner, C., Fisman, D., Havlicek, J., Lustig, Y., McIsaac, A., Van Campenhout, D.: Reasoning with temporal logic on truncated paths. In: Hunt Jr., W.A., Somenzi, F. (eds.) CAV 2003. LNCS, vol. 2725, pp. 27–39. Springer, Heidelberg (2003)
15. Eisner, C., Fisman, D., Havlicek, J., Mårtensson, J.: The $\top$, $\bot$ approach for truncated semantics. Technical Report 2006.01, Accellera (January 2006)
16. IEEE standard for property specification language (PSL). IEEE Std 1850-2005

17. Maidl, M.: The common fragment of CTL and LTL. In: Proc. 41st Annual Symposium on Foundations of Computer Science, IEEE, Los Alamitos (November 2000)
18. Manna, Z., Pnueli, A.: Temporal Verification of Reactive Systems: Safety. Springer, New York (1995)
19. Pnueli, A.: A temporal logic of concurrent programs. Theoretical Computer Science 13, 45–60 (1981)
20. RuleBase. Available from the IBM Haifa Research Laboratory, See
    `http://www.haifa.il.ibm.com/projects/verification/RB_Homepage/`
21. Vardi, M.Y.: Branching vs. linear time: Final showdown. In: Margaria, T., Yi, W. (eds.) ETAPS 2001 and TACAS 2001. LNCS, vol. 2031, pp. 1–22. Springer, Heidelberg (2001)

On the Semantics of
Matching Trace Monitoring Patterns

Pavel Avgustinov, Julian Tibble, and Oege de Moor

Programming Tools Group
Oxford University, United Kingdom

Abstract. Trace monitor specifications consist of a pattern that is matched against the trace of events of a subject system. We investigate the design choices in defining the semantics of matching patterns against traces.

Some systems use an *exact-match* semantics (where every relevant event must be matched by the pattern), while others employ a *skipping* semantics (which allows any event to be skipped during matching). The semantics of exact-match is well established; here we give a semantics to skipping by providing a translation to exact-match. It turns out the translation is *not* surjective: a pattern language with skipping semantics is strictly less expressive than one with exact-match semantics. That proof suggests the addition of a novel operator to a skipping language that makes it equivalent to exact-match.

Another design decision concerns the atoms in patterns: are these unique runtime events, or can multiple atoms match the same runtime event? Many implementations have chosen predicates for atoms, and then overlap is natural. There are some exceptions, however, and we examine the consequences of that design choice in some depth.

1 Introduction

In recent years, much research has centered on so-called *trace monitors*. The idea is simple, but powerful: a base program's execution is observed by a separate entity (the monitor), and whenever the sequence of events matches some predefined criterion, extra code is executed.

This kind of feature is useful in many situations. For example, when debugging a program, it is possible to use trace monitoring to pinpoint the exact time when something goes wrong, or even take some recovery action. One can use it to implement protocols [14] in a high-level declarative fashion. Many runtime verification concerns also have natural representations as trace specifications, either by specifying all "correct" traces (and taking action when a non-matching trace is encountered), or by specifying violating traces (and reacting to successfully completed matches). Examples of such properties are various API contracts and project-specific rules that ideally would be automatically enforced, but aren't checkable by a conventional compiler.

Investigations of trace monitoring have originated from two distinct communities. Aspect-oriented programming (AOP) is a paradigm that allows additional

O. Sokolsky and S. Tasiran (Eds.): RV 2007, LNCS 4839, pp. 9–21, 2007.

code to be triggered when certain *joinpoints* (identifiable events during program execution) are encountered. From this perspective, trace monitoring is a generalisation of the matching mechanism from single joinpoints to *sequences* of joinpoints, and a number of implementations have arisen in this area (*e.g.* [1,14,9,7]). Largely independently, the usefulness of program traces as an easily available representation of program behaviour has been exploited by the Runtime Verification (RV) and (static) fault-finding communities to implement several tools that check various constraints using this technique (*e.g.* [12,11,6,4]).

Trace monitoring is a useful and desirable feature, as evidenced by the sheer number of systems implementing it. A wide variety of formalisms for describing the patterns of interest are represented: from regular expressions [1] over context-free languages [14] to temporal logics [6] and custom query languages [12, 11]; even a general logic-independent framework [7] has been proposed. Most systems follow the intuition above by running concurrently with the base program and updating matching state as runtime events are encountered, but some [7] also support an *offline* matching mode, which dumps all events to a log file that can be analysed after the program run is complete.

Still, there are several important issues on which the various systems differ. One of them is the question of whether the trace patterns can be parameterised by *free variables*. This allows the programmer to write patterns that are quantified over cliques of interacting objects, but they significantly complicate the semantics and implementation of a trace monitoring feature [3], and so they are often not supported.

Another important aspect in which the above approaches differ is the style of semantics: some [1, 14, 9] use what we call an *exact-match semantics*, while others [12, 11, 6] use a more liberal *skipping semantics*. The distinction is that under an exact-match interpretation, each of the events of interest picked out by the monitor must be accounted for by the pattern: using the intuition suggested by temporal logics, the pattern AB means "A and next B". In contrast to this, a skipping semantics allows an arbitrary number of events to be ignored in between matched events: AB means "A and eventually B". To date, only *tracematches* have provided a formal and exhaustive account of the matching process including free variables [1], but since they are an exact-match feature, this means that there has been no formal evaluation of the implications of a skipping interpretation for a trace monitor.

In this paper, we aim to address this by examining the language design choices that need to be made when implementing a skipping feature. We start with a summary of our previous work on the semantics of tracematches in Section 2; in particular, we give a general technique for reducing the problem of matching a pattern with free variables to the more familiar problem of matching a *ground* pattern. In Section 3, we investigate the relationship of exact-match and skipping languages in detail, by defining a small skipping language, giving a semantics and exploring its expressiveness. Semantic issues regarding definitions of symbols and events are described and addressed in Section 4. We give a brief survey of related work in Section 5 and conclude with an outlook on future work in Section 6.

2   Trace Patterns with Free Variables

As the starting point of our investigation, we shall summarise our previous work on the semantics of *tracematches*, as introduced in [1]. One of the main design considerations for that particular system is tight integration with the AspectJ language. As such, events of interest are defined using the standard AspectJ mechanism for selecting runtime events (*pointcuts*), and an entire tracematch can be thought of as a more expressive pointcut for triggering an advice body as usual.

As a running example, we shall take a trace monitoring-based implementation of the well-known Observer pattern. There, a particular type of Observer object can register with a certain Subject (captured by the pcCreateObserver pointcut); subsequently any update to the Subject's state (pcUpdateSubject) should trigger a notification of each registered observer. Observers also have the opportunity to deregister with a subject to stop receiving notifications (pcRemoveObserver).

```
1   tracematch(Observer o, Subject s) {
2     sym createObserver after : pcCreateObserver(o, s);
3     sym updateSubject after : pcUpdateSubject(s);
4     sym removeObserver after : pcRemoveObserver(o, s);
5
6     createObserver updateSubject+
7
8     { o.subjectUpdated(s); }
9   }
```

Fig. 1. The Observer pattern as a tracematch

The tracematch implementing this is shown in Figure 1. It has three distinct parts: an *alphabet* of symbols (three in this case — lines 2–4), a *regular expression* over these symbols (line 6), and a *body* that is triggered on every successful match (line 8). Each symbol is defined by a standard AspectJ pointcut; moreover, the tracematch header (line 1) can declare free variables that are bound by the symbols and can be used in the body.

Intuitively, the pattern here says "We see an observer register for a particular subject, followed by one or more updates to that subject (and the observer hasn't been disassociated in the meantime)". Each time this matches, we execute the body, which makes use of the acquired bindings to notify the observer.

To perform the matching, we proceed as follows: each runtime event (or *join-point*) is matched against every symbol defined by the tracematch; the result is either a failure (in which case the joinpoint is ignored), or a successful match, which may result in some tracematch variables being bound by that symbol. We refer to the transition from the sequence of joinpoints to the sequence of matched symbols annotated with variable bindings as *filtering* the trace, as it essentially discards all events that the tracematch is not interested in.

The careful reader will have noticed that the symbols occurring in the actual tracematch pattern are *ground* — *i.e.* they do not have variable annotations. Matching a sequence of *ground* symbols against the pattern is a well-understood problem: it is just traditional regular expression matching; still, we need to obtain ground traces from the filtered trace.

Thus, after filtering the semantics performs a step called *instantiation*: For each possible valuation (that is, set of runtime values for the tracematch formal variables), the filtered program trace is projected onto the symbols compatible with that valuation. Of course, there are infinitely many possible valuations, but most of them would result in an empty projection (the projection will only be non-empty if events with matching bindings have occurred in the program history, and there are only finitely many of those at any time). However, each non-empty projection gives us a (*valuation, ground symbol trace*) pair, which we can match against the pattern in the usual way. The tracematch body is executed once for each distinct valuation that leads to a successful match.

To illustrate, consider the Observer tracematch with this sequence of events: sub.addObserver(o1); sub.foo(); sub.addObserver(o2); sub.bar(); sub.delObserver(o2); sub.update(); (here sub is a subject, and o1 and o2 are observer objects).

Filtering would discard the irrelevant events sub.foo() and sub.bar(), and match each of the remaining events with each symbol, resulting in the following *filtered trace*: createObserver(o1, sub); createObserver(o2, sub); removeObserver(o2, sub); updateSubject(sub).

Now, there are two valuations that result in non-empty projections: ($o = o1 \land s = sub$) and ($o = o2 \land s = sub$). The respective instantiated traces are just createObserver updateSubject for the former and createObserver removeObserver updateSubject for the latter. Only the former matches the pattern, so we execute the tracematch body with the first valuation, notifying o1 but not o2.

At this stage, it should be clear why we defined the additional symbol for removing an observer in Figure 1, even though it wasn't used in the pattern. Had we omitted it, any calls to the removeObserver() method would have been filtered out without affecting the matching state, and so observers would have still received update notifications after they had been deregistered. The extra symbol ensures those method calls remain in the filtered, instantiated traces; since it is not part of the pattern, no sequence of events that contains it will trigger the tracematch body.

Note that the two-step process of filtering followed by instantiation gives a general strategy for reducing the semantics of matching a trace pattern with free variables to the simpler problem of matching a ground pattern against a ground trace.

We have now summarised our formal semantics for tracematches [1]. The (equivalent) operational semantics suggests two restrictions that need to be placed on patterns so that they are useful in practice: no pattern should accept the empty sequence, and any trace that matches the pattern must guarantee all free variables bound. In the case of regular expressions, this amounts to checking that every word in the language of the regex contains at least one binding symbol for every variable. Also, some care needs to be taken when updating monitors that aren't fully bound; a full exploration of this issue is beyond the scope of the present document, and we refer the interested reader to [1].

3   Interpretation of Patterns

Trace monitoring systems have been developed by researchers in the fields of Aspect-Oriented Programming [1,14,9] and Runtime Verification and fault finding [12, 11, 6, 4]. It is interesting to observe that there seems to be a division regarding the syle of semantics used: systems with an AOP background tend to employ *exact-match semantics*, while those with roots in RV predominantly use *skipping* — perhaps due to the similarity to temporal logic expressions using 'eventually'. Arguably, this leads to nicer specificationsfor many RV properties, as essentially a pattern can be a *least counter-example* to the concern being checked.

We will now discuss skipping in-depth, investigating both semantics and expressiveness. As a preliminary motivating example, the skipping pattern one would naturally write for the *observer* concern we saw above is createObserver ∼removeObserver updateSubject. Note that we don't need to allow for several updateSubject events in the pattern, as any such events would be skipped.

3.1   A Simple Skipping Language

In order to compare the two kinds of pattern interpretation systematically, we will define two related languages. The first, which we shall call $\mathcal{L}_{em}$, is just the fragment of the tracematch language obtained by omitting the + operator, as it adds no expressive power over the standard Kleene star *. This language will be interpreted in an exact-match style, and as tracematches have a formal semantics, $\mathcal{L}_{em}$ inherits it without modification. Figure 2 illustrates its syntax.

pattern	:= term	|	seqPattern '|' pattern
term	:= simplePattern	|	simplePattern term
		|	simplePattern '*'
simplePattern	:= symbol	|	'(' pattern ')'

Fig. 2. Regular expression patterns in tracematches

The second language, $\mathcal{L}_{skip}$, is a skipping language that is as close as possible to the tracematch formalism — that is, it has an explicit alphabet of symbols that may bind free variables, and the pattern is regex-like.

A number of design considerations need to be addressed, however. Firstly, note that any skipping language must have explicit negation; in its absence it would be impossible to prohibit certain events from occurring. We borrow PQL's syntax [12] and write ∼A for the negation of a symbol A.

It is important to understand this construct fully in order to see why the restrictions we shall place upon it are necessary. This is *not* the usual complementation, as found in Extended Regular Expresions (EREs): When we write a pattern like A ∼B A, we do not mean "we see an A, followed by any sequence not matching the pattern B, followed by another A" (as would be the ERE interpretation; this would match the trace *a b b a*). Instead, the negation constrains the set of symbols we are allowed to skip. Thus, the above pattern really means "We see an A, then any number of symbols that aren't B, followed by a second A" (and does *not* match the trace *a b b a*).

The distinction is important: it is well-known that EREs can be transformed into standard regular expressions (at the cost of a non-elementary blowup in the size of the pattern), so the semantics of an exact-match ERE language (as implemented, for example, by one of JavaMOP's logic plugins [7]) do not differ significantly from the standard tracematch semantics. In a skipping setting, negation isn't matched against a part of the trace directly, but affects how the subpatterns around it are matched.

Because of this, it is not well-defined to use negation on compound patterns: The pattern ∼(A B) (while perfectly valid as an ERE pattern) makes no sense in a skipping setting. Indeed, it is common for skipping features to restrict negation — in the case of PQL [12], it is only allowed on single symbols. We will go beyond that, and allow negation of *alternations of symbols*, or, equivalently, of *symbol sets*. Thus, in our small language, it is legal to write ∼(A|B), and this allows skipping of only those events that do not match A or B.

An additional pitfall is sequential composition of patterns. Consider the following example: ∼A ∼B. This is ill-defined in the same way that ∼(A B) is ill-defined; it makes no sense with our interpretation of negation. As a consequence, we must also restrict sequential composition to prevent this kind of problem from occurring. We achieve this by allowing composition only on *fenced terms* (which are just terms that do not begin or end in negation).

pattern := fencedTerm	|	fencedTerm '|' pattern
fencedTerm := simplePattern	|	simplePattern fencedTerm
	|	simplePattern '∼' symbolSet fencedTerm
simplePattern := symbol	|	'(' pattern ')'
symbolSet := symbol	|	'(' symbol '|' symbolSet ')'

Fig. 3. Syntax of patterns in $\mathcal{L}_{\text{skip}}$

Finally, the overall pattern should also be a fenced term. The resulting skipping language, $\mathcal{L}_{\text{skip}}$, is shown in Figure 3.

Note that Kleene closure is *not* present in $\mathcal{L}_{\text{skip}}$. This is not an oversight on our part; indeed, it turns out that the traditional interpretation of the Kleene star is redundant under a skipping semantics. Suppose t is a fenced term. We can expand the Kleene closure $t*$ thrice (using alternations), and then observe that *any* sequence of events is allowed in between the two symbols tt in the penultimate disjunct, in particular $t*$.

$$t* \equiv \varepsilon \mid t \mid t\,t \mid t\,(t*)\,t$$
$$\equiv \varepsilon \mid t \mid t\,t$$

3.2 Semantics of $\mathcal{L}_{\text{skip}}$

We are now ready to give a formal semantics for $\mathcal{L}_{\text{skip}}$, the skipping language defined above. This will take the form of a syntax-directed translation of terms in the skipping language $\mathcal{L}_{\text{skip}}$ to equivalent patterns in our tracematch language $\mathcal{L}_{\text{em}}$. As the semantics of matching $\mathcal{L}_{\text{em}}$ patterns are well-understood, this procedure will capture the meaning of $\mathcal{L}_{\text{skip}}$ patterns.

$$\begin{array}{ll}
[\text{ fTerm} \mid \text{pat }] & \Longrightarrow [\text{ fTerm }] \mid [\text{ pat }] \\
[\text{ sPat fTerm }] & \Longrightarrow [\text{ sPat }] \; \Sigma* \; [\text{ fTerm }] \\
[\text{ sPat} \sim\!\alpha \text{ fTerm }] & \Longrightarrow [\text{ sPat }] \; (\Sigma \setminus \alpha)* \; [\text{ fTerm }] \\
[\text{ symbol }] & \Longrightarrow \text{symbol}
\end{array}$$

Fig. 4. Translation from $\mathcal{L}_{\text{skip}}$ to $\mathcal{L}_{\text{em}}$

The rewrite rules are given in Figure 4. We can see that alternation in $\mathcal{L}_{\text{skip}}$ is translated to alternation in $\mathcal{L}_{\text{em}}$; any particular symbol is also translated to itself. The interesting cases involve sequential composition (with or without negation). If we have a simple pattern followed by some fenced term, we evaluate this by translating the pattern, inserting $\Sigma*$ and translating the fenced term. Recall that Σ is the set of all symbols defined by the tracematch; thus the subpattern $\Sigma*$ amounts to allowing an arbitrary sequence of events, whether or not they are matched by some symbol, to occur.

Consider now negation. If a symbol set $\alpha \subseteq \Sigma$ is prohibited between a simple pattern and a fenced term in $\mathcal{L}_{\text{skip}}$, then the translation again recursively rewrites the pattern, then allows an arbitrary sequence of events that match symbols in $\Sigma \setminus \alpha$, followed by a sequence matching the fenced term. Note how the intended meaning of $[\text{ sPat fTerm }]$ (allow any events in between the two subexpressions) and $[\text{ sPat} \sim\!\alpha \text{ fTerm }]$ (allow any event except those in α between the two subexpressions) become fully explicit after the translation.

In order for the semantics of a pattern to be well-defined, recall that it needs to bind all free variables. It is not difficult to see that (based on the translation above) an $\mathcal{L}_{\text{skip}}$ pattern is permissible if and only if its translation is permissible in $\mathcal{L}_{\text{em}}$.

3.3 Expressiveness of $\mathcal{L}_{\text{skip}}$

Since we defined the semantics of $\mathcal{L}_{\text{skip}}$ by a syntax-directed translation into $\mathcal{L}_{\text{em}}$, our skipping language is no more expressive than the exact-match language. In other words, merely interpreting a formalism with the skipping paradigm does not increase the expressive power. Recall, however, that we were forced to exclude Kleene closure from $\mathcal{L}_{skip}$. It is natural to presume that in accommodating the skipping paradigm, we were forced to make our language less expressive.

In this section, we will show that this is indeed the case. We will do this by providing a backwards translation — a syntax-directed rewriting of $\mathcal{L}_{em}$ patterns into $\mathcal{L}_{skip}$— for a proper subset of $\mathcal{L}_{em}$. Indeed, the fragment we will consider contains all translations produced by the rewriting presented in Section 3.2, and will therefore be *equivalent* in expressive power to $\mathcal{L}_{skip}$.

To obtain a suitable fragment of $\mathcal{L}_{em}$, it turns out we need to restrict Kleene closure: we will allow only patterns in which the Kleene star is applied to a symbol set, rather than to a general pattern. Moreover, no two Kleene-starred expressions must appear next to each other. Note how these restrictions mirror the restrictions on negation and sequential composition that we were forced to make in designing $\mathcal{L}_{skip}$.

$$
\begin{aligned}
[\text{ term } | \text{ pat }] \quad &\Longrightarrow [\text{ term }] \mid [\text{ pat }] \\
[\text{ sPat term }] \quad &\Longrightarrow [\text{ sPat }] \sim\!\varSigma \, [\text{ term }] \\
[\text{ sPat } \alpha* \text{ term }] &\Longrightarrow [\text{ sPat }] \sim\!(\varSigma \setminus \alpha) \, [\text{ term }] \\
[\text{ symbol }] \quad &\Longrightarrow \text{symbol}
\end{aligned}
$$

Fig. 5. Translation from a fragment of $\mathcal{L}_{em}$ to $\mathcal{L}_{skip}$

The translation is shown in Figure 5. Again, alternation is mapped to alternation and symbols to themselves. When translating the sequential composition of a pattern and a term, we insert the negation of $\varSigma$ between the recursively translated subexpressions — this achieves precisely the desired effect of prohibiting all events matching a declared symbol at that point, as specified by an exact-match semantics. Finally, if there is a Kleene closure of a symbol set α in between two subpatterns, then we insert the negation of the symbol set $\varSigma \setminus \alpha$ — that is, we prohibit everything that is not in α, and hence allow everything that *is* in α.

This completes the backwards translation of a subset of $\mathcal{L}_{em}$ to $\mathcal{L}_{skip}$. Note that since skipping makes traditional Kleene closure obsolete, $\mathcal{L}_{skip}$ cannot express patterns like A(BC)* — which matches all words that start with an A, followed by any number of BC-pairs with no other symbols interspersed. Therefore, we have proved $\mathcal{L}_{skip}$ equivalent to a *proper subset* of our tracematch language $\mathcal{L}_{em}$.

Interestingly, translating the exact-match pattern from the Observer tracematch (Figure 1) does not yield the skipping pattern one would naturally write: createObserver ~removeObserver updateSubject. Applying the backward translation to the $\mathcal{L}_{em}$ pattern (rewritten to use Kleene star) yields the $\mathcal{L}_{skip}$ pattern createObserver ~(createObserver|removeObserver) updateSubject.

3.4   Making $\mathcal{L}_{skip}$ More Expressive

A natural consideration after the discussion above is the question of how we can "fix" the expressiveness of $\mathcal{L}_{skip}$— what kind of feature would we need to add to be able to express the same patterns as $\mathcal{L}_{em}$?

To give a satisfactory answer, recall that the reason we lost some expressive power was in subtle interactions between negation (as interpreted in a skipping setting) and Kleene closure. This suggests trying an extension that combines the two in some way to achieve the desired results.

As one possibility, we propose a new kind of Kleene closure-like operator, which is parameterised by a set of symbols α: $\oplus_\alpha$. It can be applied to any fenced term, and the intended interpretation is:

$$t\oplus_\alpha \ \equiv \ t \mid t \sim\alpha \ t\oplus_\alpha$$

Intuitively, $t\oplus_\alpha$ is the Kleene closure of t obtained while prohibiting all events in α between the repetitions of t. Note that $t\oplus_\alpha$ is a *fenced* term.

First of all, we shall augment the $\mathcal{L}_{\text{skip}}$ semantics with a translation rule for our new operator:

[term$\oplus_\alpha$] $\Longrightarrow$ ([term] $(\Sigma\backslash\alpha)*)*$ [term]

Intuitively, this says: match zero or more occurrences of "a trace matching the term followed by any symbols not in α", followed by a trace matching the term.

Finally, we will complete our examination by translating unrestricted Kleene closure in $\mathcal{L}_{\text{em}}$ into our extended skipping language. First of all, we rewrite the exact-match pattern (using alternations if necessary) in such a way that all occurrences of the Kleene star are replaced by the Kleene "plus" (unless they are on symbol sets, in which case the old translation already accounts for them). Then we can handle the resulting terms as follows:

[term+] $\Longrightarrow$ [term]$\oplus_\Sigma$

Recall the example pattern $A(BC)*$ that, as we argued above, can't be captured by the original skipping language. With the extension, it just becomes the following pattern: $A \mid A(B \sim(\Sigma)C)\oplus_\Sigma$.

4   Definition of Symbols and Events

Another way in which semantics of trace-monitors vary is in the relation between *symbols* and *runtime events*. To clarify, by "runtime event" we mean a joinpoint, *i.e.* a well-defined point during program execution. Such an event may or may not be relevant to a trace monitor; this is determined by matching it against the *symbols*. Now, unlike in traditional formal language theory, in this context symbols may *overlap* — that is, two or more different symbols could match the same runtime event.

One possible interpretation is suggested by temporal logics: we can view symbols as predicates that may or may not hold at the same point in time (joinpoint). If the pattern language supports it, one could then write specifications that require both symbol A and symbol B to hold at the same time, and indeed approaches that are based on temporal logics often make use of Boolean combinations of symbols. Tracematches don't allow this, but fully support overlapping symbols. The interpretation there is that if several symbols match a runtime event, then there are several filtered traces, one for each possible symbol instantiation.

An alternative view is to treat the trace monitor as a consumer of *monitor events*, which are different than runtime events in that they correspond to exactly one symbol. They are different from symbols because they may have associated variable bindings. This means that if a runtime event matches multiple symbols, then all of these instantiated symbols occur (as monitor events) in the filtered trace in some order.

To illustrate the difference, we will compare the JavaMOP and Tracematch systems on a small example, because their symbol definitions look very similar — both have adapted the pointcut language of AspectJ for this purpose. Two symbols are declared for each system in Figure 6. In both cases, 'Clear' is defined as 'immediately before calling a method named *clear*', and 'List' is defined as 'immediately before calling a method on an object of type *List*'.

JavaMOP:

Event Clear : **begin**(**call**($*$ $*$.clear())) ;

Event List : **begin**(**call**($*$ List .$*$(..))) ;

Tracematches:

sym Clear **before** : **call**($*$ $*$.clear()) ;

sym List **before** : **call**($*$ List .$*$(..)) ;

Fig. 6. Symbol declarations for JavaMOP and Tracematches

However, since these symbols overlap, the respective patterns will sometimes be matched against different traces. Consider for example this sequence of calls: someSet.clear(); someList.clear(); someList.size(), in which the first call matches the symbol *Clear*, the second matches both symbols, and the last matches *List*.

The difference is, of course, caused by the second call. Tracematches interpret symbols as predicates; correspondingly, there are two filtered traces to match against: *Clear Clear List* and *Clear List List*. In JavaMOP, on the other hand, the second call gives rise to *two* atomic, distinct events, so that the pattern is matched against *Clear Clear List List*.

Interpreting symbols as events is problematic because the number of symbols in a program trace need not be the same as the number of joinpoints in the base program. In the example above, the pattern (Clear|List)(Clear|List)(Clear|List) might be expected to match at the third call, but it would in fact also match at the second call. It is also difficult to justify the ordering of events when they are triggered by a single joinpoint. For example, why is the trace not *Clear List Clear List*? The JavaMOP designers resolved this non-determinism by specifying that events corresponding to the same cause are generated in the order that the symbols are defined in the specification.

5   Related Work

The purpose of the present paper is to relate multiple strands of research, in particular contrasting the matching semantics used in aspect-oriented programming

Table 1. Overview of some trace monitoring systems

SYSTEM	IMPLEMENTATION		SEMANTIC CHOICES	
	free variables	formalism	exact-match	overlapping
tracematches [1]	yes	regex	yes	predicates
PQL [12]	yes	CFG	no	predicates
PTQL [11]	yes	SQL	no	predicates
JavaMOP [7]	partial	multiple	yes	events
J-LO [13]	yes	LTL	no	predicates
tracecuts [14]	no	CFG	yes	events
HAWK [8]	yes	multiple	yes	predicates
Arachne [10]	yes	regex	n/a	predicates

and those in mainstream runtime verification. We have furthermore pointed out subtle variations that exist between different systems in the definition of symbols and events. So far our discussion has focussed on concepts; here we briefly relate those concepts to systems that instantiate them.

Table 1 lists some systems and, where applicable, the choices made in their design. These are often conscious choices, but sometimes the result of an accident of implementation. Concretely, we examine whether the style of semantics is exact-match or skipping, and how overlapping symbols are handled (if they are possible to define). For completeness, we also state the formalism each system uses, and whether or not free variables are supported.

PQL [12] is the principal example of a system with skipping semantics. Its patterns may be recursively defined, which is why we marked the formalism as Context Free Grammars (CFG) in the above table.

PTQL [11] also warrants some further discussion. It uses an SQL like language to write patterns, and joinpoints are regarded as records that have fields for (logical) start and end times. So to say that e_1 occurred before e_2, one states the condition $e_1.endTime < e_2.startTime$ in the query. With such a formalism, skipping is clearly the semantics of choice. Consequently the language does not provide for a Kleene star.

JavaMOP [7] is particularly interesting and relevant, because of its goal to be a framework where different specification formalisms can be plugged in. Indeed, such plugins can support both extended regular expressions and LTL variants. It supports free variables, but only as a matching context: the values bound by the variables aren't available for use when a match is completed (it is, however, possible to use *action blocks* associated with symbols to manually track bindings).

J-LO [13] represents a blend of traditional runtime verification (it uses LTL to express patterns), and aspect-oriented programming (events are specified with AspectJ pointcuts). With the use of LTL, and the focus on finding violations of properties, skipping semantics is the natural choice.

Tracecuts [14] is by contrast squarely in the aspect-oriented programming tradition. It uses an exact match semantics for context-free patterns. It splits runtime events into multiple monitor events in the same way as JavaMOP.

HAWK [8] is perhaps the most general formalism discussed here: it provides a rule based system that can express temporal logics, metric logics, extended regular expressions and it allows the user to define new logics. We hope that the present paper helps to map out the choices that designers of such logics must face.

Arachne [10] is a trace monitoring system for C. Its specification formalism is like a process algebra, restricted to the linear recursions that correspond to finite automata - hence we classified it as 'regular expressions'. The specifications are however more like definitions in process algebra, and hence the issue of skipping versus exact match does not arise: the matching process is coded by hand.

We have omitted systems from Table 1 that are so different as to be incomparable. For example, in Alpha [5], the queries are written as Prolog predicates over lists of events. Again, at that level of specification, there is no distinction between skipping and non-skipping: the programmer has to control such behaviour herself. Naturally that makes Alpha extremely expressive, but such expressivity comes at the cost of much poorer execution speed than the other systems compared here.

6   Conclusion and Future Work

The contributions of this paper are as follows:

- A reduction of the semantics of matching with variables to matching without variables, via the two-sep process of filtering and instantiation.
- A careful analysis of what pattern language constructs make sense for the skipping semantics: especially negation needs special care, as does Kleene closure.
- A formal semantics for a skipping language via a translation to an exact-match with a well understood semantics.
- A proof that skipping is strictly less expressive than exact-match.
- A proposal for a new pattern language construct (a modified form of Kleene closure) that, when included in a skipping language, makes it equivalent in expressive power to an exact-match language.

These contributions are an encouraging start to the comparative study of the semantics of matching patterns to traces, but much remains to be done. A pressing question concerns the inclusion of recursion (context-free languages) in the pattern specifications. We have seen that in the treatment of Kleene closure some subtleties arose, and it will be interesting to generalise that study to arbitrary recursive patterns.

Ultimately, it is our aim to provide a unifying framework for all these formalisms based on Datalog. In a separate strand of research, we have described a semantics of the AspectJ pointcut matching mechanism in terms of Datalog [2], and we are now extending that to richer formalisms for runtime verification, including those discussed here. We plan to use such a semantics in terms of Datalog as the basis of a single unified backend for many runtime verification systems.

References

1. Allan, C., Avgustinov, P., Christensen, A., Hendren, L., Kuzins, S., Lhoták, O., de Moor, O., Sereni, D., Sittampalam, G., Tibble, J.: Adding Trace Matching with Free Variables to AspectJ. In: Object-Oriented Programming, Systems, Languages and Applications, pp. 345–364. ACM Press, New York (2005)
2. Avgustinov, P., Hajiyev, E., Ongkingco, N., de Moor, O., Sereni, D., Tibble, J., Verbaere, M.: Semantics of static pointcuts in aspectj. In: Felleisen, M. (ed.) Principles of Programming Languages (POPL), ACM Press, New York (2007)
3. Avgustinov, P., Tibble, J., de Moor, O.: Making Trace Monitoring Feasible. In: OOPSLA 2007, ACM Press, New York (2007)
4. Barringer, H., Goldberg, A., Havelund, K., Sen, K.: Rule-based runtime verification. In: Steffen, B., Levi, G. (eds.) VMCAI 2004. LNCS, vol. 2937, pp. 44–57. Springer, Heidelberg (2004)
5. Bockisch, C., Mezini, M., Ostermann, K.: Quantifying over dynamic properties of program execution. In: DAW 2005 2nd Dynamic Aspects Workshop, Technical Report 05.01, pp. 71–75. Research Institute for Advanced Computer Science (2005)
6. Bodden, E.: J-LO - A tool for runtime-checking temporal assertions. Master's thesis, RWTH Aachen University, 2005.
7. Chen, F., Roşu, G.: A monitoring oriented programming environment for Java. In: Halbwachs, N., Zuck, L.D. (eds.) TACAS 2005. LNCS, vol. 3440, pp. 546–550. Springer, Heidelberg (2005)
8. d'Amorim, M., Havelund, K.: Event-based runtime verification of java programs. In: WODA 2005: Proceedings of the third international workshop on Dynamic analysis, pp. 1–7. ACM Press, New York (2005)
9. Douence, R., Fritz, T., Loriant, N., Menaud, J.-M., Ségura, M., Südholt, M.: An expressive aspect language for system applications with arachne. In: Aspect-Oriented Software Development, pp. 27–38. ACM Press, New York (2005)
10. Fritz, T., Ségura, M., Südholt, M., Wuchner, E., Menaud, J.-M.: An application of dynamic AOP to medical image generation. In: DAW05 2nd Dynamic Aspects Workshop, Technical Report 05.01, pp. 5–12. Research Institute for Advanced Computer Science (2005)
11. Goldsmith, S., O'Callahan, R., Aiken, A.: Relational queries over program traces. In: Proceedings of the 20th Annual ACM SIGPLAN Conference on Object-Oriented Programming, Systems, Languages and Applications, pp. 385–402. ACM Press, New York (2005)
12. Martin, M., Livshits, B., Lam, M.S.: Finding application errors using PQL: a program query language. In: Proceedings of the 20th Annual ACM SIGPLAN Conference on Object-Oriented Programming, Systems, Languages and Applications, pp. 365–383. ACM Press, New York (2005)
13. Stolz, V., Bodden, E.: Temporal Assertions using AspectJ. Electronic Notes in Theoretical Computer Science 144, 109–124 (2006)
14. Walker, R., Viggers, K.: Implementing protocols via declarative event patterns. In: ACM Sigsoft International Symposium on Foundations of Software Engineering (FSE-12), pp. 159–169. ACM Press, New York (2004)

Collaborative Runtime Verification with Tracematches

Eric Bodden[1], Laurie Hendren[1], Patrick Lam[1],
Ondřej Lhoták[2], and Nomair A. Naeem[2]

[1] McGill University, Montréal, Québec, Canada
[2] University of Waterloo, Waterloo, Ontario, Canada

Abstract. Perfect pre-deployment test coverage is notoriously difficult to achieve for large applications. With enough end users, many more test cases will be encountered during an application's deployment than during testing. The use of runtime verification after deployment would enable developers to detect and report on unexpected situations. Unfortunately, the prohibitive performance cost of runtime monitors prevents their use in deployed code.

In this work we study the feasibility of collaborative runtime verification, a verification approach which distributes the burden of runtime verification onto multiple users. Each user executes a partially instrumented program and therefore suffers only a fraction of the instrumentation overhead.

We focus on runtime verification using tracematches. Tracematches are a specification formalism that allows users to specify runtime verification properties via regular expressions with free variables over the dynamic execution trace. We propose two techniques for soundly partitioning the instrumentation required for tracematches: spatial partitioning, where different copies of a program monitor different program points for violations, and temporal partitioning, where monitoring is switched on and off over time. We evaluate the relative impact of partitioning on a user's runtime overhead by applying each partitioning technique to a collection of benchmarks that would otherwise incur significant instrumentation overhead.

Our results show that spatial partitioning almost completely eliminates runtime overhead (for any particular benchmark copy) on many of our test cases, and that temporal partitioning scales well and provides runtime verification on a "pay as you go" basis.

1 Introduction

In the verification community it is now widely accepted that, especially for large programs, verification is often incomplete and hence bugs still arise in deployed code on the machines of end users. However, verification code is rarely deployed, due to large performance penalties induced by current runtime verification approaches. Consequently, when errors do arise in production environments, their causes are often hard to diagnose: the available debugging information is very limited.

O. Sokolsky and S. Tasiran (Eds.): RV 2007, LNCS 4839, pp. 22–37, 2007.

Tracematches [1] are one mechanism for specifying runtime monitors. Tracematches enable developers to state sequences of program events and actions to take if the execution matches the sequence. Events bind objects in the heap; a tracematch only triggers if all of the events occur on a consistent set of objects.

According to researchers in industry [13], larger industrial companies would likely be willing to accept runtime verification in deployed code if the overhead is below 5%. In previous work on tracematches, we have shown that, in many cases, static analysis can enable efficient runtime monitoring by improving both the specification [3] and program under test [6]. Most often, our techniques can reduce runtime overhead to under 10%. However, our evaluation also showed that unreasonably large overheads—sometimes more than 100%—remained for some classes of specifications and programs. Other techniques for runtime monitoring also incur similar runtime overheads; for instance, the Program Query Language [10] causes up to 37% overhead on its benchmark applications (although it is intended to be a debugging tool rather than a tool for monitoring deployed programs), and JavaMOP [7] incurs up to 13% overhead on non-pathological test cases for runtime monitoring.

In this work, we attack the problem of runtime verification-induced overhead by using methods from remote sampling [9]. Because companies which produce large pieces of software (which are usually hard to analyze) often have access to a large user base, one can generate different kinds of partial instrumentation ("probes") for each user. A centralized server can then combine runtime verification results from runs with different probes. Although there are many advantages to a sampling-based approach, we are interested in using sampling to reduce instrumentation overhead for individual end users. We have developed two approaches for partitioning the overhead, *spatial partitioning* and *temporal partitioning*.

Spatial partitioning works by partitioning the instrumentation points into different subsets. We call each subset of instrumentation points a *probe* and each user is given a program instrumented with only one probe. This works very well in many cases, but in some cases a probe may contain a very hot—that is, expensive—instrumentation point. In those cases, the unlucky user who gets the hot probe will experience most of the overhead.

Temporal partitioning works by turning the instrumentation on and off periodically, reducing the total overhead. This method works even if there are are very hot probes, because even those probes are only enabled some of the time. However, since probes are disabled some of the time, any runtime verification properties of interest may be ignored while the probes are disabled.

In both spatial and temporal partitioning, the remaining instrumentation must operate correctly and, in particular, must never report false positives. The key point is that our transformations must never remove instrumentation points that can remove candidate bindings; identifying such instrumentation points can be difficult for tracematches, which may bind one or more objects and require each event to match the same objects. We have found a simple mechanism for reducing the number of these instrumentation points that appears to work well on our benchmarks.

We explored the feasibility of our approach by applying our modified trace-match compiler to benchmarks whose overheads persisted after the static anal-ysis in [6]. We first experimented with spatial partitioning. We found that some benchmarks were very suited to spatial partitioning. In these cases, each probe produced lower overhead than the complete instrumentation, and many probes carried less than 5% overhead. However, in other cases, some probes were so hot that they accounted for almost all of the overhead; spatial partitioning did not help much in those cases. We also experimented with temporal partitioning and examined runtimes when probes were enabled for 10, 30, 50, 70, 90 and 100 percent of the time. As expected, we found that the overhead increased steadily with the proportion of time that the probes were enabled, so that one can gain limited runtime monitoring by running probes only some of the time.

The remainder of this paper is structured as follows. In Section 2, we give background information on tracematches and describe the instrumentation for evaluating tracematches at runtime. In Section 3, we explain the spatial and temporal partitioning schemes. We evaluate our work in Section 4, discuss related work in Section 5 and finally conclude in Section 6.

2   Background

The goal of our research is to monitor executions of programs and ensure that programs never execute pathological sequences of events. In this project, we monitor executions using tracematches. A tracematch defines a runtime monitor using a regular expression over an alphabet of user-defined events in program executions. The developer is responsible for providing a tracematch to be verified and definitions for each event, or symbol, used in the tracematch. He provides definitions for symbols using AspectJ [8] pointcuts. Pointcuts often specify pat-terns which match names of currently executing methods or types of currently executing objects. Pointcuts may also bind parts of the execution context. For instance, at a method-call pointcut, the developer may bind the method param-eters, the caller object, and the callee objects, and may refer to these objects when the tracematch matches. If a tracematch does not bind any variables, then it reduces to verifying finite-state properties of the program as a whole.

Figure 1 presents an example tracematch. The tracematch header, in line 1, declares a tracematch variable i. Lines 2–5 declare two symbols, next and hasNext, which establish the alphabet for this tracematch's regular expression. The next symbol matches calls to an Iterator's next() method and binds the target object of the method call to i. The hasNext symbol matches calls to Iterator.hasNext(), on the same iterator i. Line 7 declares the tracematch's pattern (regular expression) and body. The pattern, next next, states that the tracematch body must execute after two consecutive calls to next(), as long as no hasNext() call intervenes.

```
1 tracematch(Iterator i) {
2     sym next before:
3       call(* java.util.Iterator+.next()) && target(i);
4     sym hasNext before:
5       call(* java.util.Iterator+.hasNext()) && target(i);
6
7     next next { /* emit error message; may access variable i */ }
8 }
```

Fig. 1. Tracematch checking that hasNext() is always called before next()

A crucial point about the semantics of tracematches' regular expressions is that intermediate events matching an explicitly-declared symbol *cannot be ignored*; that is, any occurrence of a non-matching symbol in an execution invalidates related partial matches. In our example, a sequence next hasNext next (all on the same iterator, of course) would *not* match. (Avgustinov et al. discuss the semantics of tracematches in detail in [2].)

The implementation of tracematches uses finite state machines to track the states of active partial matches. The compiler tracks variable-to-object bindings with *constraints*; each state q in the finite state machine has an associated constraint that stores information about groups of bound heap objects that must or must not be in state q. Constraints are stored in Disjunctive Normal Form as a set of *disjuncts*. Each disjunct maps from tracematch variables to objects. Note that the runtime cost of this approach comes from the large number of simultaneously-bound heap objects, and that the number of tracematch variables does not contribute to the runtime cost.

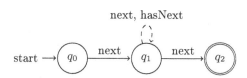

Fig. 2. Finite state machine for the tracematch of Figure 1

Figure 2 presents the automaton for the HasNext pattern; we can observe that two calls to next (on the same i) will cause the automaton to hit its final state q_2. Note that state q_1 carries a dashed self-loop. We call this loop a *skip-loop*. Skip loops remove partial matches that cannot be extended to complete matches: they delete a partial match whenever an observed event invalidates that partial match.

As an example, assume that state q_1 is associated with the constraint $\{[i \mapsto i_1], [i \mapsto i_2]\}$; that is, the program has executed next() once, and only once, on each of the iterators i_1 and i_2, following the most recent call to hasNext() on each of i_1 and i_2. If the program then executes hasNext() on i_2, then another call to next() on i_2 can no longer trigger an immediate match. Hence the skip-loop labelled hasNext will reduce the constraint on the intermediate state q_1 to $\{[i \mapsto i_1]\}$; the implementation discards the disjunct for i_2 at q_1. (In the tracematch semantics, the skip-loop implements a conjunction of the constraint at q_1 with the binding $i \neq i_2$.)

The tracematch compiler weaves code to monitor tracematches into programs at appropriate event locations. For every static code location corresponding to a potential event execution, the compiler therefore includes instrumentation code that also updates the appropriate disjuncts. This instrumentation code is called a *shadow*. In this paper, we use a previously-published static analysis that removes shadows if they can be shown to never contribute to complete matches [6]; for instance, a program which calls hasNext() but never next() would never trigger the final state of the HasNext automaton, so the hasNext shadows can removed.

3   Shadow Partitionings

Collaborative runtime verification leverages the fact that many users will execute the same application many times to reduce the runtime verification overhead for each user. The two basic options are to (1) reduce the number of active shadows for any particular run; or (2) reduce the (amortized) amount of work per active shadow. To explore these options, we devised two partitioning schemes, *spatial* and *temporal* partitioning. Spatial partitioning (Section 3.1) reduces the number of active shadows per run, while temporal partitioning (Section 3.2) reduces the amortized workload per active shadow over any particular execution.

Our partitioning schemes are designed to produce false negatives but no false positives. Our monitoring may miss some pattern matches (which will be caught eventually given enough executions), but any reported match must actually occur.

3.1   Spatial Partitioning

Spatial partitioning reduces the overhead of runtime verification by only leaving in a subset of a program's shadows. However, choosing an arbitrary subset of shadows does not work; in particular, arbitrarily disabling skip shadows may lead to false positives. Consider the following code with the HasNext pattern.

```
1 for(Iterator i = c.iterator(); i.hasNext();)
2       Object o = i.next();
```

In this case, if the iterator i only exists in this loop, one safe spatial partitioning would be to disable all shadows in the program except for those in the loop. However, disabling the hasNext skip shadow on line 1 and enabling the next shadow on line 2 on a collection with two or more objects gives a false positive, since the monitor "sees" two calls to next() and not the call to hasNext() which prevents the match.

Enabling arbitrary subsets of shadows can also lead to wasted work. Disabling the next shadow in the above example and keeping the hasNext shadow would, of course, lead to overhead from the hasNext shadow. But, on their own, hasNext shadows can never lead to a complete match without any next shadows.

We therefore need a more principled way of determining sensible groups of shadows to enable or disable. In previous work, we have described the notion of a *shadow group*, which approximates 1) the shadows needed to keep tracematches triggerable and 2) the skip-shadows which must remain enabled to avoid false positives. We will now summarize the relevant points; the complete details are given in [6]. We start by defining the notion of a static joinpoint shadow.

Definition 1 (Shadow). A shadow s of a tracematch tm is a pair $(lab_s, bind_s)$, where lab_s is the label of a declared symbol of tm and $bind_s$ is a variable binding, modelled as a mapping from variables to points-to sets. A points-to set is a set of object-creation sites in the program. The points-to set $pts(v)$ for a variable v contains the creation sites of all objects which could possibly be created at runtime and assigned to v.

In the example code above, the `hasNext` shadow in line 1 would be denoted by $(\texttt{hasNext}, \{i \mapsto \{i_1\}\})$, assuming that we denote the creation site of iterator objects that might be bound by this shadow by i_1.

Definition 2 (Shadow group). A *shadow group* is a pair of 1) a multi-set of shadows called *label-shadows* and 2) a set of shadows called *skip-shadows*. All shadows in *label-shadows* are labelled with labels of non-skip edges on some path to a final state, while all shadows in *skip-shadows* are labelled with a label of a skip-loop.

We use a multi-set for *label-shadows* to record the fact that the automaton might not reach its final state unless two or more shadows with the same label execute. For instance, the *HasNext* pattern only triggers after two `next` shadows execute; the multiplicities in the multi-set encode the number of times that a particular symbol needs to execute before the tracematch could possibly trigger.

Definition 3 (Consistent shadow group). A *consistent* shadow group g is a shadow group for which all variable bindings of all shadows in the group have points-to sets with a non-empty intersection for each variable.

For our HasNext example, a consistent shadow group could have this form:

$$label\text{-}shadows = [(next, i \mapsto \{i_1, i_2\}), (next, i \mapsto \{i_1\})],$$
$$skip\text{-}shadows = \{(hasNext, i \mapsto \{i_1\}), (hasNext, i \mapsto \{i_1, i_3\})\}$$

This shadow group is consistent—it may lead to a match at runtime—because the variable bindings for i could potentially point to the same object, namely an object created at creation site i_1. The shadow group holds two label shadows (labelled with the non-skip labels `next`). If the label shadows had disjoint points-to sets, then no execution would bind the tracematch variables to consistent objects, and the shadow group would not correspond to a possible runtime match. In addition, the shadow group holds *all* skip-shadows that have points-to sets that overlap with the label-shadows in the shadow group.

Conceptually, a consistent shadow group is the static representation of a possibly complete match at runtime. Every consistent shadow group may potentially cause its associated tracematch to match, if the label shadows execute in the proper order. Furthermore, only the skip shadows in the shadow group can prevent a match based on the shadow group's label shadows.

Our definition of a shadow group is quite well-suited to yielding sets of shadows that can be enabled or disabled in different spatial partitions. We therefore define a *probe* to be the union of all label-shadows and skip-shadows of a given consistent shadow group. (In constructing probes from shadow groups, we discard the multi-set structure of the label shadows and combine the label-shadows and skip-shadows into a single set). Probes "make sense" because they contain a set of shadows that can lead to a complete match and they are sound because they also contain all of the skip-shadows that can prevent that match. (We will explain why skip-shadows are crucial for probes in Section 3.2). Note that different probes may overlap; indeed, as Section 4 shows, many similar probes share the same hot shadows.

We can now present our algorithm for spatial partitioning.

– Compute all probes (based on the flow-insensitive analysis from [6]).
– Generate bytecode with two arrays: one array mapping from probes to shadows and one array with one entry per shadow.
– When emitting code for shadows, guard each shadow's execution with appropriate array look-ups.

The arrays, along with some glue code in the AspectJ runtime, allow us to dynamically enable and disable probes as desired. In the context of spatial partitioning, we choose one probe to enable at the start of each execution; however, our infrastructure permits experimentation with more sophisticated partitioning schemes.

3.2   Temporal Partitioning

We found that spatial partitioning was effective in distributing the workload of runtime verification in many cases. However, in some cases, we found that a single probe could still lead to large overheads for some unlucky users. Two potential reasons for large overheads are: 1) a shadow group may contain a large number of skip-shadows, if all those shadows have overlapping points-to sets, leading to large probes; or 2) if shadows belonging to a probe are repeatedly executed within a tight loop which would otherwise be quite cheap, any overhead due to such shadows would quickly accumulate. The HasNext pattern is especially prone to case 2), as calls to next() and hasNext() are cheap operations and almost always contained in loops.

In such situations, one way to further reduce the runtime overhead is by sampling: instead of monitoring a given probe all the time, we monitor it from time to time and hope that the program is executed long enough that any violations eventually get caught. However, it is unsound to disable an entire probe and then naïvely re-enable it again on the same run: missing a skip shadow can lead to a false positive.

Consider the following code and the HasNext pattern:

```
for(Iterator i = c.iterator(); i.hasNext();)
  Object o = i.next();
```

If we disabled monitoring during the call to hasNext, we could get a false positive after seeing two calls to next, since the intermediate call to hasNext went unnoticed.

Because false positives arise from disabling skip-shadows, one sound solution is to simply not disable skip-shadows at all. Unfortunately, the execution of skip-shadows can be quite expensive; we found that leaving skip-shadows enabled also leaves a lot of overhead, defeating the purpose of temporal partitioning.

However, we then observed that if a state s holds an empty constraint (i.e. no disjuncts), then skip-shadows originating at s no longer need to execute[1]. We implemented this optimization for our temporal partitioning and found it to be quite effective: Section 4 shows that our temporal partitioning, with this optimization, does not incur much partitioning-related overhead; most of the overhead is due only to the executing monitors. Intuitively, this optimization works because, while all non-skip shadows are disabled, no new disjuncts are being generated. Hence, the associated constraint will become empty after few— often, just one—iterations of the skip-shadow, practically degenerating the skip-shadow to a no-op.

We implemented the temporal partitioning as follows.

- Generate a Boolean flag per tracematch.
- When emitting code for shadows, guard each non-skip shadow with the appropriate flag.
- Change the runtime to start up an additional instrumentation control thread.

The control thread switches the instrumentation on and off at various time intervals. Figure 3 presents the parameters that the instrumentation control thread accepts; non-skip edges are enabled and then disabled after t_{on} milliseconds. Next, after another t_{off} milliseconds, the non-skip edges are enabled again.

Note that the Boolean flag we generate is independent of the Boolean array we use for spatial partitioning. If both spatial and temporal partitioning are used, a non-skip shadow is only enabled if both the Boolean array flag (from spatial partitioning) for this particular shadow and the Boolean flag (from temporal partitioning) for its tracematch are enabled. A skip shadow will be enabled if the Boolean array flag for its tracematch is enabled.

The thread can also scale the activation periods: every n periods, it can scale t_{on} by a factor i_{on} and t_{off} by i_{off}. This technique—a well-known technique from

---

[1] This optimization is only safe if all variables are known to be bound at s. However, for all patterns we used in this work, and for almost all patterns we know, this is the case for all states. Our implementation statically checks this property and only applies the optimization if it holds.

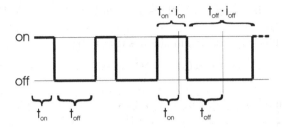

Fig. 3. Parameters for temporal partitioning, with increase period of $n = 2$

adaptive systems such as just-in-time compilers—allows us to keep non-skip edges enabled for longer as the program runs longer, which gives our temporal partitioning a better chance of catching tracematches that require a long execution time to match. Because we increase the monitoring periods over time, the cost of monitoring scales with the total execution time of the program.

4   Benchmarks

To demonstrate the feasibility of our approach, we applied our modified tracematch compiler to five of the hardest benchmark/tracematch combinations from previous evaluations [6]. These benchmarks continue to exhibit more than 10% of runtime overhead, even after we applied all available static optimizations. They all consist of tracematches that verify properties of frequently used data structures, such as iterators and streams, in the applications of version 2006-10 of the DaCapo benchmark suite [5]. As usual, all our benchmarks are available on `http://www.aspectbench.org/`, along with a version of abc implementing our optimization. In the near future we also plan to integrate this implementation into the main abc build stream. Table 1 explains the tracematches that we used.

Table 1. Tracematches applied to the DaCapo benchmarks

pattern name	description
FailSafeIter	do not update a collection while iterating over it
HasNextElem	always call hasNextElem before calling nextElement on an Enumeration
HasNext	always call hasNext before calling next on an Iterator
Reader	don't use a Reader after its InputStream was closed

4.1   Spatial Partitioning

We evaluated spatial partitioning by applying the algorithm from Section 3.1 to our five benchmark/tracematch combinations, after running the flow-insensitive static analysis described in [6]. Table 2 shows the runtime overheads with full

Table 2. Number of classes and methods per benchmark (taken from [5]), plus overhead of the fully instrumented benchmark, and number of probes generated for each benchmark

benchmark	classes	methods	complete overhead	# probes
antlr/Reader	307	3517	471.45%	4
chart/FailSafeIter	706	8972	25.08%	742
lucene/HasNextElem	309	3118	12.53%	6
pmd/FailSafeIter	619	6163	44.36%	426
pmd/HasNext	619	6163	66.53%	32

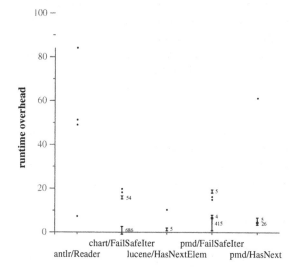

Fig. 4. Runtime overheads per probe in spatial partitioning (in percent; bars indicate clumps of probes, labelled by size of clump)

instrumentation. All of these overheads exceed 10%, and the overhead for antl-r/Reader is almost 500%. Table 2 also presents the number of probes generated for each benchmark.

Under the spatial partitioning approach, our compiler emits instrumented benchmarks which can enable or disable each probe dynamically. We tested the effect of each probe individually by executing each benchmark with one probe enabled at a time; this gave us 1210 benchmark configurations to test. For our experiments, we used the Sun Hotspot JVM version 1.4.2_12 with 2GB RAM on a machine with an AMD Athlon 64 X2 Dual Core Processor 3800+. We used the -s large option of the DaCapo suite to provide extra-large inputs, which made it easier for us to measure changes in runtimes. Figure 4 shows runtime overheads for the probes in our benchmarks. Dots indicate overheads for individual probes. For some benchmarks, many probes were almost identical, sharing the same hot shadows. These probes therefore also had almost identical overheads. We grouped these probes into clumps and present them as a bar, labelled with the number of probes in the clump.

Our results demonstrate that, in some cases, the different probes manage to spatially distribute the overhead quite well. However, spatial partitioning does not always suffice. For pmd/FailSafeIter, 9 probes out of 426 have overheads exceeding 5%, while for chart/FailSafeIter, 56 such cases exist, out of 742 probes in total. On the other hand, the lucene/HasNextElem and pmd/HasNext benchmarks contain only one hot probe each; spatial partitioning is unlikely to help in these cases.

Finally, antlr/Reader still shows high overheads, but these overheads are much lower than the original overhead of 471.45%. Interestingly, the four different overheads do not add up to 471.45%. Upon further investigation, we found that two probes generate many more disjuncts than others. In the fully instrumented program, each shadow in each probe has to look up all the disjuncts, even if they are generated by other probes, which might lead to overheads larger than the sum of the overheads for each individual probe. We are currently thinking about whether this observation could lead to an optimization of the tracematch implementation in general. (Disjunct lookup is described in greater detail in [4].)

We conclude that spatial partitioning can sometimes be effective in spreading the overhead among different probes. However, in some cases, a small number of probes can account for a large fraction of the original total overhead. In those cases, spatial partitioning does not suffice for reducing overhead, and we next explore our temporal partitioning technique for improving runtime performance.

4.2 Temporal Partitioning

To evaluate the effectiveness of temporal partitioning, we measured ten different configurations for each of the five benchmark/tracematch combinations. Figure 5 presents runtimes for each of these configurations. The DaCapo framework collects these runtimes by repeatedly running each benchmark until the normalized standard deviation of the most recent runs is suitably small.

Diamond-shaped data points depict measurements of runtimes with no temporal partitioning; the left data point includes all probes (maximal overhead), while the right data point includes no probes (no overhead). The gap between the right diamond data point and the gray baseline, which denotes the runtime of the completely un-instrumented program, shows the cost of runtime checks. Note that spatial partitioning will always cost at least as much as the right diamond.

The circle-shaped data points present the effect of *temporal partitioning*. We measured the runtimes resulting from enabling non-skip edges 10, 30, 50, 70, 90 and 100 percent of the time. Our first experiment sought to determine the effect of changing the swapping interval for temporal partitioning.

At first, we executed four different runs for each of those seven configurations, with four different increase periods n. We doubled the duration of the on/off intervals every $n = 10, 40, 160$ and 640 periods. As expected, n has no measurable effect on runtime performance. We therefore plotted the arithmetic mean of the

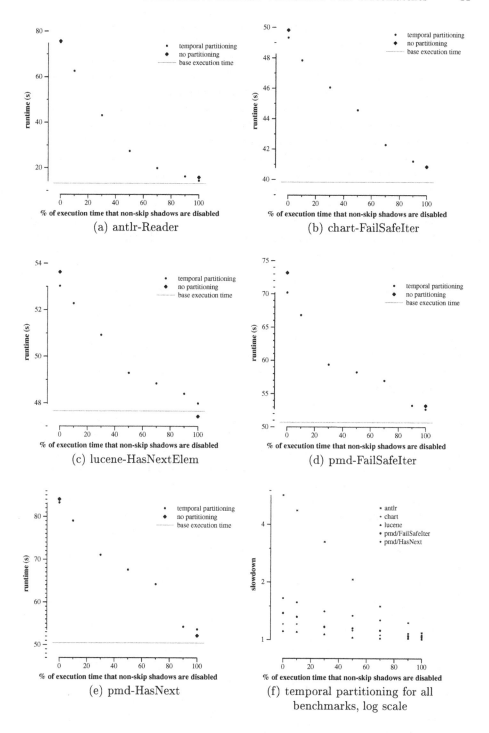

Fig. 5. Results of temporal partitioning for five benchmark/tracematch combinations

results over the different increase periods. The full set of numbers is available on our website.

Figure 5 (f) overlays the results from all of our benchmark/tracematch combinations. Note that the shape of the overhead curve is quite similar in all of the configurations. In all cases, temporal partitioning can properly scale down from 100% overhead, when all non-skip edges are always enabled, to just above 0%, when non-skip edges are never enabled. We were surprised to find that the decrease in runtime overhead did not scale linearly with a decrease in monitoring intervals. This data suggest that there might exist a "sweet spot" where the overhead is consistently lowest compared to the employed monitoring time.

The relationship between "no temporal partitioning" with all probes enabled and the 100% measurement with temporal partitioning enabled might seem surprising at first: we added additional runtime checks for temporal partitioning, and yet, in the cases of chart-FailSafeIter, lucene-HasNextElem and pmd-FailSafeIter, the code executes significantly faster. We believe that this speedup is due to the skip-loop optimization that we implemented for temporal partitioning: this optimization is applied even when non-skip edges are enabled, thereby improving overall performance.

The far right end of the graphs shows that the overhead of the runtime checks for spatial and temporal partitioning are virtually negligible. They are not zero but close enough to the baseline to not hinder the applicability of the approach.

5   Related Work

Our work on collaborative runtime verification is most closely related to the work of Liblit et al. for automatic bug isolation. The key insight in automatic bug isolation is that a large user community can help isolate bugs in deployed software using statistical methods. The key idea behind *Cooperative Bug Isolation* is to use sparse random sampling of a large number of program executions to gather information. Hence, one can amortize the cost of executing assertion-dense code by distributing it to many users, each user only executing a small randomly selected number of assertions. This minimizes the overhead experienced by each user. Although each execution report in isolation gives only very limited information, the aggregate of all such reports provides a wealth of debugging information for analysis and a high chance of finding violations of an assertion, if they exist.

Pavlopoulou et al. [12] describe a *residual test coverage* monitoring tool which starts off by instrumenting all the code. As different parts of the program are executed, the code is periodically re-instrumented, with probes added only in places which have not been covered by the testing criteria. Probes from frequently executed regions are therefore removed in the first few re-instrumentation cycles, reducing the overhead in the long term since the program spends more and more time in code regions without any probes. Such an adaptive instrumentation should be applicable to our setting, too. To avoid false positives, one would have to disable entire shadow groups at a time.

Patil *et al.* [11] propose two different approaches to minimize overhead due to runtime checking of pointer and array accesses in C programs. *Customization* uses program slicing to decouple the runtime checking from the original program execution. The second approach, *shadow processing*, uses idle processors in multiprocessor workstations to perform runtime checking in the background. The shadow processing approach uses two processes: a main process, which executes the original user program, *i.e.* without any run-time checking, and a shadow process which follows the main process and performs the intended dynamic analysis. The main process has minimal overhead (5%-10%), mostly arising from the need for synchronization and sharing of values between the two processes. Such an approach would not work for arbitrary tracematches, which might arbitrarily modify the program state, but could work for the verification-oriented tracematches we are investigating.

Recently, Microsoft, Mozilla, GNOME, KDE and others have all developed opt-in services for reporting crash data. When a program crashes, recovery code generates and transmits a report summarizing the state of the program. Recently, Microsoft's system has been extended to gather data about abnormal program behaviour in the background; reports are then automatically sent every few days (subject to user permission). Reports from all users can then be aggregated and analyzed for information about causes of crashes.

We briefly mention a number of alternative approaches for specifying properties for runtime verification. The Program Query Language [10] is similar to tracematches in that it enables developers to specify properties of Java programs, where each property may bind free variables to runtime heap objects. PQL supports a richer specification language than tracematches, since it is based on stack automata rather than finite state machines. Monitoring-Oriented Programming [7] is a generic framework for specifying properties for runtime monitoring; developers use MOP logic plugins to state properties of interest. PQL, MOP, and related approaches, can all benefit from collaborative runtime verification techniques.

6   Conclusion and Future Work

In this paper we have presented two techniques for implementing collaborative runtime verification with tracematches. The main idea is to share the instrumentation over many users, so that any one user pays only part of the cost of the runtime verification. Our paper has described the spatial and temporal partitioning techniques and demonstrated their applicability to a collection of benchmarks which exhibit high instrumentation overheads.

Spatial partitioning allocates different probes—consistent subsets of instrumentation points—to different users; probes generally have lower overheads than the entire instrumentation. Our experimental evaluation showed that spatial partitioning works well when there are no particularly hot probes.

Temporal partitioning works by periodically enabling and disabling instrumentation. We demonstrated a good correspondence between the proportion of time that probes were enabled and the runtime overhead.

We are continuing our work on making tracematches more efficient on many fronts, including further static analyses. We are also continuing to build up our benchmark library of base programs and interesting tracematches.

References

1. Allan, C., Avgustinov, P., Christensen, A.S., Hendren, L., Kuzins, S., Lhoták, O., de Moor, O., Sereni, D., Sittampalam, G., Tibble, J.: Adding Trace Matching with Free Variables to AspectJ. In: Object-Oriented Programming, Systems, Languages and Applications, pp. 345–364. ACM Press, New York (2005)
2. Avgustinov, P., de Moor, O., Tibble, J.: On the semantics of matching trace monitoring patterns. In: Seventh Workshop on Runtime Verification, Vancouver, Canada, March. LNCS, (2007)
3. Avgustinov, P., Tibble, J., Bodden, E., Lhoták, O., Hendren, L., de Moor, O., Ongkingco, N., Sittampalam, G.: Efficient trace monitoring. Technical Report abc-2006-1, (March 2006), http://www.aspectbench.org/
4. Avgustinov, P., Tibble, J., de Moor, O.: Making trace monitors feasible. In: ACM Conference on Object-Oriented Programming, Systems, Languages, and Applications (2007)
5. Blackburn, S.M., Garner, R., Hoffman, C., Khan, A.M., McKinley, K.S., Bentzur, R., Diwan, A., Feinberg, D., Frampton, D., Guyer, S.Z., Hirzel, M., Hosking, A., Jump, M., Lee, H., Moss, J.E.B., Phansalkar, A., Stefanović, D., VanDrunen, T., von Dincklage, D., Wiedermann, B.: The DaCapo benchmarks: Java benchmarking development and analysis. In: OOPSLA 2006: Proceedings of the 21st annual ACM SIGPLAN conference on Object-Oriented Programing, Systems, Languages, and Applications, pp. 169–190. ACM Press, New York, USA (2006)
6. Bodden, E., Hendren, L., Lhoták, O.: A staged static program analysis to improve the performance of runtime monitoring. In: 21st European Conference on Object-Oriented Programming, Berlin, Germany, July 30th-August 3rd. LNCS, vol. 4609, pp. 525–549. Springer, Heidelberg (2007)
7. Chen, F., Rosu, G.: MOP: An efficient and generic runtime verification framework. In: ACM Conference on Object-Oriented Programming Systems, Languages and Applications (OOPSLA) (2007)
8. Kiczales, G., Hilsdale, E., Hugunin, J., Kersten, M., Palm, J., Griswold, W.: An overview of AspectJ. In: Knudsen, J.L. (ed.) ECOOP 2001. LNCS, vol. 2072, pp. 327–353. Springer, Heidelberg (2001)
9. Liblit, B., Aiken, A., Zheng, A., Jordan, M.: Bug isolation via remote program sampling. In: Proceedings of the ACM SIGPLAN 2003 Conference on Programming Language Design and Implementation, San Diego, California, pp. 141–154 (June 2003)
10. Martin, M., Livshits, B., Lam, M.: Finding application errors using PQL: a program query language. In: Proceedings of the 20th Annual ACM SIGPLAN Conference on Object-Oriented Programming, Systems, Languages and Applications, pp. 365–383 (2005)

11. Patil, H., Fischer, C.: Low-cost, concurrent checking of pointer and array accesses in C programs. Softw. Pract. Exper 27(1), 87–110 (1997)
12. Pavlopoulou, C., Young, M.: Residual test coverage monitoring. In: ICSE 1999. Proceedings of the 21st International Conference on Software Engineering, pp. 277–284. IEEE Computer Society Press, Los Alamitos, CA, USA (1999)
13. Grieskamp, W.: Microsoft Research. In: Personal communication, (January 007)

Static and Dynamic Detection of Behavioral Conflicts Between Aspects

Pascal Durr, Lodewijk Bergmans, and Mehmet Aksit

University of Twente, The Netherlands
{durr,bergmans,aksit}@ewi.utwente.nl

Abstract. Aspects have been successfully promoted as a means to improve the modularization of software in the presence of crosscutting concerns. The so-called *aspect interference problem* is considered to be one of the remaining challenges of aspect-oriented software development: aspects may interfere with the behavior of the base code or other aspects. Especially interference between aspects is difficult to prevent, as this may be caused solely by the composition of aspects that behave correctly in isolation. A typical situation where this may occur is when multiple advices are applied at a *shared*, join point.

In [1] we explained the problem of behavioral conflicts between aspects at shared join points. We presented an approach for the detection of behavioral conflicts. This approach is based on a novel abstraction model for representing the behavior of advice. This model allows the expression of both primitive and complex behavior in a simple manner. This supports automatic conflict detection. The presented approach employs a set of conflict detection rules, which can be used to detect generic, domain specific and application specific conflicts. The approach is implemented in Compose*, which is an implementation of Composition Filters. This application shows that a declarative advice language can be exploited for aiding automated conflict detection.

This paper discusses the need for a runtime extension to the described static approach. It also presents a possible implementation approach of such an extension in Compose*. This allows us to reason efficiently about the behavior of aspects. It also enables us to detect these conflicts with minimal overhead at runtime.

1   An Example Conflict: Security vs. Logging

We first briefly present an example of a behavioral conflict. Assume that there is a base system that uses a Protocol to interact with other systems. Class Protocol has two methods: one for transmitting, sendData(String) and one for receiving, receiveData(String). Now image, that we would like to secure this protocol. To achieve this, we encrypt all outgoing messages and decrypt all incoming messages. We implement this as an encryption advice on the execution of method sendData. Likewise, we superimpose a decryption advice on method receiveData. Imagine a second aspect that traces all the methods and possible arguments. The implementation of aspect Tracing uses a condition to dynamically determine

O. Sokolsky and S. Tasiran (Eds.): RV 2007, LNCS 4839, pp. 38–50, 2007.

if the current method should be traced, as tracing all the methods is not very efficient. Aspect Tracing can, for instance, be used to create a stack trace of the execution within a certain package.

These two advices are superimposed on the same join point, in this case Protocol.sendData[1]. As the advices have to be sequentially executed, there are two possible execution orders here. Now assume that we want to ensure that no one accesses the data before it is encrypted. This constraint is violated, if the two advices are ordered in such a way that advice tracing is executed before advice encryption. We may end up with a log file that contains "sensitive" information. The resulting situation is what we call a behavioral conflict. We can make two observations; the first is that there is an ordering dependency between the aspects. If advice trace is executed before advice encryption, we might expose sensitive data. The second observation is that, although this order can be statically determined, we are unsure whether the conflicting situation will even occur at runtime, as advice trace is conditionally executed.

2   Approach Outlined

An approach for detecting such behavioral conflicts at shared join points has been detailed in [1]. A shared join point has multiple advices superimposed on it. These are, in most AOP systems, executed sequentially. This implies an ordering between the advices, which can be (partially) specified by the aspect programmer. This ordering may or may not cause the behavioral conflict. The conflict in the running example is an example of a conflict that is ordering dependent. And as such can also be resolved by changing the order. However there are conflicts, like synchronization and real-time behavior, which are independent of the chosen order. Order dependent conflicts can be resolved by changing the order either statically or dynamically. This kind of automatic resolution is beyond the scope of this paper. We have implemented such a user-defined option is our Compose* toolset.

Our approach revolves around abstracting the behavior of an advice into a resource operation model. Here the resources present common or shared interactions (e.g. a semaphore). These resources are thus potential conflicting "areas". Advices interact with resources using operations. As the advices are sequentially composed at a shared join point, we can also sequentially compose the operations for each (shared) resource. After this composition, we verify whether a set of rules accepts the resulting sequence of operations for that specific resource. These rules can either be conflict rules, i.e. patterns that are not allowed to occur, or assertion rules, i.e. pattern which must always occur. These rules can be expressed as a regular expression or a temporal logic formula.

A resource operation model is defined as follows:

Resources is the set of all resources in the system, e.g. target, sender, selector, arguments;

---

[1] In this paper we only focus on join point Protocol.sendData, but a similar situation presents itself for join point Protocol.receiveData.

Operations is the set of all possible operations in the system, e.g. read, destructive write and non-destructive write;

Alphabet(resource) is the set of operations which can be carried out on a specific resource, such that $\forall resource \in Resources \bullet Alphabet(resource) \subseteq ValidOperations$;

ResourceOperations is the set of all valid resource operations tuples on a specific resource, such that $ResourceOperations = \{(rsrc, op) \bullet rsrc \in Resources \land op \in Alphabet(rsrc)\}$;

ConflictRules(resource) is the set of conflict rules for resource *resource*;

AssertionRules(resource) is the set of assertion rules for resource *resource*.

2.1 Conflict Model

The previous described conflict detection model has been used to model the behavior of advice. In [2] we provide more detailed information about this generic model and show how this model is derived from two AOP approaches, namely AspectJ and Composition Filters. In this model, we distinguish two types of conflict, control and data related conflicts. Where the first models the effect of advice on the control flow and the latter captures conflicts that occur due to shared data. It is out of the scope of this paper to discuss all the details of this generic model, please consult [2] for this. However, we will present an overview of this generic model.

Data Conflicts. The presented resources are commonly used program elements, which can be inspected or manipulated by advice. These are usually bound via explicit context bindings or via pseudo variables, like *thisJoinPoint* in AspectJ. These resources are: caller, target, selector, arguments, returnvalue and variables.

On these resources we can execute the following operations:

read: queries the state of the resource on which it operates;

$write_n$: A nondestructive write will update the state of the resource on which it operates, e.g. compressing (lossless) or encrypting the arguments, in a reversible manner (i.e. without loss of information);

$write_d$: A destructive write will override the state of the resource on which it operates, this is normally irreversible;

unknown: Can be either a *read*, $write_n$ and $write_d$, but not known precisely.

Now that the resources and operations are defined we present the conflict rules to detect behavioral conflicts on data elements. In general, these conflict rules can be expressed in any matching language. Here, we use extended regular expressions as defined by IEEE standard 1003.1[3] to specify the conflict patterns.

- Conflict(data): $write_d$ $write_d$: The effect of the first destructive write is lost.
- Conflict(data): $read$ $write_d$: The first advice may become invalid if the data resource is changed afterwards (at the same join point).

- Conflict(data): *read write$_n$*: The first advice may become invalid if the data resource is changed afterwards (at the same join point).
- Conflict(data): *write$_n$ write$_d$*: The effect of the first nondestructive write is lost.
- Conflict(data): *unknown*: Using an unknown data manipulation operation can be potentially dangerous.

The presented conflict rules have been defined on the basis of pairs, however matching any of the rules as a sub-pattern is also considered a conflict.

Control Flow Conflicts. To capture control flow related behavioral conflicts we also instantiate the conflict detection model to capture the effects of advice on the control flow. We model control flow behavior as operations on the abstract controlflow resource. On this single resource controlflow, advice can operate using the following operations:

continue: The advice does not change the control flow, it simply passes control to the next advice, if any.

return: The advice returns immediately to either after advice or to the caller, and as such the original join point is no longer executed,

exit: The advice terminates the entire control flow, e.g. a exception is thrown or an exit call is made.

We will now show which combinations of operations on the *control flow* resource (may) yield a conflict. Again, we assume here that the (conflicting) operations are derived from two different advices.

- $Conflict(controlflow)$: *return .$^+$*: If one advice returns, another advice which should be executed after this advice, is never executed, hence if there are one or more other operations after a *return*, this will be signaled as a conflict.
- $Conflict(controlflow)$: *exit .$^+$*: Similarly, if one advice terminates the execution, the advice which should be executed after this advice is never executed. hence if an *exit* operation is followed by one or more other operations, this will be signaled as a conflict.

Note that especially these generic rules are typically conservative: i.e. they aim at detecting *potential* conflicts, and will also point out situations that are in reality not conflicting. It is important to see the resulting conflicts as warnings that something might be wrong, rather than absolute errors!

One key observation we have made, is the fact that modeling the entire system, is not only extremely complex but it also does not model the conflict at the appropriate level of abstraction. With this we mean, that during the transformation, of behavior to read and write operations on a set of variables, we might loose important information. In our example we *encrypt* the arguments of a message to provide some level of security. Our model allows for the extension of both resources and operations to capture also more domain or application specific conflicts.

2.2   Analysis Process

Imagine the following composed filter sequence on method *Protocol.sendData* in our example. The result is the following composed filter sequence:

```
1  trace : ParameterTracing = { ShouldTrace => [*.*] };
2  encrypt : Encryption = { [*.sendData] }
```

Listing 1.1. Composed filter sequence example

Filter trace traces all parameters and return value in the beginning and end of a method execution. Filter encrypt subsequently secures the data being send.

To illustrate how we can achieve automated reasoning using the declarative filter language of Composition Filters, we now present an example implementation of a filter which traces all the parameters. See [2] for more detailed information.

$$\underbrace{trace}_{Name} : \underbrace{ParameterTracing}_{Type} = \{ \underbrace{ShouldTrace}_{Condition} => [\underbrace{*}_{target} . \underbrace{*}_{selector}] \underbrace{*}_{target} . \underbrace{*}_{selector} \}$$

Name   Type   Condition   Matching   Substitution

Name: the name of this filter;

Type: the type of this filter, a filter type can thus be instantiated;

Condition: the condition is evaluated to determine whether to continue to the matching part. If this condition yields false, the filter will reject and execute its corresponding reject action. If it yields a truth value, the matching part is evaluated;

Matching: this allows for selecting a specific message. A matching part can match the *target* and/or the *selector* of a message. If a given message matches, the substitution part is executed, if any, and the filter accepts. This acceptance will result in the execution of the accept action;

Substitution: this allows for simple rewriting the target and selector of a message.

There are many steps involved in processing and analyzing a sequence of filters on a specific join point. One such step is to analyze the effects of each of the composed filters. A filter can either execute an accept action or a reject action, given a set of conditions and a message. Next, we have to determine which filter actions can be reached and whether, for example, the *target* has been read in the matching part. Filter actions perform specific tasks of a filter type, e.g. filter action *Encrypt* of filter type *Encryption* will encrypt the arguments. Likewise, filter action *Trace* of the filter type *ParameterTracing* will trace the message. Most filter types execute the *Continue* action if the filter rejects. All this domain information is gathered and a so-called message flow graph is generated. A message flow graph G_{mflow} is a directed acyclic graph and is defined as: $< V, E, L >$, where:

V is a set of vertexes representing the composition filters elements that can be evaluated. These can be filter modules, filters, matching parts, condition expressions, filter actions, etc... ;

E: is the set of edges connecting the vertexes, such that $E = \{(u,v) \bullet u, v \in V \wedge u \neq v\}$;

L: is the set of resource-operations labels attached to the edges, such that
$L = \{(e, rsrcop) \bullet e \in E \wedge rsrcop \in ResourceOperations\}$.

For each shared join point a message flow graph G_{mflow} is created. This graph is subsequently simulated to detect impossible or dependent paths through the filter set. It is out of the scope of this paper to discuss the full implementation of this simulation, please see [4] for more details. The general idea is that for each message that can be accepted by the filter we determine its effect on the filter set. If we do this for all possible messages, and once for those messages that are not accepted by the filterset, we are able to determine which filter actions can be reached and how they are reached. Impossible paths are removed and dependent paths are marked as such.

The filter sequence presented in listing 1.1 can be translated to the filter execution graph in figure 1.

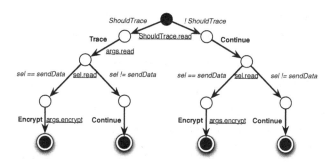

Fig. 1. Filter execution graph example

This graph is a simplified version of the actual graph, for readability purposes. The *italic* labels on the transitions are evaluations of the conditions (e.g. *ShouldTrace*), and the message matching, e.g. *message.sel(ector) == sendData*. The **bold** labels on the transitions show the filter actions. The underlined labels are resource-operations tuples corresponding to the evaluation of the conditions, matching parts and the filter actions.

Next we transform the conflict and assertion rules to graphs that are matched to the message flow graph. We require all assertion rules to be inverted, as the process for determining whether a rule matches only works for conflict rules. The assertion rules can be inverted, because we use a regular language and the alphabet is known and limited. A conflict rule graph $G_{conflict}$ is a directed acyclic graph and is defined as: $< V, E, L >$, where:

V is a set of vertexes;

E: is the set of edges connecting the vertexes, such that $E = \{(u,v) \bullet u, v \in V \wedge u \neq v\}$;

L: is the set of resource-operations labels attached to the edges, such that $L = \{(e, rsrcop) \bullet e \in E \wedge rsrcop \in ResourceOperations\}$. The label can also be a wildcard to indicate that we are that we are not interested in a certain step.

Once we have these conflict rule graphs we can intersect both graphs and see whether the intersection is empty. If so the conflict rule does not match and as such is conflict free for this rule. If the intersection is not empty, we have encountered a conflict and a trace is asked. To summarize, a shared join point contains a conflict if:

Lemma 1. $\exists g_{rule} \in G_{conflict} \bullet g_{rule} \cap G_{mflow} \neq \emptyset$

For each such conflict we have a corresponding path $P_{conflict}$, or a set of paths if there are more paths leading to the same conflicting situation. $P_{conflict}$ is a sub graph of G_{mflow}.

In this case a conflict rule stating that it is is not allowed for the arguments to be read before they are encrypted. In a regular expression: Conflict(arguments): ^*read encrypt*, this states that a conflict occurs if we encounter a situation where the arguments are read and afterwards they are encrypted. From this graph we can see that in the left most path, the *arguments* are *read* before they are *encrypted*. The intersection of the conflict rule with the message flow graph of shared join point *Protocol.sendData* is not empty, and thus the conflicting situation is detected.

Now let us elaborate on this conflict a bit more. In the example we use two filters, one of these filter uses a condition. Condition *ShouldTrace* is used to determine whether to trace this method or not. Whether this condition is true or false depends on some runtime configuration option. Statically we see that there is a possibility of a conflict, as we modeled both true and false values of the condition. This enhances our ability to reason about behavioral conflict but it also introduces possible false positives. The use of such a condition may always yield a false value, i.e. no methods should be traced. This thus requires dynamic monitoring to determine whether such a conflict actually occurs at runtime. The next section will discuss in which situations static checking is not sufficient, when using AOP.

3   Issues with Static Checking in AOP

The previous section outlined our approach to statically determine behavioral conflicts between advice. Although this provides a developer with a list of potential conflicts, not all these conflicts may occur at runtime. The simplest example of such a situation, is when the code in which the conflicting join point resides is never executed. However, there are more complex cases where static checking is not sufficient.

3.1   Dynamic Weaving

There are AOP approaches which employ dynamic weaving or proxy-base techniques to instrument an application. Although this provides some unique features over statically based weaving, it does present difficulties when statically reasoning about behavioral conflicts at shared join points. One such difficulty is that not all shared join points are known statically. As such, it becomes hard to know which advices are imposed at a shared join point. An example of such a construct is conditional superimposition found in Composition Filters. In this case one can assume a worst case situation, where each advice can be composed with any other advice. However, this can lead to large set of orders and possible combinations which have to be checked.

3.2 Dynamic Advice Execution

Most AOP approaches support conditional or dynamic properties in either pointcut or advice language. Examples of such constructs are, the *if(...)* pointcut in AspectJ and conditions in Composition Filters. In this case all shared join points are known. However, not all possible combinations of advice may occur at runtime. This can depend on some runtime state. In the running example we use condition *ShouldTrace* to determine whether to trace or not. At runtime this condition can be true or false. In our static approach, we simulate all possibilities of conditions.

3.3 Concurrency

In this paper we limit ourselves to the detection of concurrency conflicts at a single shared join point. We are aware that concurrency conflicts can also occur between join points. Concurrency conflicts between advice at a single shared join point, are caused by an unanticipated interleaving of the advices. This interleaving can occur because there is a single advice applied to a join point and that join point is concurrently executed. In this case the aspect is conflicting with itself and no resolution can be made. The interleaving can also be caused by a composition of multiple advices. In this case we may be able to resolve the conflict by changing the order. In both cases the problem can be prevented using atomic advice execution.

A single aspect or multiple aspects can cause concurrency conflicts. In either case, it is difficult to statically determine all possible interleavings. To determine the possible interleavings is not only hard, but also simulating all interleavings is very time consuming.

This section presented three situations where static checking is not sufficient. The next section will provide a runtime extension of the approach outlined in section 2. Although we focus on the second situation our approach is equally applicable to the first and third situation.

4   A Runtime Extension

As motivated by the previous section, we would like to extent our work to also capture behavioral conflicts at runtime. A naive application would be to simply instrument all advices and monitor all join points dynamically. This is required for capturing concurrency conflicts, as explained in the previous section. However, for the other two conflicting situations we can reason more efficiently. In section 2 about our approach we stated that for each possible conflict we get a set of conflicting paths called: $P_{conflict}$. This graph is translated into a DFA for checking at runtime. The nodes of this graph are elements that can be evaluated in Composition Filters. The edges represents the control flow between these nodes. Each edge has a set of labels attached to it which represent the corresponding resource operation tuples.

It should be noted that most likely the set of conflicting paths is smaller than the set of all possible paths. We only have to monitor paths that are conflicting for a specific resource and that contain dynamic elements. This will in practice reduce the number of paths to check substantially.

To informally outline our runtime extension we will use the example conflict, as presented earlier. In figure 1, we saw that the left most path was a conflicting path. This full path is: $< ShouldTrace.read >, < args.read >, < selector.read >, < args.encrypt >$. However, only part of this path is conflicting with our requirement. In this case: Conflict(args):^read encrypt. This conflict rule only limits the usage of operations for resource $args$. We can thus reduce the conflicting path to: $< args.read >, < args.encrypt >$. Where $< args.read >$ is caused by the execution of filter action Trace, and $< args.encrypt >$ is caused by filter action Encrypt. We only have to monitor the execution of these two filter actions to determine whether the conflict occurs or not. In this case, even the execution of filter action Trace is sufficient, this is however not true in the general case. There are cases where one has to monitor the evaluation of conditions, message matching and message substitutions.

4.1   Instrumentation

To be able to monitor the system while running, we have to inject monitoring code inside the advices. We assume that all code will be passed through the Compose* compiler. In our case this is always the case. However, with other more dynamic approaches this may not be a valid assumption. Our compiler will inject the bookkeeping code in the appropriate places. This ensures that the executing code will emit updates to the monitor. The next section will provide more details about this monitor.

4.2   Analysis Process At Runtime

There are multiple steps involved in checking at runtime for a behavioral conflict. Our runtime extension uses an Abstract Virtual Machine(AVM)[2] to do bookkeeping at runtime. This AVM is defined as:

ConflictingResources is the set of resources which should be monitor, where $ConflictingResources \subseteq Resources,$

---

[2] Note, that besides the name there are no similarities between the AVM and a runtime virtual machine, e.g. the JVM.

OperationSequence(rsrc) is the sequence of operations carried out on resource $rsrc$, where $\forall rsrc \in ConflictingResources$
- $OperationSequence(rsrc) \subseteq Alphabet(rsrc)$,

ConflictRules(rsrc) is the set of conflict rules for resource $rsrc$.

Now that we have defined the monitor we define the three phases that are involved while reasoning about behavioral conflicts at a shared join point.

1. **Initialization:** At the start of the first edge in conflicting path we initialize the AVM. This AVM is responsible for keeping the state of resources during the execution of this join point. It keeps track of all operations that are carried out on resources. If an operation is carried out on a resource which does not exist, this resource is created.

   In our running example the initialization is done before the filter action *Trace* or the first *continue* action is executed.

2. **Execution:** For each edge involved in a conflicting path, we execute the operations on the conflicting resources. These are carried out on the AVM, and this AVM will update its state accordingly. The execution of the operations has to be done immediately and atomically, after the filter actions, conditions and such have been executed or evaluated.

   In the example, the execution step is carried out if the edge with label $< args.read >$ attached is taken. This corresponds to the execution of operation *read* on resource *args*. The result: $OperationSequence(args) = read$. The execution step is also executed for the edge with label $< args.encrypt >$ attached is taken. This corresponds to the execution of operation *encrypt* on resource *args*. Resulting in: $OperationSequence(args) = read\ encrypt$.

3. **Evaluation:** If we reach the end of the execution path, we have to signal the AVM to verify that the rules still hold for the given execution path. We have encountered a conflict if any of the conflict rules match. In such a case we can alert the user, e.g. via a message or an exception. At the end of a join point we verify that: $\forall conf_{rule} \in ConflictRules(rsrc) \bullet rsrc \in ConflictingResources \wedge conf_{rule} \cap$
   $OperationSequence(rsrc) \neq \emptyset$.

   In the example case, this will occur after the edge, that is labeled $< args.encrypt >$, is taken. A conflict has been detected if the conflict rule matches.

The above process has to synchronize all conflict paths. Thus, start monitoring at the beginning of the first conflicting path. Similarly, at the end of the execution, the evaluation phase has to be performed at the correct time. To reduce the complexity of this, we could easily initialize the VM at the start of the join point. Similar, we could simply check at the end of the join point execution. However, these simplifications might impose a larger runtime performance hit.

Another option would be to verify the rules continuously. This would provide possibly earlier detection of the conflict. However, the runtime performance might also be decreased, due to the abundance of verifications.

5   Related Work

There is a lot of work on static analysis of AOP languages. Most of these limit themselves to detecting interaction. In some cases even the presence of a shared join point is considered a issue.

One approach to program verification is to utilize traditional model checking techniques. Krishnamurthi et. al. propose one such approach in [5]. The paper considers the base program and aspects separately. The author state that a set of desired properties, given a pointcut descriptor, can be verified by checking the advice in isolation, thus providing modular reasoning. The paper focuses on ensuring that the desired properties are preserved in the presence of aspects, in other words, the situation where applying aspects causes the desired properties of the base system to be invalidated. The paper only considers aspect-base conflicts and not conflicts between aspects.

In [6], Katz et. al. propose an approach to use model checking to verify aspects modularly. The authors create a generic state machine of the assumptions of an aspect. If the augmented system, the generic system machine with the aspect applied, satisfies certain desired properties, then all base systems satisfying the assumptions of the aspect will satisfy the desired properties. The proposed technique has several limitations, for example the restriction to a single aspect and pointcut designator, and thus can only detect base-aspect conflicts, and not conflicts between aspects at shared join points.

Another aspect verification approach is based on graph transformations. In [7], Staijen and Rensink model, part of, the Composition Filters behavior with graph based semantics. The result is a state space representation of the execution of the composed filter sequence at a shared join point. The paper proposes an interference detection approach based on the ordering of filter modules on this resulting state space. If the different orderings of the filter modules result in different state spaces, the program is considered to have a filter module (advice) composition conflict. This approach also detects aspect-aspect conflicts, but only detect an interaction. There is no way to state whether such an interaction desirable or undesirable.

In several papers (e.g. [8] and [9]), Südholt et. al. present a technique to detect shared join points, based on similarities in the crosscut specification of the aspects involved. If there is no conflict the aspects can be woven without modification, else the user has to specify the order in which the aspects should be composed. The approach does not consider the semantics of the advice on *inserts*, it just considers the presence of a shared join point to be an interaction.

There is also a lot of work about runtime verification of systems. However, these techniques are not immediately suitable for AOP languages, as these languages implement new constructs and can alter the base system even during runtime. This makes it harder to statically instrument or verify the base system and to know the exact composition of all elements. Nonetheless, especially for dynamic AOP approaches, providing runtime verification of advice and the composition of advice is important.

The notion of using resources and operations on these resources to model dependencies and conflicts has already been applied in many different fields in software engineering, e.g. for synchronization constraints [10] and for transaction systems[11].

6   Conclusion

The presented approach does not only provide feedback in an early stage of software development, i.e. while writing and compiling the aspect, it also provides an optimized way of checking whether certain conditional or dynamic conflicts actually occur at runtime. We only monitor those cases where it is known that a conflict could occur, but can not be completely statically determined. The declarative language of Composition Filters enables us to only verify those combinations that may lead to a conflict. It also enables us to reason about aspects without detailed knowledge of the base code, i.e. we only need to know the join points of the system, thus providing some form of isolated reasoning. Currently, only static verification has been implemented, in Compose*. However, we do plan to implement the proposed runtime extension in the near future.

This work has been partially carried out as part of the Ideals project under the responsibility of the Embedded Systems Institute. This project is partially supported by the Netherlands Ministry of Economic Affairs under the Senter program. This work is supported by European Commission grant IST-2-004349: European Network of Excellence on Aspect-Oriented Software Development (AOSD-Europe).

References

1. Durr, P., Bergmans, L., Aksit, M.: Reasoning about semantic conflicts between aspects. In: Chitchyan, R., Fabry, J., Bergmans, L., Nedos, A., Rensink, A. (eds.) Proceeding of ADI 2006 Aspect, Dependencies, and interactions Workshop, Lancaster University, pp. 10–18 (July 2006)
2. Durr, P.E.A., Bergmans, L.M.J., Aksit, M.: Reasoning about behavioral conflicts between aspects. Technical Report TR-CTIT-07-15, Enschede (February 2007)
3. Group, T.O.: IEEE: Regular expressions. The Open Group Base Specifications, IEEE Std 1003.1 (6) (2004)
4. de Roo, A.: Towards more robust advice: Message flow analysis for composition filters and its application. Master's thesis, University of Twente (March 2007)
5. Krishnamurthi, S., Fisler, K., Greenberg, M.: Verifying aspect advice modularly. In: SIGSOFT 2004/FSE-12: Proceedings of the 12th ACM SIGSOFT twelfth international symposium on Foundations of software engineering, pp. 137–146. ACM Press, New York, USA (2004)
6. Goldman, M., Katz, S.: Modular generic verification of ltl properties for aspects. In: Clifton, C., Lämmel, R., Leavens, G.T. (eds.) FOAL: Foundations Of Aspect-Oriented Languages, pp. 11–19 (March 2006)
7. Staijen, T., Rensink, A.: A graph-transformation-based semantics for analysing aspect interference. In: Workshop on Graph Computation Models, Natal, Brazil (2006)

8. Douence, R., Fradet, P.: Trace-based aspects. In: Filman, R.E., Elrad, T., Clarke, S. (eds.) Aspect-Oriented Software Development, pp. 201–217. Addison-Wesley, Boston (2005)

9. Ségura-Devillechaise, M., Menaud, J.M., Fritz, T., Loriant, N., Douence, R., Südholt, M.: An expressive aspect language for system applications with arachne. Transactions on AOSD I 1(1), 174–213 (2006)

10. Bernstein, A.J.: Program analysis for parallel processing. In: IEEE Trans. on Electronic Computers. EC-15, pp. 757–762 (1966)

11. Lynch, N.A., Merritt, M., Weihl, W.E., Fekete, A. (eds.): Atomic Transactions: In Concurrent and Distributed Systems. Morgan Kaufmann, San Francisco (1993)

Escaping with Future Variables in HALO

Charlotte Herzeel, Kris Gybels, and Pascal Costanza

Vrije Universiteit Brussel
{charlotte.herzeel|kris.gybels|pascal.costanza}@vub.ac.be

1 Introduction

HALO is a novel aspect language introducing a logic-based pointcut language which combines history-based pointcuts and "escape" conditions for interacting with the base language. This combination is difficult to support when escape conditions access context exposed by "future" join points. This paper introduces a weaving mechanism based on copying objects for resolving such pointcuts. Though this seems a memory consuming solution, it can be easily combined with HALO's analysis for reducing the join point history. Furthermore, pointcuts with escape conditions accessing future join point context, sometimes require *less* memory than pointcuts that don't, but otherwise implement the same functionality. In this paper, we illustrate this by measuring memory usage for simulations of an e-commerce application, switching between an implementation where the pointcut definitions contain escape conditions referring to future join point context, and an equivalent implementation that doesn't.

2 HALO by Example

In this section we give a brief introduction to HALO. HALO is a novel logic-based aspect language for CLOS [1], extending our previous work on logic-based AOP [2] with support for history-based aspects.

As a running example, we use an e-commerce application. This application, implemented using the Hunchentoot web application framework, was reported on in earlier work [3] and is used in the experiments in Section 4.2. For explanation, we use the simplified version of this application as shown in Figure 1. The classes Shop, User and Article model the e-shop, its customers and the sold articles respectively. A class Promotions simply maps articles to a discount rate, which can be changed using the method set-rate, and accessed with current-rate-for. The method singleton-instance is used to retrieve the Promotions class' only instance.

HALO is a logic-based pointcut language, meaning pointcuts are expressed as logic queries over logic facts giving information about join points. Two features of HALO are important for this paper. Firstly, it is history-based, meaning the pointcuts are not just about the "current" join point, but also about past join points. Secondly, HALO is not purely logic-based: it features an "escape" mechanism which allows methods to be called from the logic pointcuts. Space does not permit us to give a detailed discussion of HALO, we refer to earlier

O. Sokolsky and S. Tasiran (Eds.): RV 2007, LNCS 4839, pp. 51–62, 2007.

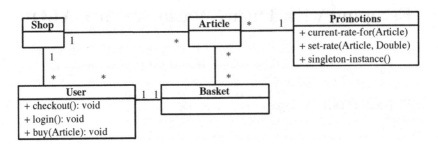

Fig. 1. Overview of the e-shop running example

work for a lengthier explanation [3] , but here we illustrate HALO by means of a few advice definitions for the running example.

Figure 2 shows an example piece of advice using the two important features mentioned above. The piece of advice expresses that logging should happen when customers buy an article for which a promotion was advertised when the customer logged in to the e-shop. In more detail, the piece of advice consists of an advice body, which simply calls the log function, and a pointcut that specifies when to execute the advice body[1].

An advice body is executed each time the conditions expressed by the pointcut are satisfied by the current join point. For this example, this means the current join point must represent a call to the method named "buy" and *before* that call, a join point representing a call to the method "login" must have occured. This "before" is expressed by means of the temporal operator `most-recent`, which is one of the three built-in temporal connectives in HALO - the others are `all-past` and `since`. Also note the `escape` condition in the pointcut. Its second argument is a piece of Lisp code that accesses the discount rate ?rate for an article ?article.

Figure 2 also depicts a sample base program, to the right. It shows a user `<kris>` logging in and purchasing a `<cd>`[2]; In addition we see that the discount rate of the `<cd>` is changed from 10 to 5 percent. When the fourth statement is

```
; advice
(at
; pointcut                                   1. (set-current-rate <promo> <cd> 0.10)
  ((gf-call buy ?user ?article)             2. (login <kris>)
   (most-recent                             3. (set-current-rate <promo> <cd> 0.05)
     (gf-call login ?user)                  4. (buy <kris> <cd>)
     (escape ?promo (singleton-instance Promotions))
     (escape ?rate (current-rate-for ?promo ?article))))
; advice body
  (log "user ~s gets a ~s % discount" ?user ?rate))
```

Fig. 2. HALO: combining temporal pointcuts with "escape"

---

[1] CLOS's and HALO's syntax are based on s-expressions: the generic function call (buy r x y) corresponds to r.buy(x,y) in Java, while the HALO logic condition (gf-call 1 ?x) corresponds to gf-call(1, X) in Prolog.

[2] The notation *<id>* is used to represent objects. E.g. `<kris>` is an instance of the class User, and `<promo>` of the class Promotions.

executed, all conditions in the pointcut are satisfied and the message "<kris> gets a 0.10 % discount" is logged. It's important to note that the discount rate will be the rate at the time <kris> logged in, not at the moment he buys the article – otherwise the `escape` condition should have been placed outside of the temporal operator. This is called *stateful* evaluation of pointcuts. This seems technically difficult, because the discount rate ?rate needs to be computed when the `login` join point occurs, but the article ?article for which to compute the discount rate is only known at the "future" `buy` join point. The remainder of the paper explains how this works in HALO in more detail.

3   The HALO Weaver

In this section we first further discuss how the join point history is actually produced and stored. We discuss the details of the HALO weaver and the specific mechanism we use for matching history-based pointcuts combined with "escape" conditions referring to "future" join point data. This mechanism is based on our own extension of the well-known Rete algorithm [4].

3.1   Weaving Schema

In aspect-oriented programming (AOP), the process that is responsible for integrating aspects and base code, is called the "weaver", and this section sketches the basic workings of the HALO weaver. The HALO weaver is an extra layer on the CLOS compiler/interpreter for processing HALO code. A schema of the weaving process is depicted in Figure 3. The black boxes represent the different weaver components, whereas the transparent boxes reflect the CLOS and HALO code respectively. The arrows depict the flow of the weaving process. As the CLOS program runs, the weaver intercepts join points, and for each of these, a representation as a logic fact is recorded (in the figure, each statement of the CLOS program is mapped to such a logic fact). Each time a logic fact is added to the fact base, the "query engine" is triggered to find *solutions* for all the pointcuts; A solution for a pointcut consists of *bindings*, mapping all variables in the pointcut to a concrete value, and they are obtained by trying to pattern match the conditions of the pointcuts to the facts in the "fact base". Next, each pointcut solution is used to replace the logic variables in the advice code associated with the pointcut. As such, the advice code can be executed and inserted in the flow of the CLOS program.

In the actual implementation of the HALO weaver, the fact base and query engine are one component. More specifically, the HALO query matching process is based on the Rete forward chaining algorithm. A full motivation for this choice is outside the scope of this paper, but we do note that due to its pre-evaluation of partial queries and caching strategies, the Rete algorithm greatly simplifies the stateful evaluation of escape conditions, and that it has been shown to be a very efficient algorithm [4]. In the next section we discuss how (an extended version of) the Rete algorithm works for matching HALO pointcuts to join point facts.

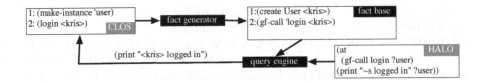

Fig. 3. HALO weaving schema

3.2   Matching Pointcuts

The Rete algorithm [4] represents queries – or pointcuts in HALO– as a network consisting of nodes with memory tables. For each condition in a pointcut, the network contains a "filter" node. For each logical connective (the logical "and", `most-recent`, `since` or `all-past`), the network contains a "join node". As an example, consider the pointcut and Rete network in Figure 4. The circle-shaped filter nodes coincide with the two conditions in the pointcut, whereas the square-shaped join node reflects the `most-recent` operator. Note that each node is associated with a " memory table".

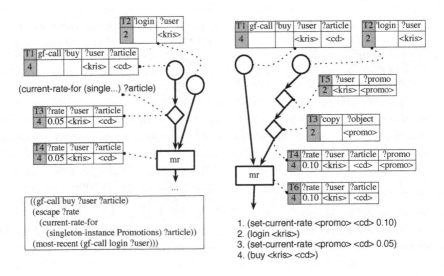

Fig. 4. Rete representation of "escape"   **Fig. 5.** Copying object state in Rete

A full explanation of the Rete networks and our extensions are beyond the scope of this paper, but using the typical graphical representation of a Rete network (cfr. Figure 4) a basic understanding of its operation can be given as: facts are inserted in the "top" of the network, the filter nodes, and these facts "trickle down" the network. When the weaver generates a fact such as (`gf-call 'login <kris>`), this is inserted in all filter nodes. A filter node for a condition such as (`gf-call 'login ?user`) checks that all the non-variable arguments of the fact and condition match. In this case, it checks that the name of the operation is `login` in both. It also binds the logical variable `?user` to the value `<kris>`. Two things then happen: an entry is made in a table, the so-called memory table of the node, to memorize this binding. The binding is also passed down to the next node in the network, a join node. Join nodes have two incoming nodes connected to them. Whenever they receive a new binding from one node, they combine these with the memorized bindings of the other node. This involves ensuring that the bindings have the same values for the same variables. If this is the case, they similarly make an entry in a memory table and pass the bindings to the next node. In our extension of Rete, the join nodes represent temporal conditions and also check these conditions before making new entries. We will not delve into further depth here, but for example a node for a `most-recent` operator will check that only the combination using the most recently created matching bindings is made.

We focus in this paper on the "escape" feature of HALO, and our experiments with a number of different implementations of this feature. This is specifically related to allowing the use of "future" variables in `escape` conditions. The problem is that an `escape` condition such as (`escape ?rate (current-promotion-for ?promo ?article)`) implies invoking the Lisp function `current-promotion-for`. For this to be possible, all of the logic variables used in the condition should have a value, but there can be conflicts between the availability of these values and the right time to evaluate the Lisp function. The different implementations define different variations of the HALO language and/or the weaver's operation.

No future variables. This is the simplest HALO variation. In this version an `escape` condition that is inside a temporal operator is limited to using the following variables: variables used in logic conditions or as the result variable of other escape conditions, but only if these conditions are also inside the temporal operator (including any conditions in a nested temporal operator). This restriction disallows "future" variables: variables that are given values only by conditions outside the temporal operator. The semantics of `escape` conditions inside a temporal operator is that the Lisp function they invoke is invoked at the moment the logic conditions inside the same operator are matched. In the Rete networks for pointcut matching, an `escape` condition is therefore represented as a node taking as input one of the nodes representing the logic conditions, and is connected to the join node representing the temporal operator. In Figure 4, the diamond-shaped node represents the escape condition in the pointcut in the same figure.

Future variables, argument copying. To increase the expressive power of HALO, we are investigating how the use of future variables in `escape` conditions can be allowed. The conflict this creates is that invocation of the Lisp function has to be postponed until the future variables are given a value. But at the same time, if the values of the other variables are objects, the state of these objects may be changed by the time the future variable is given a value. The result of the Lisp function may then not be the same as the case where it is invoked before these changes are made. Consider the pointcuts in Figure 4 and Figure 2: both capture an invocation of buy after an invocation of login and determine the discount rate of the bought article. But in the first case, this should be the rate at the time the buy invocation happens, and in the other at the time the login invocation happens. These can be different, as the rate can be changed between these invocations (using set-rate as explained in Section 2). In Figure 2, the ?article variable is a future variable for the escape condition, because it will only be given a value outside the most-recent operator. The escape can only be evaluated when the buy happens, but of course, it should still return the rate at the time of login. To solve this, this variation of HALO takes copies of the arguments that will be passed to the Lisp function. In the example of Figure 2, the value of ?promo will be copied when the login happens, the escape condition is evaluated when the buy happens, but with the copied state of the Promotions object and will thus return the right rate. Figure 5 displays the Rete network for the pointcut in Figure 2. In order to keep track of the object copies, the escape node is extended with an extra memory table.

Future variables, state change copying. Argument copying only works when the invoked Lisp function only depends on its arguments, and not on global variables. A further variation of HALO takes this into account with a more extensive copying strategy. In this strategy, the state changes of *all* objects are intercepted, by making a copy of an object whenever the object is changed. Next the CLOS slot access protocol is extended to retrieve this copy whenever the object's field is read for evaluating the escape condition.

4 Optimizing Memory Usage in HALO

An apparent drawback of history-based AOP is exactly the need to store the history. A straightforward implementation of the weaver scheme in Figure 3 would mean a quickly growing history needs to be kept forever. Several techniques can be used to optimize this history. In this section, we first classify these techniques according to the kind of history information they remove. We first further detail how HALO deals with the last kind of information, and then explain the impact of the escape extension.

Irrelevant facts. Some join point facts are not relevant to generate in the first place, because they will simply never be used to match pointcut definitions. For example, if there is only a pointcut capturing calls of the "buy" function and not of the "login" function, there is no need to generate join point facts for calls to the "login" function at all. This can be handled with static optimisation techniques, known as *shadow weaving* [5]. This is not currently done in HALO, but these techniques are orthogonal to those needed for the next two categories.

Facts relevant for one time step only. Some information is only relevant for one step in the program execution. A pointcut that captures calls to "buy" if there was a past call to "login" with matching variables, only requires the weaver to store a history of "login" calls, but not of "buy" calls. In HALO, this is handled by the same technique as for the next category.

Facts that become irrelevant. The last kind of information is the one more attention is paid to in HALO research. This is information that becomes irrelevant *after a while*. Suppose we have a pointcut that captures calls to "buy" with a certain user and article as argument, and which also gets the discount rate of that article at the *most recent* call to "login" for the same user. In this case, a history of "login" calls needs to be kept. But since only the most recent call for a particular user is accessed by the pointcut, parts of this history can be removed as the same user logs in again. This is handled in HALO by "memory table garbage collection" of the Rete nodes. The garbage collection is actually performed as part of the functionality of the nodes, there is not a separate algorithm like in memory garbage collection that intervenes once in a while. Though it can be turned on and off, and for explanative purposes we consider it separately from an explanation of node functionality.

4.1   Escape Nodes in Memory Table Garbage Collection

A full explanation of the memory table garbage collection is beyond the scope of this paper, but it can be illustrated with an example: consider the pointcut and Rete in Figure 6. The black tables labelled "LT", next to the memory tables, display the "life time" of memory table entries. The life time of a memory table entry consists of the time at which an entry was created and the time at which the entry can be removed. An entry can be removed as soon as it cannot be used anymore to derive new conclusions. The decision to remove a memory table entry depends on whether the node the entry belongs to is the input of a most-recent or all-past temporal join node. For example, the filter node labelled 1 in Figure 6 is not the right input of one of these types of temporal join nodes. This means that entries in this node will never be accessed to derive new conclusions after they're first inserted. The same is true for the nodes labelled 4, 5 and 6. As such, the life time of the entries residing at these nodes is constrained to one time step in Figure 6. If however the entry resides in a node that is the right input of a temporal join node, then it can only be removed if it is "replaced" by a new entry. For example, entries in the right input of most-recent join nodes can be removed when new entries with the same values for the memory table variables are added. In fact, only the values for the variables that are in common with the left input memory table need to be the same. This is because when an entry is added to the left input's memory table, the join node will combine it with the most recent matching entry in the right input node. The match requires that the values for the variables in common between the two input nodes are the same. Thus, if there is an older entry in the right memory table that also matches with the new entry in the left, it will still not produce a combination. Thus, such entries can be removed. E.g. in Figure 6, when the second entry in the node labeled 2 is added, the first entry is deleted, since it hase the same value <kris> for ?user.

The above scheme was developed for the version of HALO with escape conditions that cannot refer to future variables. But this extension did not require

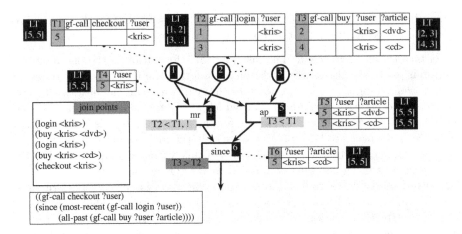

Fig. 6. Lifetime of memory table entries when garbage collected

a fundamental change to the above scheme. For `escape` nodes whose condition uses a future variable, a table needs to be kept with copies of the values of the bindings that the node takes as input, for later evaluation. The key point is how-ever that these entries are completely linked to the entries of the `escape` node's input. Therefore, the entry in the `escape` node's memory can be removed when the parent entry in its input node is removed.

4.2 Benchmarks

We have evaluated the effect of the "escape" extension on memory usage using a few simulations. These were run on the e-commerce application implemented on top of the Hunchentoot web application framework [3]. The pointcuts used in this application can be written in different ways, with or without the use of future variables in `escape` conditions. To illustrate, consider for example the two pointcuts below. They both implement the same functionality, namely comput-ing the discount rate active at login for an article bought at a later time. The first version however does not make use of a future variable. Instead, it is ensured that the `?article` variable already gets a value when the `buy` happens, by using an `all-past` to get all possible articles. In contrast, in the second pointcut in the code listing, the variable `?article` is a future variable. The Rete networks for matching both pointcuts are depicted in Figure 8.

```
((gf-call buy ?user ?article)
 (most-recent
   (gf-call login ?user)
   (escape ?promo (singleton-instance Promotions))
   (all-past (create article ?article))
   (escape ?rate (current-rate-for ?promo ?article))))

((gf-call buy ?user ?article)
 (most-recent
   (gf-call login ?user)
   (escape ?promo (singleton-instance Promotions))
   (escape ?rate (current-rate-for ?promo ?article))))
```

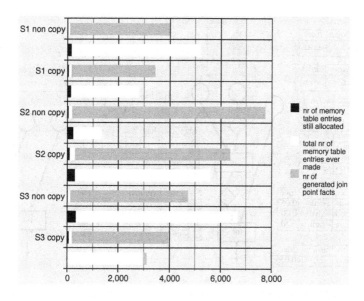

Fig. 7. Benchmarks for the memory table garbage collection

Each simulation defines a different number of articles, customers etc. and subsequently lets the customers randomly login, checkout their basket etc. for a number of times. Figure 7 depicts the total number of memory table entries made, and how many were already removed at the point the simulation stopped. In total, three different scripts were selected and run for two sets of aspects (see the labels $S1 - S3$ denoting the different scripts and (non)$copy$ denoting a different set of aspects). Both sets of aspects implement the same functionality, but in one version the aspects are rewritten to make use of the extended version of "escape", referring to "future" join point data.

Figure 8 also displays a sample base program and the content of the memory tables obtained after executing this program. As is to be expected, the network for the first pointcut contains many more entries: each time a login occurs, the promotion rate for *all* articles is computed and cached. However in the second network, at each login, a copy of the <promo> object is cached. Note that the second network keeps track of much less memory table entries than the first. A surprising conclusion is therefore that if the memory cost for a copy of the Promotions object is lower than the memory cost for keeping the many entries in the first nework, then the escape condition accessing future join point data is woven *less* costly. We found this to be actually the case in our current shop application, as the Promotions object is implemented as a hash table mapping articles to discount rates. A copy of this table takes up less memory space than a Rete memory table holding the combinations of ?article, ?user, ?promo and ?rate as is the case for the highlighted node in Figure 8. Of course, this does not mean that this is a general conclusion about the Rete networks, as this depends on the specific application and its implementation.

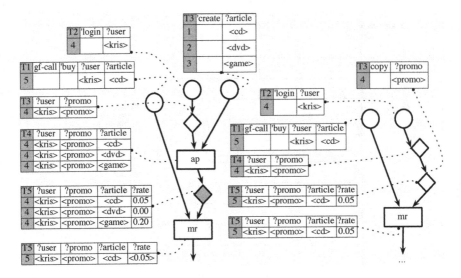

Fig. 8. Rete for pointcut avoiding the use of future variables (left) and Rete for pointcut using future variable "?article" (right)

Due to the fact that the HALO query engine records partial solutions to pointcuts, we need to take into account that additional memory is required for recording join point facts. However Figure 7 shows that the entries in the memory tables of join nodes, which represent the latter partial solutions, are also greatly reduced by the memory table garbage collection process (see second block for each simulation, where black is used to denote the remaining number of entries). Overall this means that for each join point fact that was or is memorized, the Rete network (temporarily) keeps track of partial solutions making use of it. However this is an improvement over recording all join point facts forever.

5   Related Work

Alpha [6] is a Prolog-based aspect language (for a Java-like language) for expressing pointcuts over the join point history. The language provides a built-in set of temporal relations for comparing time stamps of join points, but the programmer can define new ones. Interaction with the base language is allowed, but only for the "current" join point. Alpha's weaver performs a static analysis of source code to determine whether join point facts are necessary to generate for matching pointcuts, and at what time they can be removed from the join point history. Currently, this technique only removes join point facts when these are just used for matching pointcuts about the "current" join point. Other facts are kept indefinitely. Hence Alpha falls into the second category from Section 3.2.

Tracematches [7] is an AspectJ extension in which program traces can be formulated as regular expressions over "symbols". These symbols are AspectJ pointcuts containing "free variables", referring to join point context. The base level can be accessed through the "let" construct, but currently it is only allowed to refer to join point context exposed by its enclosing symbol. The Tracematches weaver does shadow weaving and performs a three staged static analysis to reduce the set of join point shadows [7]. As such, this falls in the first category defined in Section 3.2. Shadow weaving is orthogonal to the dynamic analysis technique in HALO, and we plan to extend the HALO weaver with shadow weaving in the near future.

6 Conclusions and Future Work

In this paper we've given an initial discussion of the use of "future" variables in `escape` conditions in the logic pointcut language HALO, and the relation to HALO's implementation using Rete networks, including how these fit into the memory table garbage collection scheme we previously developed for HALO without this feature. Supporting the feature involves copying objects to postpone the evaluation of these `escape` conditions. In the last part of the paper we presented benchmarks for the memory table garbage collection, showing the impact of the "escape" extension. Surprisingly, pointcuts written by means of this extension sometimes require less memory than their equivalents that don't. Future work consists of investigating the question of whether the Rete networks can be designed so that these differences can be removed. For example, by postponing computation of memory table combinations. There's also a need to further study the different ways in which pointcuts with a same behavior can be implemented in HALO, and the impact on memory usage.

Acknowledgements

This work was supported in part by the AOSD-Europe Network of Excellence, European Union grant no. FP6-2003-IST-2-004349. Charlotte Herzeel is funded by a doctoral scholarship of the Institute for the Promotion of Innovation through Science and Technology in Flanders (IWT-Vlaanderen), Belgium. Pascal Costanza is funded by the Institute for the Promotion of Innovation through Science and Technology in Flanders (IWT-Vlaanderen).

References

1. Bobrow, D., DeMichiel, L., Gabriel, R., Keene, S., Kiczales, G., Moon, D.: Common lisp object system specification. Lisp and Symbolic Computation 1(3-4), 245–394 (1989)
2. Gybels, K., Brichau, J.: Arranging language features for more robust pattern-based crosscuts. In: Proceedings of the Second International Conference on Aspect-Oriented Software Development (2003)
3. Herzeel, C., Gybels, K., Costanza, P.: Modularizing crosscuts in an e-commerce application in lisp using halo. In: proceedings of the International Lisp Conference (ILC) (2007)

4. Forgy, C.L.: Rete: A fast algorithm for the many pattern/many object pattern match problem. Artificial Intelligence 19(1), 17–37 (1982)
5. Masuhara, H., Kiczales, G., Dutchyn, C.: A compilation and optimization model for aspect-oriented programs. In: Hedin, G. (ed.) CC 2003 and ETAPS 2003. LNCS, vol. 2622, Springer, Heidelberg (2003)
6. Ostermann, K., Mezini, M., Bockisch, C.: Expressive pointcuts for increased modularity. In: European Conference on Object-Oriented Programming (2005)
7. Bodden, E., Hendren, L., Lhoták, O.: A staged static program analysis to improve the performance of runtime monitoring. Technical report, ABC Group (2007)

Runtime Verification of Interactions: From MSCs to Aspects

Ingolf H. Krüger[1], Michael Meisinger[2], and Massimiliano Menarini[1]

[1] Computer Science and Engineering Department
University of California, San Diego
La Jolla, CA 92093-0404, USA
{ikrueger,mmenarini}@ucsd.edu
[2] Institut für Informatik
Technische Universität München
Boltzmannstr. 3, 85748 Garching, Germany
meisinge@in.tum.de

Abstract. Runtime verification is one systematic strategy for analytical quality assurance of complex distributed systems. Model-based development approaches are promising in this context because they provide models of manageable size and complexity describing the systems under development, enabling systematic engineering processes for all development phases on various levels of detail. For runtime verification, executing implementations are monitored continuously for correctness against the specification. This requires the insertion of monitors into the software under test to gather information on system states and their evolution. In this paper we describe how we use aspect-oriented development techniques to enhance existing code with runtime monitors checking the interaction behavior of applications against their specifications. We use Message Sequence Charts (MSCs) to specify the interaction behavior of distributed systems and as basis for automatic runtime monitor generation. This uniquely ties interaction interface specifications with the monitoring infrastructure for their realization. We explain the monitor generation procedure and tool set using a case study from the embedded automotive systems domain, the Central Locking System (CLS).

1 Introduction

Designing complex distributed systems is a difficult task. They appear in application domains such as avionics and automotive control as embedded systems, as well as in telecommunications and business information systems. Sensor networks and mobile applications are growing fields where we find complex distributed systems. A property common across different applications is that distribution and complex interactions between system components are key enablers of their success. Distribution enables the creation of more modular and decentralized system architectures, contributing, for instance, to fault tolerance, component reuse, system robustness and maintainability.

O. Sokolsky and S. Tasiran (Eds.): RV 2007, LNCS 4839, pp. 63–74, 2007.

However, distributed systems can become highly complex and challenging to develop. The number of states and conditions increase exponentially with the number of distributed components. Distribution also causes significant logistics and maintenance problems. Components can be developed, maintained, extended and replaced independently, potentially harming the overall system integrity and consistency.

1.1 Problem Definition

Model-based development is a promising approach addressing the difficulties and complexities in system development; it covers all phases from requirements analysis to system execution [3]. Models provide views of systems and their designs serving specific purposes at different phases of the development process. For verification purposes, models provide the specification of a system that an implementation has to comply with.

Runtime monitoring is a verification strategy (see [6,2,1]) based on the insertion of monitors into runnable software. These monitors, for instance, gather information on system states and their change, and compare it against the specification. This type of runtime verification requires addressing two main problems. First, relating the concrete state of the running system to the abstract one in the model. Second, instrumenting the running program with code to record the state of the system and compare it to the expected run.

A simple runtime monitoring approach is to directly implement the monitors by changing the software source code. The very nature of such monitors, however, makes such modifications repetitive and scattered across the entire code base. Aspect-oriented languages [9,8] were introduced particularly to manage repetitive code changes crosscutting the code. They enable compact representation of such code modifications. Thus, using aspects to specify such monitors seams a promising avenue. Fig. 1 illustrates this concept.

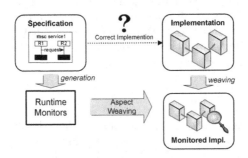

Fig. 1. Runtime Monitoring Implementations Against Specification

In this paper, we focus on distributed, loosely coupled systems, where system functions typically emerge from interactions between distributed components. Runtime verification then needs to check for compliance of the monitored component interactions with the expected communication patterns. We have developed a specification technique for distributed systems based on Message Sequence Charts (MSC) [7] capturing interaction patterns and causal communication relationships between entities. Our models are based on a thorough formal foundation (see [10,4]) and enable consistent refinement and refactoring. We make use of these message sequence models for verification and construction purposes. We apply our state machine synthesis algorithm to obtain state machines representing the full communication behavior of individual components of the system. We have applied this strategy, for instance, to test component timing conformance by runtime monitoring [1], and for efficient evaluation of multiple architecture candidates through generation of executable prototypes [13,12].

1.2   Contribution and Outline

Our models capture the communication patterns between nodes in distributed systems; this leads to a natural interface for runtime monitors. In fact, the component state of our specification is determined only by the observed communication. Therefore, we only need to identify and record all messages exchanged between nodes and can ignore the exact internal state of each component. This enables us to leverage aspects for embedding model-generated runtime monitors into existing implementations at their communication interfaces, independent of any concrete data structure used in the code to capture the node state.

In this paper, we present a combination of our interaction specification approach and aspect-oriented technologies for the purpose of efficient generation of runtime monitors. This significantly increases the efficiency of system verification efforts and keeps distributed system implementations uncluttered and easily modifiable. Our approach thus helps to develop more dependable and maintainable distributed systems. To support the approach presented we have developed a new tool and integrated it with our service-oriented toolchain [14]. We use our exiting tools to draw interactions as MSCs and generate state machines from them. The new tool adds the capability of generating monitors encoded as aspects in AspectJ.

There are several aspect-oriented languages that share similar characteristics regarding how code is modified by aspects. They extend different languages such as for example C or Java. We chose to use AspectJ [8], a Java based language, for its portability and for the ability to cater to different domains. However, the approach presented in this paper can be applied to any aspect-oriented language.

In Sect. 2, we show how we model the interactions of our running example, the automotive Central Locking System, using MSCs. In Sect. 3, we present procedures and tools that enable us to automatically generate runtime monitors from the specification, as illustrated in Fig. 1. We explain how we leverage AspectJ to weave these monitors into existing distributed Java implementations, supporting multiple different implementation styles. In Sect. 4, we report on experiences applying our approach and accompanying tools; we also provide a brief discussion. Sect. 5 shows related work and Sect. 6 summarizes and provides an outlook.

2   Specification of the CLS Interactions

We need specifications of system interactions for the verification of implementations. In this section, we show how we model the reactive behavior of the Central Locking System (CLS) as interaction patterns that will later serve as starting point for our runtime monitor generation procedure. The CLS is a well-studied and documented example of one common automotive vehicle subsystem. For reasons of brevity, we present a simplified and abstract adaptation of the CLS. In this paper, we focus on the CLS functions for locking and unlocking vehicle doors triggered by a wireless entry device; this involves user identification, signaling by flashing external lights, and user preset loading for on-board multimedia devices.

The main interacting entities – we call them roles – of the CLS are remote entry key fob (KF), controller (CONTROL), lock manager (LM), security module (SM), lighting system (LS), and database (DB) with driver presets. These logical entities communicate locally or over the network to provide the above-mentioned functions. Fig. 2 shows roles and their communication links.

We specify the interaction behavior of the selected CLS functions using a notation based on Message Sequence Charts (MSC) [7,10,17]. MSCs define sequences of *messages* as arrows between the interacting *role* vertical axes. Fig. 3 shows the specification of two interaction patterns, which are part of the "Vehicle Unlocking" function.

The MSC syntax we use should be fairly self-explanatory, especially to readers familiar with UML2 [17]. In particular, we support labeled boxes in our MSCs indicating alternatives and conditional repetitions (as bounded and unbounded loops). Labeled rectangles *on* an axis indicate actions, such as local computations; diamond-shaped boxes on an axis indicate state labels. We use high-level MSCs (HMSCs) for the purpose of specifying flows of interactions, such as sequences of, alternatives between and repetitions of interactions, in two-dimensional graphs with MSC references as graph nodes.

The CLS "Vehicle Unlocking" function requires communication through message exchange between the key fob and the controller, which, in turn, communicates with the lock manager for physical door unlocking, the lighting system for flashing the lights, and the security module to validate the driver id. We chose to

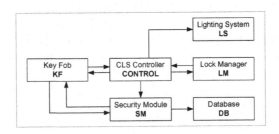

Fig. 2. Logical CLS Entities (Roles) with Communication Links

model this function as two separate interaction patterns UNLK-1 and UNLK-2 to show an application of our "join" composition, which uses common messages for synchronization.

A number of extensions to the standard MSCs warrant explanation [13,10]. First, we take each axis to represent a *role* rather than a class, object, or component. The mapping from roles to components is a design step in our approach and is described in [13]. This allows us to model our systems on a higher level of abstraction independent of any deployment configurations. Furthermore, our MSC dialect provides an extended set of operators that help us make specifications smaller and more precise. Examples are operators for specifying preemptions, liveness properties and synchronized composition. We use the *join* operator [10] extensively for composing *overlapping* interactions, such as the two unlocking interactions presented in Fig. 3; this operator *synchronizes* otherwise fully interleaved interactions on their shared messages. We refer the reader to [13,10] for more details about our specification technique and formal semantics definitions.

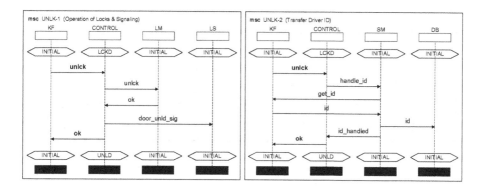

Fig. 3. CLS Function "Vehicle Unlocking" Specification with two MSCs

Our MSC-based models provide complete system interaction specifications. We interpret the MSC specifications – composed and arranged by HMSCs – *universally* [10]. This means that our MSCs specify the full set of permitted and required behaviors, instead of documenting only exemplary runs. Such complete interaction behavior specifications are the starting point for further system development, including deployment on selected target architectures. Furthermore, we can simulate the model, verify and model-check it, and generate code for prototypical implementations. Often, however, we want to be able to relax the *universal* interpretation of our models enabling verification of partial specifications. We achieve this by excluding messages not present in the specification from the verification, enabling us to verify implementations that use a larger set of messages than the ones captured in the MSCs. A system is deemed correct as long as the specified messages follow the defined protocol.

3   Generation of Aspect-Oriented Runtime Monitors

Fig. 4 outlines the process and tool-chain for runtime monitoring. It starts with the availability of an interaction specification; we use our modeling tool *M2Code* [1] to specify systems using MSCs. In this work, we are creating runtime monitors for existing distributed applications written in Java, in order to verify them against the interaction specifications. Using Java as implementation language gives us the ability to use AspectJ [8], a Java based aspect-oriented language, to instrument programs with the monitors. To embed generated runtime monitors within such implementations, we have to identify the communication interfaces of the communicating components in the code. The interfaces should match the definitions given in the specification.

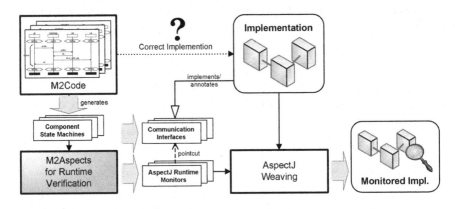

Fig. 4. Runtime Monitor Generation and Weaving into Implementation

Aspect-oriented languages insert and run code at particular points in the program called join-points [8]. These languages extend normal programming languages and allow the definition of a set of join-points (called pointcuts). Examples of pointcuts match calls to methods with a particular name or from a particular class, and access to properties. To identify the communication interface of the implementations' components we need to establish some relation between method calls and messages sent/received. To this end, we have experimented with different approaches. The approaches that provide most flexibility are (1) using interfaces to identify methods that send and receive messages, and (2) using Java annotations to identify these methods.

First, we analyze how to use Java interfaces to identify suitable join-points for capturing the communication interface. We have to arrange the code such that each role of the interaction model is implemented by one or more distinct classes in the program. Message sending and receiving is then performed by calling specific methods of such a class. When defining pointcuts, we need to have an interface for each role. A class that performs the communication of such a role implements the interface. For instance, based on the interactions it engages in in Fig. 3, the interface we define for the keyfob role in our CLS case study is:

```
public interface IRKF {
  public void ok(IRole src);
  public void get_id(IRole src); }
```

Using this implementation strategy enables defining suitable pointcuts in AspectJ. Pointcuts identify communication between two roles by identifying methods calls performed by a class playing one role to a method representing a message. Examine, for example, the following pointcut:

```
pointcut pcCONTROL_ok_KF():
  call(void IRKF.ok(IROLE)) && this(CLS.roles.IRCONTROL)
                           && target(CLS.roles.IRKF);
```

It defines a pointcut that identifies when the role CONTROL sends the message *ok* to the role KF. The method name matches the message name. The class that calls the method must implement the sending role interface (IRCONTROL for the CONTROL role) and the class implementing the receiving role must implement the receiving role interface (IRKF).

The second approach uses Java annotations to establish suitable pointcuts in the code to identify the communication interface. Annotations were introduced in Java version 5 to enable adding arbitrary meta-information to the code. With annotations we can add information about roles played by classes and messages transported by methods to the code. This eliminates the need to follow special naming conventions and class/interface hierarchies. An annotation example is:

```
@Role("KF")public class CKeyFob {
  @Message("get_id") public void get_id(IRole s){ //...
```

A pointcut for such a programming style to identify the code, where role CONTROL sends *ok* to role KF, is:

```
pointcut CONTROLokKF(Message m,Role s,Role d):
  execution(* * (*)) && @this(d) && @annotation(m) &&
  cflowbelow(call(* * (*)) && @this(s)) &&
  if(m.value()=="ok") && if(s.value()=="CONTROL") && if(d.value()=="KF");
```

This pointcut, like the previous one, also identifies when the role CONTROL sends the message *ok* to the role KF. This definition style for the communication interface is more flexible at the cost of a more complex definition of the pointcut. However, the ability to explicitly insert the interface definition into the code, without the need to encode it using particular naming conventions, is beneficial, in our opinion, independently from its usage in runtime verification. Therefore, we recommend to define the roles in the code using this style. Note that in the approach we present here the user only writes the annotation whereas the pointcut is generated automatically.

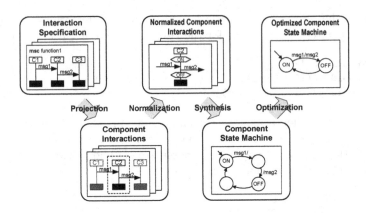

Fig. 5. Component State Machine Generation Process from MSCs

Now that we have established the communication interface and the means to instrument the program, we need to create the code that monitors the program at runtime and verifies its compliance to the specification. To this end we generate monitors (one per role) that contain the implementation of a state machine defining the acceptable communication interface for the role. The generation of such automata is based on our synthesis algorithm [11] to transform MSCs into state machines. We briefly outline the main steps of this transformation here; we refer the reader to [11] for a complete treatment of the subject. Fig. 5 depicts the five steps of our algorithm.

The algorithm takes an *interaction specification* as input in form of a set of MSCs and HMSCs, as described in Sect. 2. These MSCs need to be consistent and *causal* to yield reasonable results. A causal MSC imposes a restriction on the order of messages exchanged such that the next send/receive action can be locally determined by each role. This restriction avoids the well-known "non-local choice" phenomenon of generic MSC specifications [15]. Component state markers, hexagonal labels depicted in Fig. 3, help to specify a seamless flow of interactions also in models of larger size. As explained above, we interpret the set of MSCs universally by applying a *closed world assumption* when executing our algorithm. We apply our algorithm for each role in the specification, thus generating the same number of state machines as there are roles in the specification. The *projection* operation restricts the set of messages considered; only messages sent or received by a single role are used to create its state machine. Therefore, by *projection*, we eliminate all interactions not relevant for any given component. Subsequently we *normalize* the resulting component-specific interactions. Normalization, for instance, adds missing start and end state markers. The resulting normalized interactions are the input for component state machine *synthesis*. We translate each state label and guard appearing in any of the interactions into corresponding automaton states. We identify the MSCs as transition paths and convert all message send/receive events into respective transitions between added intermediate states. The synthesis algorithm works fully automatic for *causal*

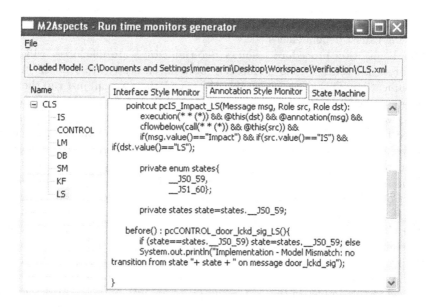

Fig. 6. M2Aspects Screenshot – Generation of AspectJ Runtime Monitors

MSCs and can handle choice, repetition, and concurrency/interleaving [10]. Finally, we apply *optimization* algorithms to the resulting state machine. We have implemented this algorithm in our M2Code tool.

Our algorithm transforms MSCs to state machines without the need for other intermediate frameworks such as *JavaMOP* or *tracematches*. This gives us maximum freedom in defining the exact semantics of our MSC dialect and allows us to ensure that the generated code respects it. To generate the AspectJ code, we use the tool *M2Aspects - Run time monitor generator*, depicted in Fig. 6. It takes the state machines generated by M2Code as input and generates all necessary AspectJ files. In particular, the figure shows an example of advice that implements a transition of the state machine that represents the monitor for the LS role.

The generated monitors observe all messages sent and received by each role. This is done using advice run when the pointcuts that identify the messages (defined in one of the two styles described earlier) are encountered. The state machine implemented in the monitor takes the transition corresponding to the message identified. If, from the current state in the monitor, there is no transition matching the observed communication, an error is flagged and the verification fails.

4   Evaluation and Discussion

The current translation of our interaction specifications generates state machines with guarded transitions. Each transition is marked with a message name and a message direction (send/receive). This allows us to detect duplicated and out-of-order messages. It is, however, impossible to use this approach to detect missing messages; we would need to extend the translation to support timeouts besides capturing causal dependencies.

Our translation procedure assumes deterministic state machines, which enable direct inference of the monitoring automaton states from observing the communication. This greatly simplifies the translation: we can just run the state machine in parallel with the implementation. With non-deterministic state machines, we would need to track sets of possible current states and examine all enabled transitions for a match, complicating the runtime monitor significantly. However, we are observing message traces, and the language of the traces specified in our MSC notation is regular. Because it is always possible to find a deterministic state machine that recognizes a given regular language, we can restrict ourselves to generating monitors from deterministic state machines.

We have applied our runtime monitoring procedure to a Java implementation of the CLS specification of Sect. 2. Although the implementation was simple and straightforward, we were able to detect several interaction related errors violating the specification, for instance incorrect message orderings and incorrect causal relations between method calls. We were able to apply runtime monitoring iteratively while implementing – an example of an automatic test first strategy; the resulting error messages pointed us to defects in the code, which we could fix subsequently. The error trace in our implementation logs the sequence of messages detected from the monitor. In the future we plan to map those traces back to the MSC that was not satisfied by the run. At no point was the insertion of the runtime monitors intrusive or obstructing the implementation. We see the non-intrusiveness as one particular strength of our approach. Implementations need only slight modifications to match one of the supported styles. Interaction properties can be specified easily and intuitively using our graphical modeling tool, M2Code. The automatic runtime monitor generation facility and the aspect weaving with the implementation work efficiently and smoothly.

Our case study was too simple to conduct extensive performance evaluation analysis. However, given that we use AspectJ to inject simple transitions in a state machine and that our pointcuts only select classes and method signatures (or annotations on classes and methods), we do not expect performance issues also in larger systems.

5   Related Work

In our approach, we separate a system architecture into logical and implementation models. The logical model as described in this paper contains the interaction specifications of system functions. The implementation model contains the target component architecture. Thus, our approach is related to Model-Driven Architecture (MDA) [16] and architecture-centric software development (ACD) [17], in particular in using synthesis algorithms to obtain state machines for our monitors. In contrast to MDA and ACD, however, we consider system functions (services) and their defining interaction patterns as first-class modeling elements of *both* the abstract and the concrete models. Furthermore, we see the implementation model as a strict refinement of the logical model and require consistency of the mapping. Our models make use of MSCs as notation and are independent from any programming language constructs.

We see scenarios as aspects in the sense of AOP [9] at the modeling level, by focusing on inter-component interaction patterns. In Aspect-Oriented Modeling [5], the crosscutting concerns are captured as *design* aspects, while our approach models these concerns as scenarios.

Runtime verification approaches differ in the techniques they apply to specify verified properties. Havelund et al. [6] categorize different runtime verification strategies and give an overview of existing approaches. Our approach is a *Specification-Based Runtime Verification* and fits their *temporal assertions* category for monitoring approaches. In particular, our specification allows both location quantification (methods calls) and temporal quantification (sequence of messages captured by the generated automata). The benefit of our technique is that it allows us to distribute the verification of complex interactions on separate monitors localized in each role class.

6   Summary and Outlook

In this paper we have combined our model-based approach for distributed system design focusing on interactions and logical architectures, with aspect-oriented implementation technologies for the purpose of runtime verification of executable systems against the specification. Interaction patterns specify the required behavior of the implementation and are blueprints for the generation of runtime monitors. To combine monitors with existing implementations, we use AspectJ and its aspect weaver. Implementations must fulfill one of two possible communication styles, so that the aspect weaver can directly insert the monitors into the implementation.

More work is needed to have a complete and general translation to aspects implemented in the M2Aspects tool. Moreover, experiments are currently in progress to establish the practicality and usability of this approach in larger applications. Finally, we are investigating the integration of runtime verification, based on the outlined technique, with a full service oriented development process for fail safe systems. We expect this integration to allow us to specify and integrate failure management code into existing systems, to increase the reliability of distributed systems without the risks introduced by substantial refactoring.

Acknowledgments

Our work was partially supported by NSF grant CCF-0702791. Financial support came also from the UC Discovery Grant and the Industry-University Cooperative Research Program, as well as from the California Institute for Telecommunications and Information Technology (Calit2). Further funds were provided by the Deutsche Forschungsgemeinschaft (DFG) through the project *InServe*.

References

1. Ahluwalia, J., Krüger, I., Meisinger, M., Phillips, W.: Model-Based Run-Time Monitoring of End-to-End Deadlines. In: EMSOFT. Proceedings of the Conference on Embedded Systems Software (2005)
2. Barringer, H., Finkbeiner, B., Gurevich, Y., Sipma, H. (eds.): RV'2005. Proceedings of the Fifth International Workshop on Runtime Verification ENTCS 144, Edinburgh, Scotland. Elsevier, Amsterdam, UK (2005)
3. Broy, M.: The Impact of Models in Software Development. In: Hutter, D., Stephan, W. (eds.) Mechanizing Mathematical Reasoning. LNCS (LNAI), vol. 2605, pp. 396–406. Springer, Heidelberg (2005)
4. Broy, M., Krüger, I., Meisinger, M.: A Formal Model of Services. ACM Transactions on Software Engineering and Methodology (TOSEM) 16(1) (2007)
5. France, R., Georg, G., Ray, I.: Supporting Multi-Dimensional Separation of Design Concerns. In: The 3rd AOSD Modeling With UML Workshop (2003)
6. Havelund, K., Goldberg, A.: Verify Your Runs. In: Proceedings of the Grand Verification Challenge Workshop Verified Software: Theories, Tools, Experiments, Zurich, Switzerland (2005)
7. ITU-TS. Recommendation Z.120: Message Sequence Chart (MSC). Geneva (1996)
8. Kiczales, G., Hilsdale, E., Hugunin, J., Kersten, M., Palm, J., Griswold, W.G.: An overview of AspectJ. In: Knudsen, J.L. (ed.) ECOOP 2001. LNCS, vol. 2072, pp. 327–353. Springer, Heidelberg (2001)
9. Kiczales, G., Lamping, J., Mendhekar, A., Maeda, C., Lopes, C., Loingtier, J.-M., Irwin, J.: Aspect Oriented Programming. Technical report, Xerox Corp (1997)
10. Krüger, I.: Distributed System Design with Message Sequence Charts. PhD thesis, Technische Universität München (2000)
11. Krüger, I., Grosu, R., Scholz, P., Broy, M.: From MSCs to Statecharts. In: Rammig, F.J. (ed.) Distributed and Parallel Embedded Systems, pp. 61–71. Kluwer Academic Publishers, Dordrecht (1999)
12. Krüger, I., Lee, G., Meisinger, M.: Automating Software Architecture Exploration with M2Aspects. In: SCESM. Proceedings of the ICSE 2006 Workshop on Scenarios and State Machines (2006)
13. Krüger, I., Mathew, R., Meisinger, M.: Efficient Exploration of Service-Oriented Architectures using Aspects. In: ICSE. Proceedings of the 28th International Conference on Software Engineering (2006)
14. Krüger, I.H., Ahluwalia, J., Gupta, D., Mathew, R., Moorthy, P., Phillips, W., Rittmann, S.: Towards a Process and Tool-Chain for Service-Oriented Automotive Software Engineering. In: SEAS. Proceedings of the ICSE 2004 Workshop on Software Engineering for Automotive Systems (2004)
15. Leue, S.: Methods and Semantics for Telecommunications Systems Engineering. PhD thesis, University of Berne, Switzerland (1994)
16. OMG (Object Management Group). Model Driven Architecture (MDA). MDA Guide 1.0.1, omg/03-06-01 (2003), http://www.omg.org/mda
17. OMG (Object Management Group). UML, Version 2.0. OMG Specification formal/05-07-04 (superstructure) and formal/05-07-05 (infrastructure) (2005)

Towards a Tool for Generating Aspects from MEDL and PEDL Specifications for Runtime Verification

Omar Ochoa, Irbis Gallegos, Steve Roach, and Ann Gates

The University of Texas at El Paso, Computer Science Department,
500 W. University Avenue, El Paso TX, 79912, USA
{omar,irbisg}@miners.utep.edu, {sroach,agates}@utep.edu

Abstract. This paper describes an approach to generate AspectJ aspects from formal specifications written for the Monitoring and Checking (MaC) runtime verification tool. The aspects can serve as the foundation for instrumentation of programs that can be verified at runtime. To demonstrate the practicability of the proposed approach, the authors used a benchmark from the MaC research. The benchmark is based on a safety-critical railroad crossing system comprised of a train, a gate, and a controller. Finally, the paper describes the results from generating Java-MaCs specification scripts to AspectJ aspects, and it compares the proposed approach to related approaches and ones that use aspects.

Keywords: Runtime Verification, Java-MaC, Aspect Oriented Programming, Runtime Monitoring, Software Assurance.

1 Introduction

With the ubiquity of software, especially in safety-critical systems, avoiding software failures *must* be emphasized. The failure of safety-critical systems, such as airplane controllers or railroad crossing systems can result in monetary loss, injury, or death. Software testing, the most commonly used verification technique, cannot provide complete test coverage; furthermore, designing effective comprehensive test suites for complex systems is difficult. A complementary technique called runtime verification examines actual execution paths, not possible paths. In this approach, a monitor system observes the behavior of a system and determines if it is consistent with specified properties. A monitor takes a software system and specifications of software properties and checks that the execution meets the properties, i.e., that the properties hold for the given execution [1].

A programming paradigm called Aspect Oriented Programming (AOP) [2] allows developers to encapsulate cross-cutting concerns that are needed to develop effective runtime verification approaches that require instrumentation of specifications in software code. This paper examines the integration of AOP into the runtime verification approach called Monitoring and Checking (MaC) [3]. MaC was chosen because it supports the separation of monitoring and specification

O. Sokolsky and S. Tasiran (Eds.): RV 2007, LNCS 4839, pp. 75–86, 2007.

requirement level concerns by using two distinct languages, one that deals with details of implementation and another one that deals with requirements.

MaC is a framework for run-time correctness and assurance of real-time systems. Currently a prototype implementation for programs written in the Java language exists (Java-MaC) [4]. MaC offers well-defined specification languages based on Linear-time Temporal Logic (LTL) in which the underlying structure of time is a totally ordered set (S, <) isomorphic to the natural numbers with their usual ordering (ℕ, <). Under this definition, time is discrete, it has an initial moment with no predecessors, and it is infinite into the future.

The *goal of the proposed approach* is to enhance runtime verification by developing a tool that translates the MaC specifications into AspectJ aspects. This is important because it removes the need for an instrumentation system, such as the one included in MaC, while maintaining MaCs unique features, i.e., the MEDL and PEDL specification languages that support specification of the properties to be monitored and the events and conditions that trigger monitoring. The proposed approach allows the runtime verification community to benefit from research advances in AOP and to reduce the need to maintain instrumentation code, which is managed by AspectJ in our approach.

The paper is divided as follows: Section 2 presents a detailed overview of Java-MaC and AOP. Section 3 describes the proposed approach and an example illustrating it. Section 4 presents the related work. Finally, Section 5 provides concluding remarks.

2   Background

In this section, an overview is provided of the most relevant features of Java-MaC and Aspect Oriented Programming.

2.1   Java-MaC

The Java-MaC framework allows users to specify system states to be monitored, define high-level events based on run-time system states, and describe correctness properties in terms of high-level events. The framework uses a runtime component called a *filter* to track the collection of probes inserted into the target program, and a separate runtime component called an *event recognizer* to detect events from the state information received from the filter.

The Meta-Event Definition Language (MEDL), based on an extension of LTL, is used to express a large subset of safety properties of systems, including real-time properties such as when a train is crossing, the gate is down. The Primitive Event Definition Language (PEDL) is used to describe events and conditions in terms of system objects such as methods and variables. PEDL specifications define the events recognized by the event recognizer, and these event definitions are used to automatically instrument the original program. The event recognizer emits event streams to the run-time checker that verifies the sequence of events with respect to the specified MEDL properties [6]. Fig. 1. depicts a data flow diagram for the Java-MaC framework.

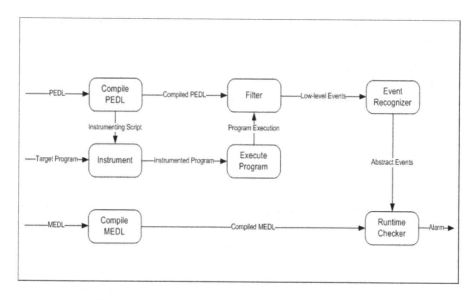

Fig. 1. Data flow diagram for the Java-Mac Framework

Property and Behavior Specifications. Java-MaC defines two types of state information, *events* and *conditions*. *Events* are asserted instantaneously during the system execution, whereas *conditions* represent information that holds true for a duration of time [6]. The distinction between the two determines what the monitor can infer about the execution. The monitor can conclude that an event does not occur at any moment until it receives an update from the filter. By contrast, once the monitor receives a message from the filter, it will determine if a state change has occurred.

In Java-MaC, PEDL is closely related to the target programming language because events are defined using program entities such as variables and methods [7]. Each declaration identifies an object that needs to be monitored. The object resides in a memory location. Since the exact memory location of the object is not known during the static phase, this object is specified in a monitoring script as a chain of references that starts in a fixed place in the object graph of the Java program, i.e., either a static variable of a class, a local variable of a static method, or the beginnings and endings of methods. When such a chain of references in a monitoring script is specified, it becomes a name for the memory location of the monitored objects [7]. PEDL allows the monitoring of fields and variables of the primitive type, but it does not allow objects to be monitored directly in order to minimize monitoring overhead.

Additionally, domain specific safety requirements are written in MEDL. Primitive events and conditions in MEDL specifications are imported from PEDL specifications. The correctness of the system is described in terms of safety properties and alarms. Safety properties are conditions that must always be true during execution. Alarms are notifications that a violation has occurred. Alarms and safety properties are complementary ways of expressing the same thing. Having both provides the user with flexibility in expressing how properties are to be expressed and handled.

Java-Mac Instrumentation. Java-MaC monitors global primitive variables, local primitive variables, and the start and end of methods. The Java-MaC instrumentor detects instructions that update monitored variables, or instructions located at the beginning and ending of methods by placing bytecode instructions to overlook updates of the entities of interest.

During the static analysis phase, the Java-MaC instrumentor identifies candidate update instructions for the monitored variables. Once the instrumentor recognizes an update instruction for a monitored variable, the instrumentor inserts a method call to Java-MaCs monitoring methods, acting as a probe at the bytecode level. The probe appears immediately before the instruction and consists of the following methods: *monitorEnter(), Filter.lock()* and *sendObjMethod(Object parentAddress, <T> value, String varName)*, where *parentAddress* is an address of an object whose field *varName* is monitored. When sendObjectMethod() is called at runtime, it checks if the variable being probed is a monitored variable by matching *parentAddress* with the address of a monitored object in the address table, i.e., a variable of interest. If the variable is a variable of interest, *sendObjMethod()* sends it to the event recognizer; otherwise, the variable is ignored.

The instrumentor inserts *monitorExit(), Filter.lock()* after the variable being monitored. The pair of *monitorEnter()* and *monitorExit()* ensures that the update to a variable and the sending of its new value are executed atomically. For execution points (i.e., calls and exits from methods) the instrumentor inserts probes at the starting point of a method and at the ending points of a method [7].

2.2 Aspect-Oriented Programming

AOP aids programmers in the encapsulation of cross-cutting concerns, i.e., specific requirements that span different modules in a system and that cannot be modularized into one component. An *aspect* is a class that includes constructs to support cross-cutting encapsulation through pointcuts and advice as described in the following paragraph. Aspects can include fields and methods that are merged with classes by a program called a *weaver*. Aspect weaving can occur at the source code level, at post compilation, or at class-load time [8, 9]. Aspects provide the benefit of good modularity, leading to code simplicity, ease of development and maintenance, and potential for reuse [10].

AspectJ. AspectJ [11] is an AOP implementation for the Java programming language. A *join point* is a place in the code where additional behavior is required. A *pointcut* is a specification of a set of join points. There are two types of pointcuts: primitive and user-defined. *User-defined pointcuts* are boolean combinations of primitive pointcuts. Pointcuts may match a method invocation at either the call site or the method site, at an assignment or read from a field, or at a point where some condition holds. For example, one could verify if variable x is updated by using the construct: *pointcut checkx() : set(int Class.x)*, where *checkx()* identifies the aspect, *set()* recognizes when the specified non-private variable is updated, and *int Class.x* specifies variable x in class *Class* as the variable of interest. The behavior of the program can be changed at each join point by specifying a construct called *advice*, i.e., code to be executed at a join point. The constructs *before()*, *after()*, direct when the *advice* is going to be executed, either before entering the join point or after exiting the join point, respectively. Additionally, the construct *around()* executes before entering the join point like a *before()* and optionally using a *proceed()* to execute the join point or to return and not execute the join point.

3   Proposed Approach

Primitive events in PEDL correspond to transfer of control between methods or assignments to variables. PEDL events describe join points in a program. MEDL properties correspond to safety and liveness requirements; therefore, the advice at each pointcut is checked against the MEDL specification. As mentioned earlier, an aspect is comprised of pointcut declarations and advice associated with each pointcut. Recall that the goal of the proposed approach is to enhance runtime verification by developing a tool that translates the MaC specifications into AspectJ aspects. This section describes the generation of an aspect from PEDL and MEDL, and it provides an example of how the approach can be used to provide assurance to a safety-critical system.

3.1   Description

PEDL lists the variables and method calls that are going to be used to generate events as well as the conditions to be used for monitoring. As a result, each listed variable and method must have a corresponding join point specified. Events that are described by the PEDL keywords *update, IoM, start, end, startM, endM*, are mapped to corresponding AspectJ constructs (see Table 1). For example, *startM* and *endM* correspond to the beginning of a method and the ending of a method, and they map to the *before()* and *after()* directives given to the advice modifier.

Recall that conditions are a combination of variables and booleans that when true emit an event. The proposed tool takes a condition and creates an auxilliary method that checks the current state of the system with respect to the condition. If the condition is true, then an appropriate aspect variable will contain the boolean value true; otherwise, it will contain the value false. MEDL states the conditions on high-level events that must be checked on the low-level events and conditions given by a PEDL specification. Because PEDL field methods are created for conditions and low-level events, MEDL specifications will be expressed as a method inside the aspect. Such methods are called on the advice

Table 1. Mapping from Java-MaC to AspectJ

Java-MaC	AspectJ
update(x)	set(x)
startM()	pointcut: before()
endM()	pointcut: after()
IoM()	pointcut: around()

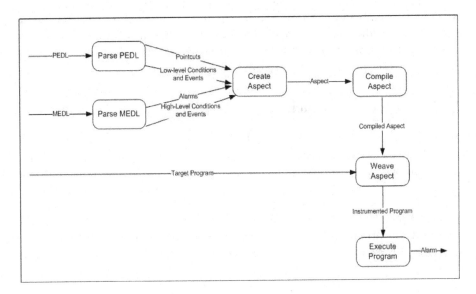

Fig. 2. Data flow diagram using AOP and MaC specifications

corresponding to the pointcuts extracted from PEDL, i.e., when this method gets called, it will check the boolean value of the aspect fields that represent the conditions described by PEDL. The diagram in Fig. 2 illustrates how data flows in the proposed tool.

3.2 Example

The described approach is applied to the simulation of railroad crossing gates, and it is a benchmark that was used by MaC [12]. The code, conditions, and events from the MaC example were reused in order to demonstrate that the behaviour of both approaches remained unchanged for this example. The safety property used was: when the train crosses the railroad crossing, the gates must be down. The railroad-crossing example was the modified example that is provided with the distribution of Java-MaC, which included the MEDL and PEDL specification files. The purpose of this example is to demonstrate instrumentation using the generated AspectJ aspect and to show how the specified properties, as captured by the aspects, are verified at runtime.

The PEDL file for this example contains the following conditions: *startIC* denotes a train reaching the rail road crossing; *endIC* denotes the train passing the crossing; *startGD* denotes the gate closing; and *endGD* denotes the gate starting to rise. The MEDL file contains the conditions *IC*, which denotes a train is crossing, and *GD*, which denotes a gate is down. These conditions are represented as $CondIC = [startIC, endIC]$ and $CondGD = [startGD, endGD]$, with the safety property $safeRRC = !IC||GD$. The aspect generated from this specification consists of the safety condition $safeRRC = !IC||GD$. Two point-cuts are generated to monitor each part of the condition. Pointcut *IC* is triggered when $train_x + train_{length} > cross_x \&\& train_x <= cross_x + cross_{length}$, which represents the train crossing. Pointcut *GD* is triggered after $Gate.gd()$ is executed, but before $Gate.gu()$ is called, which represent the gate going down or up, respectively.

The aspect monitors the safety condition and, if it is violated, an alarm is raised. Once the aspect is generated, it is woven into the railroad-crossing application. The simple aspect-instrumented version detected the same violations as the Java-MaC-monitored version.

The following PEDL code excerpt provides the pointcuts for the AspectJ aspect. The *MonVarDcl* heading indicates that the variable declarations following the heading are to be monitored. So in this case, the variables: $train_x$, $train_{length}$, $cross_x$ and $cross_{length}$ in the class RRC are of interest. Similarly, the MoMethodDcl heading indicates that the methods following the heading are to be monitored, which in this instance are the methods: $gd()$ and $gu()$ in the class *Gate*.

PEDL Code excerpt used to provide the pointcuts for the AspectJ Aspect

```
MonVarDcl:
      float RRC.train_x;
      int RRC.train_length;
      int RRC.cross_x;
      int RRC.cross_length;

MonMethodDcl:
      Gate.gd();
      Gate.gu();
```

The MEDL code excerpt below was used to provide the advice for the AspectJ aspect. In this excerpt, four events are imported: *startIC, endIC, startGD, endGD*. The events are monitored based upon the properties defined later in the MEDL script. The *CondDef* heading denotes the area in which the conditions to be associated with events are declared. In this case, the *InCrossing* specifies that there is a train in the crossing. Similarly, *GateDown* specifies that the gate in the crossing is down. Next the user specifies the safety properties that use the *CondDef* specification. The specification appears after the *SafePropDef* heading. For this property, it is the case that whenever a train is in the crossing (*InCrossing*), it must always be the case that the gate is down (*GateDown*).

MEDL code excerpt used to provide the advice for the AspectJ Aspect

```
ReqSpec RailroadCrossing

    import event startIC, endIC, startGD, endGD;

    CondDef:
        Cond InCrossing = [startIC, endIC];
        Cond GateDown = [startGD, endGD];

    SafePropDef:
        SafeProp safeRRC = InCrossing -> GateDown;

    End
```

In this small example, the proposed tool used the MEDL and PEDL specifications and successfully generated the AspectJ aspect matching the MEDL and PEDL specifications as illustrated in the following code. The generated aspect behaved as expected.

AspectJ Aspect Matching the MEDL and PEDL Specifications

```
//PEDL equivalent section

before(RRC trgt) : set (float RRC.train_x) &&
                   target(trgt)

before() : call(void Gate.gd(int))

after() : call(void Gate.gd(int))
        GD=true;
        monitor();

before() : call(void Gate.gd(int))
        GD=false;
        monitor();


//MEDL equivalent section
IC =
    aRRC.train_x + aRRC.train_length > aRRC.cross_x && aRRC.train_x
    <= aRRC.cross_x + aRRC.cross_length;
```

4   Related Work

Several approaches have exploited the cross-cutting and instrumentation mechanisms of AOP to provide runtime verification and fault recovery capabilities.

This section provides a short description of some of these efforts, and it describes how each differs from the described approach.

4.1   Monitoring Oriented Programming (MOP)

The University of Illinois at Urbana-Champaigns Monitoring Oriented Programming (MOP) framework [13] allows users to check conformance of implementation to specifications at runtime. Similar to the proposed approach, the framework uses an AOP-based instrumentation package that allows monitors to be generated as AspectJ aspects. In MOP, monitors are viewed as added functionality because user-defined code is executed at user-specified places within the code of the existing system and violations are reported at runtime. MOP also extends programming languages (Java, for instance) by adding logics that can be added anywhere in the program. So far, MOP supports logic plug-ins for future-time and past-time temporal logics, extended regular expressions and JASS, all available through a web repository.

The difference between MOP and the proposed approach lies in that MEDL and PEDL are used as specification languages. Mondragon et al. [14] showed that patterns and scopes can be used to generate formal specification in Future Interval Logic (FIL) that can be converted into MEDL provide support to users without deep training in formal specifications. In addition, MOP requires generation of a separate monitor for every specification, which can consume intensive computation power when large sets of specifications exist. With the proposed approach, one monitor is generated as an aspect for all specifications.

4.2   TRAP/J

TRAP/J [15] from Florida International University is a software tool that enables autonomic computing in existing Java programs by generating adapt-ready versions of the original programs at compile time, i.e., programs in which behavior can be managed at runtime. The generation process is transparent to the user, and there is no need to modify the original source code manually. In TRAP/J, new behavior is introduced to the adapt-ready programs at runtime using the wrapper- and meta-language classes. First, the adapt-ready application is loaded by the JVM. At the time each meta-object (entities of interest in the code) is instantiated, it registers itself with the Java RMI registry using a unique ID. Next, if an adaptation is required, the composer (entity that requests an adaptation to the code) dynamically adds new code to the adapt-ready application at runtime, using Java RMI to interact with the meta-objects. As part of the behavioral reflection provided in the adaptation infrastructure, a meta-object protocol is supported in TRAP/J that allows interception and reification of method invocations targeted to objects of the classes selected at compile time to be adaptable. To reduce overhead, TRAP/J enables the developer to select, at compile time, a subset of classes to be adaptive at runtime.

To support dynamic adaptation in existing Java programs, TRAP/J benefits from aspect-oriented programming (AspectJ) and the ability of programs to reason and alter their own behavior (behavioral reflection). TRAP/J generates specific aspects and reflective classes associated with the selected classes. A case study is presented by Sadjadi et al. [15] in which TRAP/J is used to enable an existing audio-streaming application to perform self-optimization in a wireless network environment by adapting to changing conditions automatically. Because TRAP/Js main goal is not to provide verification, but to provide fault recovery capabilities, it does not support automatic integration of formally specified properties into existing code.

4.3 Temporal Assertion Using AspectJ

Stolz and Bodden [16] present Java Logical Observer (JLO), a runtime verification framework for Java programs. In the JLO approach, properties are specified in LTL over AspectJ pointcuts. These properties are checked during program execution by an automaton-based approach in which transitions are triggered through aspects and violations are detected when the automaton enters an error state.

No Java source code is necessary since AspectJ works on the byte-code level, permitting instrumentation of third-party applications. The current implementation supports the full formalism without access to the runtime state. The difference between JLO and the proposed approach is that JLO uses AspectJ to determine whether code execution causes the automaton to enter an invalid state while the proposed approach uses AspectJ to instrument the program and monitors the execution of the code itself.

4.4 jMonitor

jMonitor [17] is a pure Java library and runtime utility that allows users to specify event patterns to monitor runtime execution of Java applications. jMonitor works by overloading the dynamic class loader by instrumenting the class bytecode of the monitored Java program on the fly according to externally specified event patterns and event monitors.

During the execution of an instrumented application, each Java bytecode instruction that matches any of the specified event patterns triggers the call of one or more associated monitor methods. The monitor methods get called with the following runtime context information regarding the triggering event: the type of event, its target object, the call stack representing the method in which the event occurred, and the arguments to the method which collectively defines the full call context when the event occurred.

jMonitor events correspond to fundamental Java programming abstractions such as reading or writing of a field in a class, method invocation, method return or throw of an exception, and creation of a new object or array. Each event is also qualified with a Java application context such as the name of the field or the method as well as the names of the class and method context. The names are specified as strings representing POSIX compliant regular expressions.

Several distinct event monitors can be associated with any event. jMonitor instruments applications to capture the call context and call the monitor function with this information. Each monitoring function is called before, after, or instead of the associated event depending on the event specification.

Both jMonitor and the proposed approach are building instrumentors that instrument at the bytecode level, however, jMonitor is not using aspects to support instrumentation. By using aspects, the proposed approach has the support of the AOP community for maintaining, improving, and porting the instrumentor to other languages.

5   Summary

The *goal of the proposed approach* is to enhance runtime verification by developing a tool that translates the MaC specifications into AspectJ aspects. This is important because it removes the need for an instrumentation system, such as the one included in MaC, while maintaining MaCs unique features, i.e., the MEDL and PEDL specification languages that support specification of the properties to be monitored and the events and conditions that trigger monitoring. The proposed approach allows the runtime verification community to benefit from research advances in AOP and to reduce the need to maintain instrumentation code, which is managed by AspectJ in our approach. The AOP community has been focused on the development of next-generation aspect weavers, and this work will benefit software instrumentation.

The tool described in this paper converts MEDL and PEDL files to AspectJ aspects. The results show the effectiveness of using AspectJ as the foundation for instrumentation because of the cross-cutting nature of instrumentation. Future work includes support for all features in the MEDL and PEDL languages and demonstration of the equivalence of the weaving process of AspectJ to Java-MaC instrumentation. Other work includes determining whether the proposed approach can be applied to runtime verification of services used in a service-oriented environment and implemented in a variety of AOP-supported languages.

Acknowledgments. This work was partially supported by NSF grant nos. CNS-0540592 and EIA-0080940.

References

1. Delgado, N., Gates, A., Roach, S.: A Taxonomy and Catalog of Runtime Software-Fault Monitoring Tools. IEEE Transactions on Software Engineering 30(12), 859–872 (2004)
2. Kiczales, G., Lamping, J., Mendhekar, A.: Aspect-Oriented Programming. In: Aksit, M., Matsuoka, S. (eds.) ECOOP 1997. LNCS, vol. 1241, pp. 220–242. Springer, Heidelberg (1997)
3. MaC: Run-time Monitoring and Checking (MaC) (2006),
   http://www.cis.upenn.edu/rtg/mac/index.php3

4. Emerson, E.: Temporal and Modal Logic. Handbook of theoretical computer science: formal models and semantics B, 995–1072 (1990)
5. Palo Alto Research Center: ÒThe AspectJ Programming GuideÓ (October 1, 2006) [Online] available,
   `http://www.eclipse.org/aspectj/doc/released/progguide/index.html`
6. Kim, M., Kannan, S., Lee, I., Sokolsky, O.: Java-MaC: A Run-time Assurance Tool for Java. In: Proc. 1st International Workshop on Run-time Verification (2001)
7. Kim, M., Viswanathan, M., Kannan, S., Lee, I., Sokolsky, O.: Java-MaC: A Runtime Assurance Approach for Java Programs. Formal Methods in System Design 24(2), 129–155 (2004)
8. Hilsdale, E., Hugunin, J.: Advice Weaving in AspectJ. In: Proc. Aspect-oriented Software Development 2004, pp. 26–35 (2004)
9. Alto, P.: Research Center: The AspectJ Programming Guide (2006),
   `http://www.eclipse.org/aspectj/doc/released/progguide/index.html`
10. Kiczales, G., Lamping, J., Mendhekar, A.: Aspect-Oriented Programming. In: Aksit, M., Matsuoka, S. (eds.) ECOOP 1997. LNCS, vol. 1241, pp. 220–242. Springer, Heidelberg (1997)
11. Kiczales, G., Hilsdale, E., Hugunin, J., Kerten, M., Palm, J., Griswold, W.G.: An overview of AspectJ. In: Proc. European Conference on Object- Oriented Programming 2001 (2001)
12. Heitmeyer, C., Mandrioli, D. (eds.): Formal Methods for Real-Time Systems. Number 5 in Trends in Software. John Wiley & Sons, Chichester (1996)
13. Chen, F., D'Amorim, M., Rosu, G.: A Formal Monitoring-based Framework for Software Development and Analysis. In: Davies, J., Schulte, W., Barnett, M. (eds.) ICFEM 2004. LNCS, vol. 3308, Springer, Heidelberg (2004)
14. Mondragon, O., Gates, A.Q., Roach, S., Mendoza, H., Sokolsky, O.: Generating Properties for Runtime Monitoring from Software Specification Patterns. International Journal of Software Engineering and Knowledge Engineering 17, 107–126 (2007)
15. Sadjadi, M., McKinley, P.K., Stirewalt, R.E.K., Cheng, B.H.C.: Generation of Self-Optimizing Wireless Network Applications. In: ICAC-04. Proc. International Conference on Autonomic Computing (2004)
16. Stolz, V., Bodden, E.: Temporal Assertions using AspectJ. In: RV 2005. Proc 5th Workshop on Runtime Verification (2005)
17. Karaorman, M., Freeman, J.: Java Runtime Event Specification and Monitoring Library. Electronic Notes in Theoretical Computer Science 113(3), 181–200 (2005)

ARVE: Aspect-Oriented Runtime Verification Environment

Hiromasa Shin, Yusuke Endoh, and Yoshio Kataoka

Corporate Research & Development Center, Toshiba Corporation,
(1 Komukai-Toshiba-cho, Saiwai-ku, Kawasaki-shi, Kanagawa 212-8582, Japan)
hiromasa.shin@toshiba.co.jp

Abstract. Software quality assurance activities consume a large amount of effort in industrial software developments. Actually, industrial software development sometimes requires a larger amount of testing/verification assets than the product code itself. Appropriate management of the testing/verification assets will effectively reduce the software quality assurance effort. We propose a verification asset reuse environment based on the aspect-oriented programming paradigm. Our tool, ARVE (Aspect-oriented Runtime Verification Environment), enables efficient verification asset reuse thanks to the aspect-oriented scripting language. ARVE also promotes the efficiency of the verification process by automating the verification script weaving.

1 Introduction

The more important the role of software becomes in everyday life, the more severe the requirement for software dependability becomes. Therefore, software quality assurance activities are consuming a large portion of resources, a tendency that is especially marked in the case of industrial software development. For instance, it is often observed that the number of lines of verification software for a certain software product is significantly larger than the one of the product software itself. One of the major reasons is that the verification software is usually for the target software product's exclusive use. Therefore, the verification software should be prepared from scratch for each newly developed software product, although the product itself is usually developed with reusable components. We found that the major obstacle to the reuse of verification software is the fact that verification software often relates with the target product software in a crosscutting manner. In addition, verification software is often developed in an ad hoc manner, or without reference to any reusability policy.

Aspect-oriented programming attempts to deal with crosscutting functionality by means of modules. We studied the aspect-oriented paradigm and designed a framework to deal with verification software in the aspect-oriented manner. In this paper, we introduce the practical realization of the aspect-oriented verification framework. From the practical viewpoint, we chose C/C++ platform to realize the framework although most of the aspect-oriented tools available

O. Sokolsky and S. Tasiran (Eds.): RV 2007, LNCS 4839, pp. 87–96, 2007.

are designed for Java. We did so because most industrial software products are written in C/C++, and are developed with well-matured C/C++ tools such as compilers, symbolic debuggers and performance profilers. Our tool, ARVE (Aspect-oriented Runtime Verification Environment), utilizes those existing development tools to improve the reusability of verification software following the aspect-oriented paradigm.

In the following sections, we first introduce the overview of ARVE, followed by the usage of ARVE. Then we explain the details of ARVE from some technical viewpoints. We also discuss the relation with previous research and mention our plans for future work.

2 Overview

The aim of ARVE is to realize the "Write once, run anywhere" (WORA) environment in runtime verification. A verification asset, or verification intellectual property (VIP), is defined as a reusable part of verification software. The WORA environment is helpful for accumulating and reusing the verification asset. ARVE is designed to provide the WORA environment in runtime verification by operating in combination with an existing proven tool, a symbolic debugger.

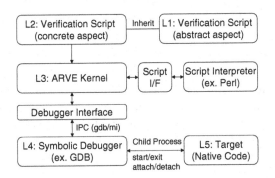

Fig. 1. Suggested usage of ARVE

We introduce ARVE as a solution to realize the WORA environment in runtime verification. The main features of ARVE are as follows.

- ARVE provides an aspect-oriented script language to describe verification asset.
- ARVE provides a platform-independent interpreter for the verification script. In other words, the same verification script runs on a variety of platforms.
- ARVE dynamically weaves the scripts into the target by using a symbolic debugger. In other words, we can start a verification session on an already running target.

– ARVE has a debugger driver interface to support multiple debuggers. In other words, we can easily add the new debugger supported by ARVE.

For writing verification script, ARVE provides an aspect-oriented script programming language. In our prototype system (see Fig. 1), this script is the Perl language extended with aspect-oriented syntax that is a subset of AspectJ [1]. ARVE controls a symbolic debugger for virtually weaving the verification script into the verification target. The detail of the control is explained in a later section.

3   Usage

As an illustration of a usage of ARVE, we describe a trace checker written in the script language.

3.1   Abstraction Layer

ARVE proposes a 5-layered structure (see Fig. 1), to improve reusability and portability of verification scripts.

– The L1 layer is a verification script that should describe "how to verify" as an abstract aspect in AOP. For example, the L1 script describes a reusable algorithm for verification.
– The L2 layer is also a verification script that should describe "what to verify" as a concrete aspect in AOP. For example, the L2 script extends the L1 script, and describes customizing information for verification.
– The L3 layer is ARVE that works as both an interpreter and a dynamic weaver for the L1 and L2 scripts. The L3 interacts with the L4 via the debugger driver interface that ensures the independence from the underlying debugger.
– The L4 and the L5 are platform-dependent parts. The L5 is a verification target and is a debuggee for the L4.

3.2   Trace Checker

The following script *FileChecker* gathers events of file handling operations during a target execution, and checks whether the operation sequence satisfies a pattern specified in the script. The pattern is written in regular language. Having found an operation deviating from the specified pattern, this checker breaks the target execution and dumps an execution stack.

A script listed below is written in a Perl-based language equipped with aspect-related syntax similar to AspectJ [1]. The concrete aspect *FileChecker* extending the abstract aspect *TraceChecker* specifies monitoring events by the pointcut *mark()* and a *normal* pattern by an argument of the constructor *new(...)*.

```
import "./lib/TraceChecker.pl";
aspect FileChecker extends TraceChecker {
  pointcut mark() :
    call(fopen) || call(fread) || call(fwrite) || call(fclose);
  sub new ($$) {
    my $class = shift;
    my $self = TraceChecker->new(
        "A-fopen[-1] (B-fread[3]|B-fwrite[3])* B-fclose[0]");
    return bless $self, $class;
  }
}
```

The parent aspect *TraceChecker* is a reusable aspect listed below, which contains an algorithm to generate a DFA (Deterministic Finite Automaton) from a regular expression and to drive the DFA by invocation of advice related with pointcut *mark()*. An event symbol in the regular expression is defined by the syntax *(after or before)-(name of joinpoint)[location of handler]*. Like these examples, the *TraceChecker* implements a reusable algorithm, and the *FileChecker* implements a disposable detail for each verification.

```
# outline of algorithm
abstract aspect TraceChecker {
  private state for DFA
  abstract pointcut mark();
  sub new ($$) {
    construct a DFA from regular expression
    Initialize the state of DFA
  }
  sub DESTROY($) {
    if DFA is not in acceptance state, report error
  }
  before() : mark() {
    drive DFA by the current location
    if there is no transition then report error
  }
  after() : mark() {
    ...
  }
}
```

We applied the aspect *TraceChecker* to monitor the API usage of socket handling in the server process, such as Apache or Squid, and conformed that it worked properly.

3.3   Other Examples

The followings are other examples of the verification assets for ARVE.

- *Tracer* monitors the execution of a target and prints the call graph. This is one of the most popular applications in AOP, and is also one of the most useful scripts for ARVE.

- *Profiler* counts the frequency of the subroutine calls and measures their execution time.
- *LeakChecker* records the usage of resources in the process. At the end of the verification, this checker shows the list of resources, which were acquired but were not released.

The *Tracer* or the *Profiler* may be useful but is too simple to call a verification asset. These kinds of useful scripts can be written in portable and reusable ways, and become a part of verification assets. By reusing useful verification assets, we can easily construct the customized runtime verification system (see Fig. 2).

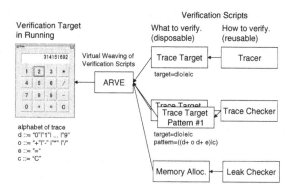

Fig. 2. Application example of ARVE

4   Details

4.1   Optimization

ARVE uses a symbolic debugger to weave verification script and to evaluate expression in the target context. ARVE interacts with the debugger by inter-process communication, which causes sizable runtime overhead. For reducing the interaction with the debugger, ARVE has a static optimizer to minimize the number of breakpoints, and to simplify the pointcut expression at each breakpoint. We briefly explain these optimization techniques.

The join point model in AOP defines the potential locations where aspect acts on. ARVE takes a join point as a breakpoint addressed by symbol name.

A verification script has pointcut expressions for selecting breakpoints. The pointcut expression ($pcut ::= prim \mid pcut \wedge pcut \mid pcut \vee pcut \mid \neg pcut$) is a logical formula, whose atomic proposition is primitive pointcut ($prim ::= prim_s \mid prim_d$). The primitive pointcut is classified into two categories, a static one ($prim_s ::= call(patt) \mid \cdots$) and a dynamic one ($prim_d ::= if(expr) \mid \ldots$). The former is defined to depend on the static context (ex. breakpoint location), and the latter is defined to depend on the dynamic context (ex. execution state). In the following description, SC denotes the whole set of static context, and DC denotes the whole set of dynamic context in the target program.

The minimum set of breakpoints for pointcut $pc(x, t)$ is defined as $BP(pc) \equiv \{x \in SC \mid \exists t \in DC.\ pc(x, t) = true\}$, whose element is a breakpoint where pointcut pc is possibly true. Applying the definition to the dynamic pointcut leads to $BP(prim_d) = SC$ and $BP(\neg prim_d) = SC$. The similar application to the static pointcut leads to $BP(prim_s) = P$ and $BP(\neg prim_s) = SC - P$, where P is defined as a subset of SC selected by $prim_s$. The application to the logical operator leads to $BP(pc_1 \wedge pc_2) = BP(pc_1) \cap BP(pc_2)$ and $BP(pc_1 \vee pc_2) = BP(pc_1) \cup BP(pc_2)$. The minimum set of breakpoints for arbitrary pointcut expression in negation normal form (NNF) can be computed by recursive application of the previous rules. Having computed the minimum set of breakpoints, ARVE reduces the pointcut expression at each breakpoint.

For an illustration, we explain the case with $SC = \{x1, x2, y1, y2\}$ and $pc = call(x*) \wedge \neg(call(x1) \wedge if(e)) = call(x*) \wedge (\neg call(x1) \vee \neg if(e))$. The minimum set of breakpoints is computed as $BP(pc) = BP(call(x*)) \cap (BP(\neg call(x1)) \cup BP(\neg if(e))) = \{x1, x2\}$. The pointcut expressions at each breakpoint can be reduced as follows, $pc|_{x1} = \neg if(e)$ and $pc|_{x2} = true$. The latter expression does not need to evaluate e in the target context, and thus ARVE reduces the interaction with the debugger.

We evaluated the runtime performance of ARVE in a laptop computer (Dynabook TECRA 9000, Pentium-III 1.2 GHz, Linux 2.4.20 and gdb 6.4). According to this experiment, one empty subroutine with one empty advice took about 6 microseconds, whereas one empty subroutine without advice took about 10 nanoseconds. The relatively large overhead is due to the inter process communication (IPC) between ARVE and the debugger, and the cost of one advice call is comparable to the cost of one operating system call.

The overhead in microseconds is not acceptable for timing- or performance-critical applications, but is acceptable for network communication or user-interactive applications, whose time scale is larger than milliseconds. For limiting the target, ARVE can be used for the verification.

4.2 Debugger Control

ARVE interacts with symbolic debugger via debugger driver interface defined in Table 1. This interface located between the L3 and L4 in Fig. 1, ensures the independence of ARVE from a debugger. Any debugger satisfying this interface can work in the ARVE system. In the current implementation, we can use two popular debuggers, GNU's gdb and Microsoft's WinDbg. In order to add a new debugger, we have only to add a new debugger driver for it.

ARVE starts a debugger by *start*, and selects a verification target by *load* (or *attach*). ARVE parses and analyzes the verification script, and computes the minimum breakpoint by calling symbol *lookup*. ARVE installs the initial breakpoints by *insert*, starts the target by *run* (or *cont*) and waits for the target event by *wait*. Having found the target stopped at a breakpoint, ARVE evaluates the pointcut to decide whether to call the advice or not. Having finished the work at the breakpoint, ARVE continues the target execution by *cont*. Having received

Table 1. Debugger interface in ARVE

Name	In	Out	Function
start	—	—	start a debugger
stop	—	—	stop the debugger
query	$com	$ret	query $com to the debugger
load	@arg	—	load a target with @arg
attach	$pid	—	attach to a target with $pid
detach	—	—	detach from the target
return	—	—	return from the subroutine
run	—	—	start the target
cont	—	—	continue the target
wait	—	$bp	wait for a breakpoint
insert	$id	$bp	insert a breakpoint $id
remove	$bp	—	remove the breakpoint $bp
lookup	$reg	@vec	query symbols @vec matching $reg

the signal to stop the session, ARVE removes the breakpoints by *remove*, and calls *stop* (or *detach*) to close the session.

Some more details are explained below. The *before* advice is called at the entrance breakpoint of the subroutine, whereas the *after* advice is called at the returned breakpoint of the subroutine. Therefore, ARVE does not distinguish between pointcuts *call* and *execution*. The returned breakpoint used for *after* advice is installed at the entrance of the subroutine, and is removed after the advice is called.

4.3   Target Abstraction

ARVE works a runtime environment for verification scripts, and the environment provides primitive service calls for the scripts to use debugger. The script can use any debugger service by these service calls listed in Table 2. However, most scripts should not use them directly, because they are so primitive that their direct use spoils the platform portability of the scripts.

Table 2. Primitive service for verification script

Name	In	Out	Function
eval	$exp	$val	evaluate expression $exp
call	$com	$ret	query command $com
this	—	$jp	retrieve join point signature

For example, in order to retrieve a return value of subroutine on Intel x86 architecture, the script has to read the value of a register named $eax. For localizing this kind of platform-dependent code, we introduced target abstraction script, which provides platform-independent methods to access context information at join point. The following is an example of this script, which hides details of the target architecture. Most verification scripts access the join point information by this script.

```
# ThisJP Class for x86 architecture
class ThisJP {
  sub getArgv ($$) { # get an argument value
    my ($ref, $idx) = @_;
    my $exp = sprintf('"*(int*)($fp + %d)"', ($idx + 2)<<2);
    return gdb::eval($exp);
  }
  sub getRetv ($) {   # get a return value
    return gdb::eval('$eax');
  }
  ...
}
```

5 Related Work

Dynamic weaving AOP systems for Java were reported in several articles [2,3]. ARVE uses a symbolic debugger for weaving and works on multiple debuggers. ARVE is able to take an executable file compiled from C/C++ language as a weaving target.

Dynamic binary instrumentation techniques reported in articles [4,5] take an executable file as a patching target. ARVE only uses a script language to describe a patching source. Compared to their binary approach, our script approach has a disadvantage in runtime efficiency, but has advantages in portability and changeability of the patching software.

The aspect of ARVE is written in script language. ARVE has a definite interface with the symbolic debugger, and can use a different symbolic debugger for each platform. These features are derived from the ARVE design policy, improving portability and portability of a verification script.

6 Future Work

We are working on three plans. The first plan is to extend the ARVE kernel to support multi-process environments. In our experiment on an Apache server, we had difficulty in tracing many processes forked by the server. If ARVE supports an aspect among multi-processes and automatically attaches to multiple processes, the runtime verification aspect concerning IPC (Inter Process Communication) can be naturally described in a single aspect.

The second plan is to prototype more useful examples of a verification assets. One instance of a verification asset will be simple but useful scripts for visualizing the target execution like the *Tracer*. Another instance will be slightly more complex script for monitoring an execution trace by a formal specification.

A regular expression used in *TraceChecker* is one of the formal specifications, but is limited in descriptive power for monitoring. The more powerful specification methods for monitoring are reported in articles [6,7], and will serve as useful references.

The third plan is to apply ARVE to an execution environment for model-based testing [8]. In order to perform effective runtime verification, we need some way of generating verification scripts from upstream design specifications. In model-based testing, we can generate test cases from a formal specification. By converting these test cases to verification script, ARVE automates conformance testing. ARVE cannot only monitor the relations between input and output in the testing, but also can monitor internal events and states of IUT (Implementation Under Test) by controlling the debugger.

7   Summary

We have presented a concept of verification assets and have explained ARVE as a means of realizing verification assets. ARVE enables development of a test program in script language and in the aspect-oriented paradigm, and achieves independence from an underlying symbolic debugger. We have presented two examples of verification assets, namely an execution tracer and a trace checker. We have shown some details of optimization for reducing runtime overhead.

References

1. Kiczales, G., Hilsdale, E., Hugunin, J., Kersten, M., Palm, J., Griswold, W.: An Overview of AspectJ. In: Knudsen, J.L. (ed.) ECOOP 2001. LNCS, vol. 2072, pp. 327–355. Springer, Heidelberg (2001)
2. Popovici, A., Gross, T., Alonso, G.: Dynamic Weaving for Aspect-Oriented Programming. In: AOSD 2002: Proceedings of the 1st International Conference on Aspect-Oriented Software Development, pp. 141–147. ACM Press, New York (2002)
3. Suvée, D., Vanderperren, W., Jonckers, V.: JAsCo: an aspect-oriented approach tailored for component based software development. In: AOSD 2003: Proceedings of the 2nd International Conference on Aspect-Oriented Software Development, pp. 21–29. ACM Press, New York (2003)
4. Buck, B., Hollingsworth, J.: An API for Runtime Code Patching. Int. J. High Perform. Comput. Appl. 14(4), 317–329 (2000)
5. Luk, C.-K., Cohn, R., Muth, R., Patil, H., Klauser, A., Lowney, G., Wallace, S., Reddi, V., Hazelwood, K.: Pin: building customized program analysis tools with dynamic instrumentation. In: PLDI 2005: Proceedings of the 2005 ACM SIGPLAN Conference on Programming Language Design and Implementation, pp. 190–200. ACM Press, New York (2005)
6. Barringer, H., Goldberg, A., Havelund, K., Sen, K.: Rule-Based Runtime Verification. In: Steffen, B., Levi, G. (eds.) VMCAI 2004. LNCS, vol. 2937, Springer, Heidelberg (2004)

7. Stolz, V., Bodden, E.: Temporal Assertions using AspectJ. In: Fifth Workshop on Runtime Verification (RV 2005), Electronic Notes in Theoretical Computer Science, Elsevier Science Publishers, Amsterdam (2005)
8. Barnett, M., Grieskamp, W., Nachmanson, L., Schulte, W., Tillmann, N., Veanes, M.: Towards a Tool Environment for Model-Based Testing with AsmL. In: Petrenko, A., Ulrich, A. (eds.) FATES 2003. LNCS, vol. 2931, pp. 252–266. Springer, Heidelberg (2003)

From Runtime Verification to Evolvable Systems

Howard Barringer[1], Dov Gabbay[2], and David Rydeheard[1]

[1] School of Computer Science, University of Manchester,
Oxford Road, Manchester, M13 9PL, UK
{howard.barringer,david.rydeheard}@manchester.ac.uk
[2] Department of Computer Science, Kings College London,
The Strand, London, WC2R 2LS, UK
dov.gabbay@kcl.ac.uk

Abstract. We consider evolvable computational systems built as hierarchies of evolvable components, where an evolvable component is an encapsulation of a supervisory component and its supervisee. Here, we extend our prior work on a revision-based logical modelling framework for such systems to incorporate programs within each component. We describe mechanisms for combining programs, possibly in different languages, from separate components and outline an operational semantics for programmed evolvable systems. We show how supervisory components extend run-time verifiers/monitors with capabilities for diagnosis and change. We illustrate the logical modelling using an example of an automated bank teller machine.

1   Introduction

We are interested in developing theories and tools to support the construction and running of safe, robust and controllable systems that have the capability to evolve or adapt their structure and behaviour dynamically according to both internal and external stimuli. Many computational systems have this capability. Examples include: supervisory control systems for, say, reactive planning, modelling evolving business processes, systems for adaptive querying, responsive memory management, dynamic network routing, autonomous software repair, data structure repair, and adaptive hybrid systems.

Runtime verification techniques show considerable promise (and some return) for establishing the correctness of systems at runtime by monitoring system behaviour against a behavioural specification. This is particularly useful for systems that are too large for static verification techniques. Typically, in runtime monitoring and verification, when conformance fails, an error is reported and the system halted, possibly with some diagnostic data returned. This is fine for runtime verification applied during system simulation. However, for real-time on-line systems, fault diagnosis and system recovery is required, which in general will mean modification of the running system. When such additional capabilities are in place, the overall dynamically-monitored system becomes an *evolvable* system. The notion of evolvability which we explore here shares some features with Aspect-Oriented Programming [5].

O. Sokolsky and S. Tasiran (Eds.): RV 2007, LNCS 4839, pp. 97–110, 2007.
© Springer-Verlag Berlin Heidelberg 2007

In [1,3,4], we introduced evolution at a level of abstraction that allows us to describe systems that are constructed as a hierarchical assembly of evolvable (software and/or hardware) components. We model (and implement) evolvable components as a pairing of a supervisor and its supervisee component, where the supervisor dynamically monitors its supervisee as a runtime verifier, and possibly changes the supervisee so that its behaviour accords with that required by the supervisor. This approach is a generalisation of the software architecture principles that have been developed over a number of years, largely in the context of business process modelling [7]. Figure 1 depicts the pairing of a supervisor component with its supervisee as a new (evolvable) component. Figure 2 depicts a small hierarchical assembly of components. It shows both the *horizontal* composition of communicating components, namely

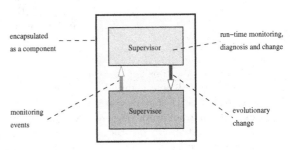

Fig. 1. An Evolvable Component Pairing

EC1, C2 and EC3 yielding the component C, and the *vertical* composition of supervisors and their associated supervisees, namely E1 and C1 as EC1, E3 and C3 as EC3, and E and C as EC. Thus instead of one overall runtime verifier for a system, verification and evolution is localised to, and embedded within, components in a system hierarchy. This improves the manageability of runtime verification and system evolution for large systems and also enables us to use evolutionary behaviour as part of system design.

We provide a logical account of these evolvable systems in which the supervisor theory is described as a *meta-level* theory to the object-level supervisee

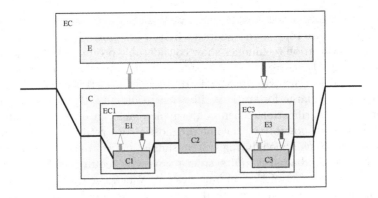

Fig. 2. An Example Hierarchical Assembly

theory. In other words, the supervisor theory has access to the logical structure of the theory of the supervisee, including its predicates, formulas, state, axioms, logical revision actions, and its subcomponent theories. This technically equips the supervisor with sufficient capability both to observe supervisee behaviour and to describe evolutionary object-level supervisee changes. Thus, not only can supervisor states record observations of its own state of computation, but they can also record observations about the object-level supervisee system. Actions at the meta-level update the state of the supervisor and, as a consequence of being meta to the supervisee, may also induce a transformation of the object-level supervisee system. This provides a logical account of how systems may evolve their structure during computation.

In this paper, we outline how the logical modelling can be extended to components which contain programs of actions. All components may be active with programs running in concert, but we may also model passive service-provider systems in this approach. Components within one system may use different programming languages: this is common in practice, for example using a separate verification language, but seldom do such combinations come equipped with a logical account of the combined systems. We present a structural operational semantics for the various ways that component programs may be combined, including, in particular, the vertical supervisor-supervisee combination of evolvable components. This provides not only a foundation for static proof analysis of an evolvable component hierarchy but also a natural setting for dynamic, reasoned and programmed, control of a system's evolution as a generalization of standard runtime verification.

2   Upgrading ATMs

To illustrate our modelling approach to evolvable systems, we visit the world of banking and automated teller machines (ATMs). We focus, in particular, on how runtime monitoring programs for supervisors and basic supervisee component programs are semantically integrated. The Bank of New Island's old form of ATM, although comprising distinct hardware components, such as magnetic strip readers, note counters, keypads, displays, etc., had its local software built in an unstructured, monolithic fashion. Only limited security checks were programmed and certainly not easily changed (indeed the whole ATM network would need to be shutdown for at least a day to perform even minor upgrades). The design of the new system is such that each individual ATM will monitor, adapt and evolve its behaviour, in particular its security checking, to fit best with the bank's and their customers' desires and expectations. The individual software components used in the ATM will themselves also be evolvable and the network of ATMs will naturally support dynamic co-evolution.

The old banking system is modelled as a component assembly comprising a banking centre which holds the records and a number of automated teller machines (ATMs). Figure 3 shows an ATM linked to a central bank component; the ATM component has four communicating sub-components. In [1], we out-lined specifications for the overall structure of the banking system, its ATMs, together with simplified card-reader and note-

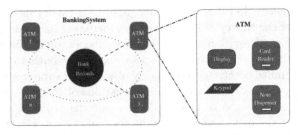

Fig. 3. The banking system component structure

dispenser components. Only basic actions were specified. In particular, we did not present a formalisation of the programs controlling the actions of the card reader and note dispenser. Here, we introduce programs over the specified actions of a component and incorporate these within the component. Given the differing roles of the supervisor and supervisee, different programming languages for these components may be appropriate. We first consider just the card-reader component and describe the control of its actions via a (very basic) guarded command style program. We then consider a supervisor component for the card reader, whose role is to monitor the patterns of acceptances and rejections of cards and, should the behaviour fall outside acceptable norms, modify, i.e. upgrade, the card reader's security level and associated card checking mechanisms. The temporal nature of the supervisory program can readily be captured via a combination of *declarative* temporal logic runtime monitors with *imperative* guarded command programs for the diagnosis and possible evolutionary change.

The card-reader component for security level 0, $CardReader_0$, is simplified to holding the account number and PIN for the card currently in the card reader and any cards that have not been returned to the customer. The $cardIn$ action, defined when no card is present, makes the account number and PIN of the card a state observation. The action $getUserPin(\_)$ is a shared action with the keyboard component (not specified here) and yields the user supplied PIN value. Validation of the current card is performed by the $checkPin$ action; each call increments the number of attempts to verify the card's PIN and then, if the user supplied PIN is the same as the PIN of the current card, $cardAccepted$ is added to the current state. The $cardOut$ action simply removes the observation from the state. The $swallowCard$ action removes the $currentCard$ observation and adds the fact that the card is swallowed as well as its rejection.

The card reader's control program loops endlessly. It first reads the account number and PIN from the input card, gets a user supplied PIN and attempts to validate it. If validation succeeds in less than three attempts, the card is returned (we are not concerned with other account actions that may then have followed). If validation does not succeed within three attempts, the card is swallowed and the reader becomes ready to accept another card.

$CardReader_0$

OBSERVATION PREDICATES
  $currentCard : Account \times Pin$
  $attempts : 0..3$
  $cardAccepted, cardRejected$
  $swallowedCard : Account \times Pin$

CONSTRAINTS
  $unique \stackrel{dfn}{=}$
      $\forall a_1, a_2 : Account, p_1, p_2 : Pin \cdot$
          $((currentCard(a_1, p_1) \wedge currentCard(a_2, p_2))$
              $\Rightarrow (a_1 = a_2 \wedge p_1 = p_2)) \wedge$
      $\neg(cardAccepted \wedge cardRejected) \wedge$
      $\forall a : Account, p_1, p_2 : Pin \cdot$
          $((swallowedCard(a, p_1) \wedge swallowedCard(a, p_2)) \Rightarrow (p_1 = p_2))$

ACTIONS
  $cardIn(acc : Account, pin : Pin)$

pre	$\{\neg\exists a : Account, p : Pin \cdot currentCard(a, p)\}$
add	$\{currentCard(acc, pin), attempts(0)\}$
del	$\{cardAccepted, cardRejected, attempts(n) \mid n \in 1..3\}$

  $cardOut()$

pre	$\{currentCard(acc, pin)\}$
add	$\{\}$
del	$\{currentCard(acc, pin)\}$

  $getUserPin(userPin : Pin)$

pre	$\{\}$
add	$\{\}$
del	$\{\}$

  $checkPin(userPin : Pin)$

pre	$\{attempts(n), n < 3, currentCard(acc, pin)\}$
add	$\{attempts(n + 1)\} \cup \{cardAccepted \mid pin = userPin\}$
del	$\{attempts(n)\}$

  $swallowCard()$

pre	$\{currentCard(acc, pin), \neg cardAccepted\}$
add	$\{swallowedCard(acc, pin), cardRejected\}$
del	$\{currentCard(acc, pin)\}$

PROGRAM
  $[\ cardIn(?acc, ?pin);$
    $[\neg(cardAccepted \vee cardRejected) \rightarrow$
        $getUserPin(?userPin);$
        $checkPin(userPin);$
        $[\neg cardAccepted \wedge attempts(3) \rightarrow swallowCard()$
        $\| cardAccepted \rightarrow cardOut()$
        $]$
    $]^*$
  $]^*$

The new banking system is to be dynamically upgradable. The card reader is therefore reconstructed as an *evolvable* component by pairing it with a supervisory component and encapsulating the pair as a single component. A specification for the structure and actions of the supervisor component is given below. There are a number of different types of temporal criteria that may be dynamically monitored. For example, the system may monitor the ratio of rejected to accepted cards over a rolling 24-hour period, or on a daily basis, or over a fixed number of night-time hours, etc. The supervisor thus contains a predicate *criterion* pairing a criterion type and value – the latter may represent time-series data in order to compute rolling ratios, etc.

$CardReaderSupervisor$ META TO $cid : CardReader_{level}$

TYPES

$\quad CriterionType \overset{dfn}{=} \{rejectsPerHour, usersPerHour, \ldots\}$

$\quad CriterionValue \overset{dfn}{=} \ldots$

FUNCTIONS

$\quad updateCriterion : CriterionType \times CriterionValue \times Int \times Time$
$\qquad\qquad\qquad\qquad \to CriterionValue$

OBSERVATION PREDICATES

$\quad clock : Time$

$\quad criterion : CriterionType \times CriterionValue$

$\quad securityUpgrade : Int \times$ STATETRANSFORMER $\times$
$\qquad\qquad\qquad\qquad$ COMPONENTTRANSFORMER $\times$ SCHEMATRANSFORMER

$\quad holds :$ FORMULA $\times ConfigName$

$\quad current : ConfigName$

CONSTRAINTS $\ldots$

ACTIONS

$observeAccept(X : 2^{CriterionType})$

pre	$\{current(c), clock(t), \bigwedge_{ct \in X} criterion(ct, cv_{ct})\}$
add	$\{holds(cid.cardAccepted, s(c)), current(s(c)),$ $\bigwedge_{ct \in X} criterion(ct, updateCriterion(ct, cv_{ct}, 1, t))\}$
del	$\{current(c), \bigwedge_{ct \in X} criterion(ct, cv_{ct})\}$

$observeReject(X : 2^{CriterionType})$

pre	$\{current(c), clock(t), \bigwedge_{ct \in X} criterion(ct, cv_{ct})\}$
add	$\{holds(cid.cardRejected, s(c)), current(s(c)),$ $\bigwedge_{ct \in X} criterion(ct, updateCriterion(ct, cv_{ct}, 0, t))\}$
del	$\{current(c), \bigwedge_{ct \in X} criterion(ct, cv_{ct})\}$

$upgradeSecurityChecking()$

pre	$\{current(c), securityUpgrade(level, st, ct, cs),$ $component(thisComp \text{ as } [cid \mapsto \langle CardReader_{level}, \_, \_, \_\rangle])\}$
add	$\{current(s(c)), component(ct(thisComp))$ $evolve(st, ct(thisComp), cs(CardReader_{level}), s(c))\}$
del	$\{current(c), component(thisComp)\}$

Before presenting the supervisor's monitoring program, a few words of explanation on the above actions are necessary. The basic monitoring actions update the *criterion* predicate according for the associated criteria types. The evolutionary action *upgradeSecurityChecking*() specifies the potentially complex operation of updating the card reader's security checking procedures. To keep things simple, we suppose that the card reader supervisor has pre-programmed transformations that it can apply to the card reader. Recall that the card reader component performed very basic checking. A higher level vetting may include, for example, a check with the bank on the card's recent transaction history to determine whether its current use is out of the norm, and then, if so, to proceed through further security checks, e.g. via questions agreed previously with the customer. It may also be possible to invoke other forms of unique customer identification, e.g. finger prints, iris prints, etc., depending upon hardware capability and information stored on chip. The *upgradeSecurityChecking*() action schema abstracts the update via three transformations that are stored in the supervisor's state. The predicate *securityUpgrade(level, st, ct, cs)* records the fact that *st*, *ct* and *cs* are, respectively, state, component instance and component schema transformers which yield a card reader at security level *level*. These transformers are applied in the appropriate way to the observation state, component instance map and schema map of the object-level configuration for the card reader component by the addition of a suitably instantiated *evolve* predicate in the supervisor's observation state.

From past analyses of card use, the bank finds that it is acceptable for (i) the hourly average of retries on PINs not to exceed one during daytime unless there's been very high usage over the past 24 hour period, and (ii) the hourly average of retries to be no more than 2 during the wee night hours, again unless the usage has been exceptionally low over the past 24 hours. The Bank of New Island governors believe that patterns of behaviour falling outside these norms warrant a higher level of security checking. We can capture this monitoring via a supervisor program in which temporal formulas, for example EAGLE formulas [2], are used to define the acceptable norms. The program construct

> MONITOR USING ⟨Actions⟩ WHERE ⟨Bindings⟩
> BEHAVIOUR ⟨Formula⟩
> [ON SUCCESS ⟨Program⟩]
> [ON FAILURE ⟨Program⟩]

describes a runtime monitor that checks conformance of the supervisor's state against the given formula whenever any of the specified actions are executed. As soon as the observed temporal behaviour matches the specified logical formula, the (optional) success continuation program is executed. On the other hand, as soon as the run-time behaviour can be determined not to match the specified behaviour, the (optional) failure continuation program is executed. As an example, we give a simple card reader monitoring program:

PROGRAM
[MONITOR USING *observeAccept*, *observeReject* WHERE

$$a \overset{dfn}{=} \iota x \text{ ST } criterion(rejectsPerHour, x)$$
$$u \overset{dfn}{=} \iota y \text{ ST } criterion(usersPerHour, y)$$
$$t \overset{dfn}{=} \iota z \text{ ST } clock(z)$$
$$daytime(t) \overset{dfn}{=} 3 \leq hour(t) \wedge hour(t) < 22$$

BEHAVIOUR
ALWAYS($(daytime(t) \Rightarrow a \leq 1 \vee \text{OVERPASTDAY}(t, u > 20)) \wedge$
$(\neg daytime(t) \Rightarrow a \leq 2 \vee \text{OVERPASTDAY}(t, u < 2)))$
ON SUCCESS [STATUS(STOP) $\rightarrow$ STOP
‖ STATUS(ABORT) $\rightarrow$ *resetCardReader*()]
ON FAILURE *upgradeSecurityChecking*()
]*

The card reader supervisor observes the accepts and rejects of the card reader via *observeAccept*() and *observeReject*() actions. The bindings define the average number of rejects per hour and of users per hour given by the *criterion* predicate, and also the time given by the *clock* predicate. The temporal formula characterises the desired behaviour. Because it is an ALWAYS formula, it can evaluate to true only when the program of the card reader terminates. For normal termination with status STOP, the monitoring program also stops. For abnormal termination with status ABORT, the supervisor resets the card reader (we do not define this here). On the other hand, should the sequence of observations lead to criterion values that do not satisfy the temporal formula, then the failure continuation program, the *upgradeSecurityChecking*() action of the card reader supervisor, is executed to upgrade the card reader to a higher security level. As the monitor construct is embedded within a loop, once the upgrade is complete, monitoring will be resumed.

3   A Logical Framework

We now give an overview of a revision-based logical framework which provides an interpretation for descriptions of evolvable component systems, such as that of the ATM above. A full description of this framework may be found in [1].

3.1   States, Configurations and Revision Actions

States of systems are expressed in terms of sets of formulas which are ground, i.e. no free variables, and atomic, i.e. consisting only of applications of predicates to terms. Such formulas are 'observations' of a system's computational state. For example, the set $\{currentCard(5435123456789012, 1234), attempts(3)\}$ is a possible state of the card reader described above.

Computations are expressed in terms of actions which 'revise' states. For states which are sets of formulas, these revisions take on a particularly simple form, namely the addition of new formulas, possibly with the deletion of some existing formulas. For example, the *swallowCard* action of the card reader revises the above state to become the state:

$$\{swallowedCard(5435123456789012, 1234), cardRejected, attempts(3)\}.$$

When a state Δ is updated by an action α to become state Δ', we write $\Delta \xrightarrow{\alpha} \Delta'$.

A *configuration* corresponds to the full logical structure of a component hierarchy. A configuration $\Gamma = \langle \Delta, \Theta, \Sigma, \Pi, \chi \rangle$ consists of a tree-structured state Δ, i.e. a set of ground atomic formulas allocated to each node of the hierarchy, a component instance hierarchy Θ and a schema hierarchy Σ. Access to elements of these hierarchies are provided by well-formed *paths*. Full details of this structure are found in [1]. New to this account are the remaining elements of the configuration, consisting of a program structure Π and a program status χ. The form of these is described in the next section. The definition of revision by actions may be extended to tree-structured states, using paths to identify the location of a revision.

3.2   Meta-view Relations

In the description of an evolvable card reader consisting of an object-level component, $CardReader_0$, and a meta-level component, $CardReaderSupervisor$, the states of the two components must be in accord, in that what is asserted to hold at the meta-level of the object-level system, must indeed hold. Moreover, the supervisor state may assert the existence of constraints, actions and programs at the object-level, which therefore must exist. Further, when an *evolve* predicate is present in the meta-level state, the required change of object-level structure must occur. These requirements are expressed as 'meta-view' relations.

Definition 1 (State meta-view). *Let W^M and W be the typed first-order theories for meta-level and object-level systems respectively. We say that Δ^M (from a configuration Γ^M of W^M) is a state meta-view of a configuration $\Gamma = \langle \Delta, \Theta, \Sigma, \Pi, \chi \rangle$ of theory W if, for any valid non-empty path of basic (i.e. non-evolvable) component identifiers p in Δ^M*

- *for all object-level formulas φ and any configuration name c, if $p.\{current(c), holds(\varphi, c)\} \subseteq\ \downarrow \Delta^M$, then $\downarrow \Delta \models_W \varphi$;*
- *for all component instance maps θ, if $p.component(\theta) \in\ \downarrow \Delta^M$, then $\theta \subseteq \Theta$;*
- *for all schema definition maps σ, if $p.schema(\sigma) \in\ \downarrow \Delta^M$, then $\sigma \subseteq \Sigma$;*
- *for all program structures π, if $p.program(\pi) \in\ \downarrow \Delta^M$, then $\pi = \Pi$.*

We also say that Γ^M is a meta-configuration *for Γ.*

Here, $\downarrow \Delta$ is the flattened form of the tree-structured state Δ. When this relationship is extended to all levels of a component hierarchy in a configuration, we say that the configuration is *state meta-consistent*.

Definition 2 (Transition meta-view). *Given meta-level configurations,* $\Gamma^{M} = \langle \Delta^{M}, \Theta^{M}, \Sigma^{M}, \Pi^{M}, \chi^{M} \rangle$ *and* $\Gamma^{M\prime} = \langle \Delta^{M\prime}, \Theta^{M\prime}, \Sigma^{M\prime}, \Pi^{M\prime}, \chi^{M\prime} \rangle$ *of component theory* W^{M}, *and, at object-level,* $\Gamma = \langle \Delta, \Theta, \Sigma, \Pi, \chi \rangle$ *and* $\Gamma' = \langle \Delta', \Theta', \Sigma', \Pi', \chi' \rangle$ *of component theory* W, *such that* Δ^{M}, $\Delta^{M\prime}$ *are, respectively, state meta-views of* Γ, Γ', *we say that the pair* $\langle \Delta^{M}, \Delta^{M\prime} \rangle$ *is a* transition meta-view *of* $\langle \Gamma, \Gamma' \rangle$, *if whenever for any valid non-empty path of basic (i.e. non-evolvable) component identifiers* p *in* Δ^{M},

$$p.\{evolve(\delta, \theta, \sigma, \pi, c), current(c)\} \subseteq \downarrow \Delta^{M\prime}$$

and $\Delta' = \delta(\Delta)$ *is consistent in theory* W', *where* W' *is the component theory* W *with component instance map* Θ *updated to* $\Theta' = \Theta \dagger \theta$, *component schema definitions* Σ *updated to* $\Sigma' = \Sigma \dagger \sigma$, *and program structure updated* Π *updated to* $\Pi' = \pi(\Pi)$, *then* $\Gamma' = \langle \Delta', \Theta', \Sigma', \Pi', \text{RUN} \rangle$.

Furthermore, we say that the configuration pair $\langle \Gamma^{M}, \Gamma^{M\prime} \rangle$ *is a* transition meta-configuration pair *for* $\langle \Gamma, \Gamma' \rangle$ *and write* $tmcp(\Gamma^{M}, \Gamma^{M\prime}, \Gamma, \Gamma')$.

4   Including Programs in Component Theories

4.1   Evolvable Component Structures

We now consider how to incorporate programs into a hierarchy of evolvable components. There are several issues which need to be addressed when each individual component has a program associated with it:

- In an assembly of components, how do we determine the overall computation from that of the individual programs?
- In cases where programs may terminate normally or abort their computation abnormally, how does this behaviour in a component affect the overall computational behaviour of the system?
- How are the monitoring, diagnostic and evolutionary aspects of a supervisor expressed in terms of a program?

To formalise answers to these, we (1) introduce combinators for programs corresponding to way we assemble components, (2) present an operational semantics of these combinators, (3) include explicitly the notion of the 'status' of a program in the semantics, so that the effect of the status of individual programs on the overall computation can be expressed, and (4) introduce a specific monitoring language for supervisors.

For evolvable systems, there are two ways that components may be combined. The 'horizontal' combination of components allows components to communicate via synchronised joint actions. The corresponding combination of programs is

$$\Pi \text{ WITH } \Pi_1, \Pi_2$$

denoting the main program Π of a component instance C with sub-component programs Π_1 and Π_2 of sub-component instances C_1 and C_2 of C.

The 'vertical' combination of components is that of the supervisor/supervisee pairing used to model evolvable components. We write

$$\Pi_M \text{ META TO } \Pi_O$$

for the combination of a supervisor's program Π_M (at a meta-level) with that of the program Π_O of its supervisee (at an object-level).

To make the semantics specific and to correspond to the example above of automated bank teller machines, we introduce two simple programming languages. The first is a language of guarded commands, built from basic actions α, and standard constructs:

$$\Pi ::= \alpha \mid \text{STOP} \mid \Pi_1; \Pi_2 \mid [\,]_i g_i \rightarrow \Pi_i] \mid \Pi^*$$

The second language is that of supervisory control for meta-level components. We reuse the language of guarded commands, extending it with a monitoring construct:

$$monitor(A, \varphi, \Pi_1, \Pi_2)$$

This is abstract syntax for the monitoring programs that we introduced in the banking example above. The set A is that of supervisor actions at which the monitoring events take place, φ is the monitoring formula (in the above example we use a temporal logic to express monitoring formulas, but other logics may be used instead), Π_1 is the program that runs in the case when the monitoring succeeds i.e. the formula becomes satisfied, and Π_2 is the program that runs when the monitoring fails i.e the formula becomes falsified.

4.2   An Operational Semantics

We provide an SOS-style [6] transition semantics. The semantics of a program structure Π is a labelled relation between configurations which we write as

$$\Gamma \xrightarrow{\alpha} \Gamma',$$

where α is the current action undertaken to transform configuration Γ to Γ'. For a component configuration $\Gamma = \langle \Delta, \Theta, \Sigma, \Pi, \chi \rangle$, we write $\Gamma[\Pi', \chi']$ for the configuration $\langle \Delta, \Theta, \Sigma, \Pi', \chi' \rangle$. Much of the semantics follows standard guarded-command language semantics [6]. We concentrate here on monitoring programs and the combinators corresponding to component assembly.

The first rule states that the semantic relation $\xrightarrow{\alpha}$ is indeed an extension of the revision relation and we introduce the RUN program status. Thus, for a program which consists of a single action α with precondition pre-α[1]:

$$\frac{\downarrow \Delta \models \text{pre-}\alpha \qquad \Delta \xrightarrow{\alpha} \Delta'}{\langle \Delta, \Theta, \Sigma, \alpha, \text{RUN} \rangle \xrightarrow{\alpha} \langle \Delta', \Theta, \Sigma, \text{NULL}, \text{RUN} \rangle}$$

---

[1] For the case of an action for which the precondition is *not* satisfied, the resulting program status is not RUN but is ABORT, with suitable rules for the ABORT status.

The semantics of monitoring programs of the form $monitor(A, \varphi, \Pi_1, \Pi_2)$ require us to 'unfold' the monitoring formula φ as the computation proceeds. The exact form of this depends upon the logic used to express monitoring formulas, in particular, temporal operators unfold as future obligations become satisfied. Techniques for this are well-known (see e.g [2]). We thus assume a relation of the form $\Gamma, \varphi \xrightarrow{\alpha} \Gamma', \varphi'$ where φ' is the unfolding of φ after the action α in the context of the two configurations Γ and Γ'. The rules for monitoring are:

$$\frac{\alpha \in A, \qquad \Gamma, \varphi \xrightarrow{\alpha} \Gamma', \varphi', \qquad \varphi \notin \{\top, \bot\}}{\Gamma[monitor(A, \varphi, \Pi_1, \Pi_2), \text{RUN}] \xrightarrow{\alpha} \Gamma'[monitor(A, \varphi', \Pi_1, \Pi_2), \text{RUN}]}$$

$$\frac{\alpha \in A, \qquad \Gamma, \varphi \xrightarrow{\alpha} \Gamma', \top}{\Gamma[monitor(A, \varphi, \Pi_1, \Pi_2), \text{RUN}] \xrightarrow{\alpha} \Gamma'[\Pi_1, \text{RUN}]}$$

$$\frac{\alpha \in A, \qquad \Gamma, \varphi \xrightarrow{\alpha} \Gamma', \bot}{\Gamma[monitor(A, \varphi, \Pi_1, \Pi_2), \text{RUN}] \xrightarrow{\alpha} \Gamma'[\Pi_2, \text{RUN}]}$$

The first rule is the case when monitoring continues with a revised formula, the second and third rules are the cases when monitoring succeeds and the formula is satisfied, and the case when monitoring fails and the formula is falsified. There are also rules for the case where the object-level system terminates, either normally or with failure.

We now turn to evolvable components, i.e. the supervisor/supervisee pairing of a a meta-level to an object-level system. The actions of such a combination are of three forms:

$\langle \alpha_{observe}, \alpha \rangle$, a *paired action* consisting of a meta-level observation action $\alpha_{observe}$ executed in synchrony with an object-level component action α;

$\langle \alpha_{query}, \rangle$, a meta-level *query* action[2] α_{query} executed in isolation of the object-level component, but leaving the object-level system unchanged;

$\langle \alpha_{evolve}, \rangle$, a meta-level *evolution* action α_{evolve} with no explicit object-level action, but inducing an object-level system change.

The semantics of paired actions is:

$$\frac{\uparrow_{\mathcal{M}} \Gamma[\Pi_M, \text{RUN}] \xrightarrow{\alpha_M} \uparrow_{\mathcal{M}} \Gamma'[\Pi_M', \chi_M'] \qquad \uparrow_{\mathcal{O}} \Gamma[\Pi_O, \text{RUN}] \xrightarrow{\alpha_O} \uparrow_{\mathcal{O}} \Gamma'[\Pi_O', \chi_O'] \qquad \text{where } tmcp(\uparrow_{\mathcal{M}} \Gamma, \uparrow_{\mathcal{M}} \Gamma', \uparrow_{\mathcal{O}} \Gamma, \uparrow_{\mathcal{O}} \Gamma')}{\Gamma[\Pi_M \text{ META TO } \Pi_O, \text{RUN}] \xrightarrow{\langle \alpha_M, \alpha_O \rangle} \Gamma'[\Pi_M' \text{ META TO } \Pi_O', \chi_M']}$$

Here, for a configuration Γ of a supervisor/supervisee pairing, $\uparrow_{\mathcal{M}} \Gamma$ is the configuration of the supervisor (at the meta-level) and $\uparrow_{\mathcal{O}} \Gamma$ is the configuration of the supervisee (at the object-level). This rule says: if the supervisor program makes an α_M transition, and the supervisee program makes an α_O transition, then the combination program may make a $\langle \alpha_M, \alpha_O \rangle$ transition, provided that

---

[2] The query action is typically used when the supervisee program has terminated and the supervisor needs to query the reason for termination.

the configurations of the supervisor before and after the transition, and those of the supervisee, are related as a *transition meta-configuration pair* (see Definition 2), i.e. the action of the supervisor tracks that of the supervisee so that the required relationship holds. The program status of the final system is that of the *supervisor* after its action, giving the supervisor overall control of the computation. The rule for query actions is similar, except that there is no α_O action and therefore the configuration of the supervisee remains unchanged.

The *evolution action* is a key to the whole account. Here an action is undertaken by the supervisor which *induces a change* in the supervisee, without an explicit supervisee action. The semantics of this is expressed in the following rule.

$$\frac{\uparrow_{\mathcal{M}} \Gamma[\Pi_M, \text{RUN}] \xrightarrow{\alpha_M} \uparrow_{\mathcal{M}} \Gamma'[\Pi'_M, \chi'_M] \qquad \Pi'_O = \Pi(\uparrow_O \Gamma'), \text{ where } tmcp(\uparrow_{\mathcal{M}} \Gamma, \uparrow_{\mathcal{M}} \Gamma', \uparrow_O \Gamma, \uparrow_O \Gamma')}{\Gamma[\Pi_M \text{ META TO } \Pi_O, \text{RUN}] \xrightarrow{\langle \alpha_M, \rangle} \Gamma'[\Pi'_M \text{ META TO } \Pi'_O, \chi'_M]}$$

Again, the crucial condition linking the configuration of the supervisee before and after the supervisor's evolution action is the transition meta-view relation.

We now look briefly at the semantics of the horizontal composition of components. For a configuration Γ consisting of a component with configuration $\uparrow_0 \Gamma$ which has two immediate subcomponents with configurations $\uparrow_1 \Gamma$ and $\uparrow_2 \Gamma$ several actions are possible. We consider here only one case, the action of a component which consists of a 'communication' between its two subcomponents. In this case, the action α of the component is defined to be the joint action $\alpha_1 || \alpha_2$ of the two subcomponents, with semantics:

$$\frac{\uparrow_0 \Gamma[\Pi, \text{RUN}] \xrightarrow{\alpha} \uparrow_0 \Gamma'[\Pi', \chi'_0] \qquad \uparrow_1 \Gamma[\Pi_1, \text{RUN}] \xrightarrow{\alpha_1} \uparrow_1 \Gamma'[\Pi'_1, \chi'_1]}{\uparrow_2 \Gamma[\Pi_2, \text{RUN}] \xrightarrow{\alpha_2} \uparrow_2 \Gamma'[\Pi'_2, \chi'_2] \qquad \chi' = (\chi'_1 = \text{ABORT}?\chi'_1 : \chi'_2)}{\Gamma[\Pi \text{ WITH } \Pi_1, \Pi_2, \text{ RUN}] \xrightarrow{\alpha} \Gamma'[\Pi' \text{ WITH } \Pi'_1, \Pi'_2, \chi']}$$

As an example of the semantics, consider the specification of an evolvable bank card reader in Section 2. The *CardReaderSupervisor* has a monitoring program which, when the monitoring fails because the pattern of activities falls outside its requirements, invokes the *upgradeSecurityChecking* action. To interpret this, the *evolution action* rule applies. This says that, if the supervisor's status is RUN, then the result of the *upgradeSecurityChecking* action is a supervisor/supervisee configuration Γ' whose object-level configuration $\uparrow_O \Gamma'$ is related to the meta-level as a transition meta-configuration pair (Definition 2). This relation says that the object-level card reader is that provided by the *evolve*-formula added to the state by the *upgradeSecurityChecking* action, i.e. a new card reader with an upgraded security vetting system. The rule says that the program for the supervisor is the continuation after the evolution step and the program of the card reader is that supplied with the new card reader.

We have thus demonstrated how programmed monitoring and evolutionary change may be described in terms of a revision-based logic and a transition-based operational semantics.

5   Conclusions

One starting point for this work lies in the relationship between supervisory control systems and runtime monitoring and verification. To explore this link, we have shown how programs may be incorporated into a logical account of evolvable component systems, using a transition-based operational semantics to capture the interaction of programs amongst components, in particular for components which have supervisory monitoring and control. We are currently developing a corresponding trace-based denotational semantics.

As a revision-based logic, the framework may be implemented to provide a *logical abstract machine*. The implementation requires automated reasoning tools to establish the validity of action application and of meta-view relations. Such a machine can be used to prototype evolvable systems, or, when run alongside an actual evolvable system, it can provide a mechanism for runtime verification. This work thus provides not only a foundation for static proof analysis but also a natural setting for dynamic, reasoned and programmed, control of system evolution as a generalization of standard runtime verification.

References

1. Barringer, H., Gabbay, D., Rydeheard, D.: Logical modelling of evolvable component systems: Part (I) A logical framework. Submitted for publication (2007), See `http://www.cs.manchester.ac.uk/evolve`
2. Barringer, H., Goldberg, A., Havelund, K., Sen, K.: Program monitoring with LTL in Eagle. In: Proceedings of PADTAD 2004, Parallel and Distributed Systems: Testing and Debugging, Santa Fe, New Mexico, USA (2004)
3. Barringer, H., Rydeheard, D., Gabbay, D.: A logical framework for monitoring and evolving software components. In: TASE 2007. Proceeding of the First Joint IEEE/IFIP Symposium on Theoretical Aspects of Computer Science, Shanghai, China, June 2007, IEEE Computer Society Press, Los Alamitos (2007)
4. Barringer, H., Rydeheard, D., Warboys, B., Gabbay, D.: A revision-based logical framework for evolvable software. In: SE 2007. Proceeding of IASTED Multi-Conference: Software Engineering, Innsbruck, Austria, pp. 78–83 (2007)
5. Kiczales, G., Lamping, J., Mendhekar, A., Maeda, C., Lopes, C., Loingtier, J.-M., Irwin, J.: Aspect-oriented programming. In: Aksit, M., Matsuoka, S. (eds.) ECOOP 1997. LNCS, vol. 1241, pp. 220–242. Springer, Heidelberg (1997)
6. Plotkin, G.D.: A structural approach to operational semantics. Technical Report, DAIMI FN-19, University of Aarhus (1981)
7. Warboys, B.C., Snowdon, R.A., Greenwood, R.M., Seet, W., Robertson, I., Morrison, R., Balasubramaniam, D., Kirby, G., Mickan, K.: An active architecture approach to cots integration. IEEE Software - Special Issue on Incorporating COTS into the Development Process 22(4), 20–27 (2005)

Rule Systems for Run-Time Monitoring: From EAGLE to RULER

Howard Barringer[1], David Rydeheard[1], and Klaus Havelund[2,*]

[1] School of Computer Science, University of Manchester, Oxford Road, Manchester, M13 9PL, UK
{Howard.Barringer,David.Rydeheard}@manchester.ac.uk

[2] NASA's Jet Propulsion Laboratory, California Institute of Technology, Pasadena, CA 91109, USA
Klaus.Havelund@jpl.nasa.gov

Abstract. In [3], EAGLE was introduced as a general purpose rule-based temporal logic for specifying run-time monitors. A novel and relatively efficient interpretative trace-checking scheme via stepwise transformation of an EAGLE monitoring formula was defined and implemented. However, application in real-world examples has shown efficiency weaknesses, especially those associated with large-scale symbolic formula manipulation. In this paper, after briefly reviewing EAGLE, we introduce RULER, a primitive conditional rule-based system, which we claim can be more efficiently implemented for run-time checking, and into which one can compile various temporal logics used for run-time verification.

1 Introduction

In earlier work, the rule-based temporal logic EAGLE [3] was developed as a generalisation of the plethora of logics which have been used for the specification of behavioural system properties and which can be dynamically checked either on-line throughout an execution of the system or off-line over an execution trace of the system. We showed that EAGLE supported future and past time logics, interval logics, extended regular expressions, state machines, logics for real-time and data constraints, and temporal-based logics for stochastic behaviour.

The EAGLE logic is a restricted first order, fixed-point, linear-time temporal logic with chop (concatenation) over *finite* traces. As such, the logic is highly expressive and, not surprisingly, EAGLE's satisfiability (validity) problem is undecidable; checking satisfiability in a given model, however, is decidable and that is what's required for run-time verification. The syntax and semantics of EAGLE are succinct. There are four primitive temporal operators: $\bigcirc$ — next, $\odot$ — previously, $\cdot$ — concatenation, and ; — chop (overlapping concatenation, or sequential composition). Temporal equations can be used to define schema

---

* The work of this author was carried out at the Jet Propulsion Laboratory, California Institute of Technology, under a contract with the National Aeronautics and Space Administration.

O. Sokolsky and S. Tasiran (Eds.): RV 2007, LNCS 4839, pp. 111–125, 2007.

for temporal formulas, where the temporal predicates may be parameterized by data as well as by EAGLE formulas. The usual boolean logical connectives exist. For example, the linear-time $\Box$, $\Diamond$, $\mathcal{U}$ and $\mathcal{S}$ (always, sometime, until and since) temporal operators can be introduced through the following equational definitions.

$$\textbf{max Always(Form } F) = F \wedge \bigcirc \text{Always}(F)$$
$$\textbf{min Sometime(Form} F) = F \vee \bigcirc \text{Sometime}(F)$$
$$\textbf{min Until(Form } F_1, \textbf{Form } F_2) = F_2 \vee (F_1 \wedge \bigcirc \text{Until}(F_1, F_2))$$
$$\textbf{min Since(Form } F_1, \textbf{Form } F_2) = (F_2 \vee (F_1 \wedge \odot \text{Since}(F_1, F_2)))$$

The qualifiers **max** and **min** indicate the positive and, respectively, negative interpretation that is to be given to the associated temporal predicate at trace boundaries — corresponding to maximal and minimal solutions to the equations. Thus $\bigcirc\text{Always}(p)$ is defined to be true in the last state of a given trace, whereas $\bigcirc\text{Until}(p, q)$ is false in the last state. Thus the formula $\text{Always}(p)$ will hold on a finite sequence from, say index i, if and only if p holds in every state from index i up to and including the final state. Whereas, if $\text{Until}(p, q)$ holds at index i then q must be true at some state with index $j \geq i$ and p true on all states from i up to but not including j.[1]

Even without data parametrization, the primitive concatenation temporal operators together with the recursively defined temporal predicates take the logic into the world of context-free expressivity thus enabling simple grammatical-like specification of parenthesis, call return, or login logout matching. Assume *call* and *return* are propositions denoting procedure call and return events. The temporal formula $\text{Match}(call, return)$ where

$$\textbf{min Match(Form } C, \textbf{Form } R) =$$
$$C \cdot \text{Match}(C, R) \cdot R \cdot \text{Match}(C, R) \vee \text{Empty}()$$

with $\text{Empty}()$ true just on the empty sequence captures the behaviour that every *call* has a matching *return* — a call may be followed by a (possibly empty) sequence of matched calls and returns, followed a return, followed by another (possibly empty) sequence of calls and returns. Parametrization of temporal predicates by data values allows us to define real-time and stochastic logical operators. To address real-time, for example, we assume that EAGLE is monitoring time-stamped states, where the state contains a variable *clock* holding the associated real time. Then it becomes straightforward to define real-time qualified temporal operators such as *happens before real time u.*

$$\textbf{min HappensBefore(Form } F, \textbf{double } u) =$$
$$clock < u \wedge (F \vee (\neg F \wedge \bigcirc \text{HappensBefore}(F, u)))$$

It should be clear how more complex real-time, and even probabilistic, temporal operators can be recursively defined.

We still claim that EAGLE presents a natural rule/equation based language for defining, even programming, monitors for complex temporal behavioural

---

[1] Arguments for using other interpretations over finite traces have been put forward. However, we have found that this simple interpretation has been adequate for our monitoring purposes.

patterns. EAGLE is, however, expressively rich and in general this comes with a potentially high computational cost, practically speaking. So one might ask whether EAGLE presents the most appropriate set of primitive temporal operators for run-time monitoring. The non-deterministic concatenation operator, as used above in the matching parentheses example, requires considerable care in use. In order to achieve the expected temporal behaviour pattern, the formulas passed to Match should specify single state sequences. If that is not the case, the concatenation operator may choose an arbitrary cut point, and therefore skip unmatched Bs or Es in order to give a positive result. Later, but currently unpublished, work developed such arguments further and proposed a variety of deterministic versions of temporal concatenation and chop for run-time monitoring, using different forms of cut, e.g. left and right minimal, left and right maximal, etc..

With respect to the computational effectiveness of algorithms for EAGLE trace-checking, in [3] we showed how trace-checking of full EAGLE can be undertaken on a state-by-state basis without recording the full history, even though the logic has the same temporal expressiveness over the past as over the future; basically, our published trace-check algorithm maintains sufficient knowledge about the past in the evolving monitor formulas. Furthermore, we have shown that for restricted subsets, we can achieve close to optimal complexity bounds for monitoring; one such fragment for which we computed complexity results was the LTL (past and future) fragment of EAGLE [4]. However, considerable care must be taken with the presence of data arguments in temporal predicates, for an explosion in the size of the evolving monitor formula may occur.

What was clear to us at the time was that there were some practically useful and efficiently executable subsets of EAGLE. Despite the pleasing features of EAGLE, we still believe we should continue to search for a powerful and simpler "core" logic, one that is easy and efficient to evaluate for monitoring purposes. To that end, we present in the remainder of this paper a seemingly simpler, lower-level, rule-based system RULER. In Section 2 we introduce RULER and a simple evaluation algorithm by example. Section 3 then provides a more formal semantic treatment and indicates how propositional temporal logic (with past and future operators) can be compiled into RULER. In Section 4, we then briefly consider RULER with rule parameters and then present brief conclusions and indicate further work in Section 5.

2 RULER by Example

A RULER monitoring program comprises a collection of named rules. A rule is formed from a condition part (antecedent) and a body part (consequent). The rule's condition may be a conjunctive set of literals, whereas the body is a disjunctive set of conjunctive sets of literals, a literal being a positive or negative occurrence of a rule name or an observation name. The idea is that rules can be made active or inactive. For each active rule, if the condition part evaluates to true for the current state (formed from the current observations and previous obligations of the rule system), then the body of the rule defines what rules are active and what observations must hold in the next state. As a very simple example, consider the rule named r below in the context of some observation named a.

$$r : \multimap a, r$$

The rule has a vacuous condition. The rule's body is the conjunctive set containing observation a and rule name r. If r is active at the start of monitoring, r's body asserts that the observation a must hold in next monitoring state and the rule r must be active again, thus effectively asserting that observation a must hold in all subsequent monitoring states. If, at some future state, a fails to hold, then there will be a conflict between obligations and actuality. In this simple case, the rule will fail at that particular point.

Figure 1 outlines a basic algorithm for monitoring a sequence of observation states with a set of named rules. Essentially, the algorithm unfolds the active rules according to the given input observation states. As rule bodies are disjunctive, the algorithm computes sets of possible future states in order to avoid the need for backtracking when a rule failure occurs. A rule activation state is a set of rule name literals and observation literals. We demonstrate this algorithm in Example 1 where we consider a set of rules that capture both past time conditions and future time obligations. We will assume that we wish to monitor some temporal behaviour of a system in terms of two properties, a and b. Thus, we arrange for the system to be instrumented to produce an ordered sequence of observation states and that the letters a and b denote particular propositions over an observation state. In effect, we'll treat an observation trace as a sequence of sets of literals[2].

```
create an initial set of initial rule activation states
WHILE observations exist DO
  obtain next observation state
  merge observation state across the set of rule activation states
  raise monitoring exception if there's no self-consistent merged state
  for each of the current and self-consistent merged states,
     use activated rules to generate a successor set of activation states
  union successor sets to form the new frontier of rule activation states
OD
```

Fig. 1. The basic monitoring algorithm

Example 1. We wish to monitor the constraint that whenever property a occurs both now and in the immediate previous state then b must occur as a later observed property. We can characterise this by the linear time temporal logic formula $\Box((a \wedge \bigodot a) \Rightarrow \Diamond b)$ where $\Diamond$ is the strict "eventually in the future" temporal operator, or using the EAGLE temporal predicates defined in Section 1

---

[2] We don't allow both x and $\neg x$ to occur in an observation state, for any x.

by the monitoring formula $\texttt{Always}((a \wedge \odot a) \Rightarrow \bigcirc \texttt{Sometime}(b))$. In RULER the following set of rules characterise the required temporal behaviour

$$r_0 : \multimap r_0, r_1, r_3 \qquad r_1 : a \multimap r_2 \qquad r_2 :$$
$$r_3 : a, r_2 \multimap b \mid \neg b, r_4 \qquad r_4 : \multimap b \mid \neg b, r_4$$

assuming that the monitoring algorithm starts with an initial set of rule activation sets as $\{\{r_0, r_1, r_3\}\}^3$. Rule r_0 acts as a generator rule; it ensures persistent activity of itself together with r_1 and r_3, i.e. the three rules are always to be active. The empty rule r_2 is used to represent that the temporal constraint $\odot a$ holds (hence it is initially inactive). The rule r_1 is then a generator for r_2 and can be viewed as the temporal rule "if we have a today then tomorrow we have yesterday a". Rule r_4 captures the obligation $\diamondsuit b$, either b holds in the next observation state or $\neg b$ holds together with a continued obligation to $\diamondsuit b$.

For the example observation trace in the table below, we see that in step 4, both a and $\odot a$ are true (in the merged state, both a and r_2 are present) and hence rule r_3 yields two possibilities for step 5. The choice with b holding true conflicts with the observation in step 5 and therefore is eliminated. Rule r_4 is thus active and remains activated until step 7 when b is observed to hold.

Step	Obs.	Rule Activations	Merged States
0	$\{\}$	$\{\{r_0, r_1, r_3\}\}$	$\{\{r_0, r_1, r_3\}\}$
1	$\{a, b\}$	$\{\{r_0, r_1, r_3\}\}$	$\{\{a, b, r_0, r_1, r_3\}\}$
2	$\{\neg a, b\}$	$\{\{r_0, r_1, r_2, r_3\}\}$	$\{\{\neg a, b, r_0, r_1, r_2, r_3\}\}$
3	$\{a, b\}$	$\{\{r_0, r_1, r_3\}\}$	$\{\{a, b, r_0, r_1, r_3\}\}$
4	$\{a, b\}$	$\{\{r_0, r_1, r_2, r_3\}\}$	$\{\{a, b, r_0, r_1, r_2, r_3\}\}$
5	$\{\neg a, \neg b\}$	$\{\{b, r_0, r_1, r_2, r_3\}, \{\neg b, r_0, r_1, r_2, r_3, r_4\}\}$	$\{\{\neg a, \neg b, r_0, r_1, r_2, r_3, r_4\}\}$
6	$\{a, \neg b\}$	$\{\{b, r_0, r_1, r_3\}, \{\neg b, r_0, r_1, r_3, r_4\}\}$	$\{\{a, \neg b, r_0, r_1, r_3, r_4\}\}$
7	$\{\neg a, b\}$	$\{\{b, r_0, r_1, r_2, r_3\}, \{\neg b, r_0, r_1, r_2, r_3, r_4\}\}$	$\{\{\neg a, b, r_0, r_1, r_2, r_3\}\}$
8	$\{\neg a, \neg b\}$	$\{\{r_0, r_1, r_3\}\}$	$\{\{\neg a, \neg b, r_0, r_1, r_3\}\}$

But how do we determine whether any generated temporal existential obligations, such as $\diamondsuit b$, have indeed been satisfied? Essentially, the rule system structure notes those rules that correspond to such obligations and then, at the end of monitoring, one must check whether the final merged state set contains states without those noted rules active. If there are no such states, then the given (finite) observation trace fails to satisfy the rule set. If there is at least one of the possible final states not containing such noted rules, the observation trace satisfies the rule set. The approach is exactly that of the minimal and maximal rule interpretations used in EAGLE. In the above, the final set of merged states has just one state that does not contain the noted rule r_4 and hence the observation satisfies the given rule set.

The rule set in fact contained an optimisation; the choices appearing in rules r_3 and r_4 were made deterministic, either b or $\neg b \wedge$ .... The determinisation thus

---

[3] The absence of r_2 from this set gives $\neg r_2$ a positive interpretation; this is not the case, however, for observation literals a and b where absence is taken as meaning "undetermined".

reduced the number of possible successor states that are generated at any one time. For example, if the rules r_3 and r_4 had been defined as

$$r_3 : a, r_2 \rightarrow\!\!\!\!\!\cdot\ b \mid r_4 \qquad\qquad r_4 : \rightarrow\!\!\!\!\!\cdot\ b \mid r_4$$

the rule activations for step 7 would be $\{\{b, r_0, r_1, r_2, r_3\}, \{r_0, r_1, r_2, r_3, r_4\}\}$, yielding merged states $\{\{\neg a, b, r_0, r_1, r_2, r_3\}, \{\neg a, b, r_0, r_1, r_2, r_3, r_4\}\}$. Then, step 8 would have had $\{\{r_0, r_1, r_3\}, \{b, r_0, r_1, r_3\}, \{r_0, r_1, r_3, r_4\}\}$ for rule activations and $\{\{\neg a, \neg b, r_0, r_1, r_3\}, \{\neg a, \neg b, r_0, r_1, r_3, r_4\}\}$ for its merged states, one of which does not contain the noted (minimal) rule r_4 and so the observation trace, as is to be expected, satisfies the rule set.

2.1   Inhibiting Rule Activation

The informal semantics we've used above has rules being activated in the next step if they appear positively in some applied consequent of some currently applicable rule. In particular, rules that are not mentioned in a consequent of some rule can not be activated by that rule; however, some other rule may indeed activate them. Consider, for example, the contrived (sub)set of rules below.

$$r_0 : \rightarrow\!\!\!\!\!\cdot\ r_2 \mid r_3 \qquad\qquad r_1 : \rightarrow\!\!\!\!\!\cdot\ r_3 \mid r_4$$

Assume at some stage that r_0 and r_1 are activated in the same step. Rule r_0 therefore generates the partial successor states $\{r_2\}$ and $\{r_3\}$. Rule r_1 will then extend these states to yield the possible (partial) states $\{r_2, r_3\}$, $\{r_2, r_4\}$, $\{r_3\}$ and $\{r_3, r_4\}$. Suppose it was desired that rules r_2 and r_3 were mutually exclusive. One way would be to modify the rules as below.

$$r_0 : \rightarrow\!\!\!\!\!\cdot\ r_2, \neg r_3 \mid r_3, \neg r_2 \qquad\qquad r_1 : \rightarrow\!\!\!\!\!\cdot\ r_3 \mid r_4$$

Assuming again both r_0 and r_1 active, the possible successor activation sets are now $\{r_2, \neg r_3, r_4\}$, $\{\neg r_2, r_3\}$ and $\{\neg r_2, r_3, r_4\}$ — since the potential rule activation set $\{r_2, \neg r_3, r_3, \neg r_2\}$ is inconsistent. The negation of a rule should be interpreted as a forced "non-activation" of the rule.

In the examples above, we indicated how various temporal conditions could be translated into collections of these low-level single-shot (or step?) rules. In a certain sense, rule names can be viewed as propositions denoting temporal subformulas. However, it is important to emphasise that a negated rule name does not correspond to the negation of a subformula that the rule name may be viewed as representing. More strictly, one should view a positive occurrence of a rule name as meaning that the rule will be applied and in doing so will generate possible traces that satisfy the associated subformula. A negative occurrence of a rule name (in the rule activation state) simply means that the rule is NOT applied and hence places no constraints on the generation of traces.

In summary, we can use rules to activate other rules (positive appearance of a rule in a consequent), to not inhibit activation (no mention of a rule in a consequent), and to inhibit activation (negative appearance of a rule in a consequent).

3 Propositional RULER Trace Semantics

We now present a formalization of propositional rule systems and an evaluation semantics over traces of observations.

Preliminary definitions. Let X denote a set of atoms. We then use X^- to denote the set of negated atoms of X, i.e. $X^- = \{\neg x \mid x \in X\}$, and let $X^{\pm}$ denote the set of literals of X, i.e. $X \cup X^-$. We use the term X-literal to refer to a member of $X^{\pm}$. A set of X-literals L is said to be *self-consistent* if and only if for any $x \in X$ it is not the case that both $x \in L$ and $\neg x \in L$. Let L_X^{-*} denote the negative closure of L with respect to the atoms X, i.e. the set $L \cup \{\neg l \mid l \notin L, l \in X\}$. Given LS_1 and LS_2 as sets of self-consistent sets of literals, the product $LS_1 \times LS_2$ is the set $\{ls_1 \cup ls_2 \mid ls_1 \in LS_1, ls_2 \in LS_2, \text{ and } ls_1 \cup ls_2 \text{ is self-consistent}\}$.

Rule Systems. Given disjoint sets of rule names R and observations O, a *rule* ρ is a pair $\langle C, B \rangle$ where C, the condition part, is a conjunctive set of $(R \cup O)$-literals, and B, the body part, is a disjunctive set of conjunctive sets of $(R \cup O)$-literals. A *named rule* is then an association $r : \rho$ where $r \in R$ is a rule name and ρ is a rule. A *rule system* RS is a tuple $\langle R, O, P, I, F \rangle$ where R and O are, respectively, disjoint sets of rule names and observations, and P is a set of disjointly R-named rules over R and O, $I \subseteq O^{\pm} \cup R$ is a self-consistent subset of observation literals and rule names, and $F \subseteq R$ is a set of terminally excluded rule names (rule names that may not appear in the very final monitoring state). A *configuration* γ for a rule system RS is a pair $\langle A, \Theta \rangle$ where A is a consistent set of R-literals, called the activity set, and Θ is a consistent set of O-literals, called the observation state. We also write $A(\gamma)$ to denote the activity set of a configuration γ, similarly $\Theta(\gamma)$ for the observation state.

We next define the interpretation of a set of literals in a configuration. The presence of a positively signed rule name r in the activity set means that the rule ρ associated with r is active. On the other hand, the presence of a negatively signed rule name r, or the absence of r, in the activity set means that the rule ρ associated with r is not active. For observation atoms, however, undefinedness of an O-literal o, i.e. the absence of o from the observation state of the configuration, means that the observation literal o may be either true or false.

Modelling and step relation. Let $RS = \langle R, O, P, I, F \rangle$ be a rule system. A self-consistent set of literals L from RS holds in a configuration γ for RS, which is denoted by $\gamma \models L$, if and only (i) the set of rule name literals mentioned in L is contained in the negative closure of $A(\gamma)$, i.e. $(L - O^{\pm}) \subseteq A(\gamma)_R^{-*}$, and (ii) observation literals within L are contained in the configuration's set of observations $(L - R^{\pm}) \subseteq \Theta(\gamma)$. We can now define a single step relation over configurations for a given named rule. This relation can then be used to define a single step relation for a rule system. An *$r{:}\rho$-step relation* $\xrightarrow{r{:}\rho}$ between configurations is such that $\gamma \xrightarrow{r{:}\rho} \gamma'$ if and only if (i) $r \in A(\gamma)$, (ii) $\gamma \models C(\rho)$, and (iii) there is a $\theta \in B(\rho)$ such that $A(\gamma') \cup \Theta(\gamma') = \theta$. Then for a set of rule names R, let Γ' be an *R-indexed set of outcome configurations* such that for each

$r \in R$, $\gamma \xrightarrow{r:\rho} \Gamma'_r$. We then define the step relation $\longrightarrow$ between configurations such that $\gamma \longrightarrow \gamma'$ if and only γ' is a consistent union of an $(A(\gamma) \cap R)$-indexed set of outcome configurations from γ. Note that an empty union set is treated as being an inconsistent union.

The single step relation for the rule system can now be used to define the notion of an accepting run of a rule system over a given observation trace. This requires matching obligations against actual observations. As we have adopted a classical interpretation for observation literals (which is not the case for rule name literals), we thus have the following.

Matching. An actual set of observation literals X is said to *match* an obligatory set of literals Y if and only if $X \cup Y$ is self-consistent and $Y \subseteq X$.

Finally, we can define the language accepted by a rule system.

Language acceptance. An accepting run of a rule system $RS = \langle R, O, P, I, F \rangle$ on an observation trace $\tau = o_1 o_2 \ldots o_n$ is a sequence of configurations $\gamma_1 \gamma_2 \cdots \gamma_n \gamma_{n+1}$ such that (i) $A(\gamma_1) \in I$, (ii) for all $i \in 1..n$ the actual and obligated observations, o_i and $\Theta(\gamma_i)$ respectively, match and $\langle A(\gamma_i), \Theta(\gamma_i) \cup o_i \rangle \longrightarrow \gamma_{i+1}$, and (iii) $A(\gamma_{n+1}) \cap F = \{\}$. Thus, the language accepted by a rule system RS, $\mathcal{L}(RS)$, is the set of all finite observation traces τ accepted by RS. Furthermore, we say a rule system RS is violated by an observation trace τ if RS has no accepting run on τ, alternatively, $\tau \notin \mathcal{L}(RS)$.

We now claim that the monitoring algorithm of Section 2 accepts an observation trace τ for a rule system RS if and only if $\tau \in \mathcal{L}(RS)$. Indeed, the steps of the algorithm closely reflect the semantic construction we have given.

3.1 Propositional Linear Temporal Logic as a Rule System

Having formally defined propositional rule systems, we are now in a position to show how linear-time temporal logic formulas for monitoring over finite traces can be encoded in RULER. Our translation is based on the separation result of Gabbay (originally 1981 but elaborated in [8]), which can then be used to show that any mixed past, present and future linear-time temporal formula can be translated into a collection of universal implications of the form *non-strict past formula* implies *pure future formula*, a minor variation of the rule forms used in the executable temporal logic METATEM [2]. Our starting point is thus to show how such separated temporal implications can be represented in RULER.[4]

The Pure Future Part. The pure future linear-time temporal formulas are built from propositions, the boolean connectives and, or, and negation, $\wedge$, $\vee$ and $\neg$, respectively, and a strict until and unless operator, $\mathcal{U}^+$ and $\mathcal{W}^+$. All other standard future time operators are definable from this set. Without loss

---

[4] Fisher's SNF representation for temporal logic [6] is close to RULER rule forms and an alternative translation to a rule system could be given via SNF. However, we believe our direct translation has interest in its own right and might lead to an easier SNF translation.

of generality, we assume formulas are further transformed in negation normal form (NNF[5]), i.e. negation operators pushed inwards to propositional literals and cancellations applied. Let WFF^+ denote the set of well-formed strict future time formulas in NNF and WFF denote the set of well-formed future time formulas in NNF (which may include the present, i.e. propositions under no future time operator).

We define a translation $\overrightarrow{T} : WFF \rightarrow RuleSystem$ inductively over the structure of the temporal formulas. Let ϕ and ψ denote arbitrary members of WFF. The base cases of the translation are straightforward, e.g. for an atom p, we have $\overrightarrow{T}(p) = \langle\{\}, \{p\}, \{\}, \{\{p\}\}, \{\}\rangle$, indicating a rule system with an atom p with an initial set of active rule names containing the singleton set $\{p\}$. Negated atoms translate in a similar way. The propositional constant **true** gives rise to the rule system $\langle\{\}, \{\}, \{\}, \{\{\}\}, \{\}\rangle$ whereas **false** translates to a system with an empty set of initial states. As one might expect, the logical conjunction (disjunction) of formulas ϕ and ψ translate to the obvious product (union) operations that can be defined for rule systems. This leaves the most interesting part of the translation, namely an until formula $\phi \mathcal{U}^+ \psi$. Recall that the semantics of the strict until operator gives the temporal equivalence $\phi \mathcal{U}^+ \psi \Leftrightarrow \bigcirc(\psi \vee (\phi \wedge (\phi \mathcal{U}^+ \psi)))$.

$$\overrightarrow{T}(\phi \mathcal{U}^+ \psi) = \text{LET } \langle R_\phi, O_\phi, P_\phi, I_\phi, F_\phi\rangle = \overrightarrow{T}(\phi) \text{ AND}$$
$$\langle R_\psi, O_\psi, P_\psi, I_\psi, F_\psi\rangle = \overrightarrow{T}(\psi)$$
$$\text{IN } \langle R_\phi \cup R_\psi \cup \{r_{\phi \mathcal{U}^+ \psi}\},$$
$$O_\phi \cup O_\psi,$$
$$P_\phi \cup P_\psi \cup \{r_{\phi \mathcal{U}^+ \psi} :-\!\!\circ\!\!\rightarrow I_\psi \cup (I_\phi \times \{\{r_{\phi \mathcal{U}^+ \psi}\}\}),$$
$$\{\{r_{\phi \mathcal{U}^+ \psi}\}\},$$
$$F_\phi \cup F_\psi \cup \{r_{\phi \mathcal{U}^+ \psi}\}\rangle$$

For ease of understanding, we have subscripted the rule names by the subformulas they represent. As the until operator has a strong interpretation, requiring its second argument to be satisfied, the associated rule name for the until formula must be included in the F set of the rule system. As might be expected, the translation of the unless formula differs from the until translation just in the non-inclusion of the rule for the unless formula in the F set.

Example 2. Assume a, b, c and d are atomic propositions. The translation of $a \mathcal{U}^+ b$ yields the rule system

$$\langle\{r_{a\mathcal{U}^+b}\}, \{a, b\}, \{r_{a\mathcal{U}^+b} : -\!\!\circ\!\!\rightarrow b \mid a, r_{a\mathcal{U}^+b}\}, \{\{r_{a\mathcal{U}^+b}\}\}, \{r_{a\mathcal{U}^+b}\}\rangle$$

Similarly, the translation of $a \wedge (c \mathcal{W}^+ d)$ yields the rule system

$$\langle\{r_{c\mathcal{W}^+d}\}, \{a, c, d\}, \{r_{c\mathcal{W}^+d} : -\!\!\circ\!\!\rightarrow d \mid c, r_{c\mathcal{W}^+d}\}, \{\{a, r_{c\mathcal{W}^+d}\}\}, \{\}\rangle$$

Thus the translation of $(a \mathcal{U}^+ b) \mathcal{U}^+ (a \wedge (c \mathcal{W}^+ d))$ yields the rule system

$$\langle\{r_0, r_1, r_2\}, \{a, b, c, d\}, \left\{\begin{array}{l} r_0 : -\!\!\circ\!\!\rightarrow b \mid a, r_0 \\ r_1 : -\!\!\circ\!\!\rightarrow d \mid c, r_1 \\ r_2 : -\!\!\circ\!\!\rightarrow a, r_1 \mid r_0, r_2 \end{array}\right\}, \{\{r_2\}\}, \{r_0, r_2\}\rangle$$

---

[5] Some authors refer to this as positive normal form.

where

$$r_0 = r_{a\mathcal{U}+b}, \quad r_1 = r_{c\mathcal{W}+d}, \quad r_2 = r_{(a\mathcal{U}+b)\mathcal{U}+(a\wedge(c\mathcal{W}+d))}$$

Past Time Temporal Queries. The pure past time fragment of linear-time temporal logic is constructed in a mirror fashion to the pure future part, i.e. from propositions, the boolean connectives ($\wedge$, $\vee$ and $\neg$), and just the temporal operators $\mathcal{S}^-$ (the strict *since*, false at the beginning of time) and its weak version $\mathcal{Z}^-$ (true at the beginning of time). Without loss of generality, we assume that past time temporal formulas are in negation normal form, i.e. with negations pushed inwards to atomic propositions/literals and double negations cancelled. Let us first consider the translation of pure past time temporal queries. The temporal equivalence $\phi\mathcal{S}^-\psi \Leftrightarrow \odot(\psi \vee (\phi \wedge (\phi\mathcal{S}^-\psi)))$ should serve as a reminder of the semantics that needs to be captured by the translation. The basic idea for handling the past is an old one, namely, we use the translation rules to calculate the value of the temporal query as we proceed in time (rather than evaluating the query over the history). We will use the presence of the rule name $r_{\phi\mathcal{S}^-\psi}$ in the rule activation state to denote whether the temporal formula $\phi\mathcal{S}^-\psi$ held in the previous moment (similarly for r_ϕ and r_ψ). We then use a rule, named $r_{\psi:\psi\mathcal{S}^-\phi?}$, to calculate whether $r_{\phi\mathcal{S}^-\psi}$ should be made active because ψ held in the previous moment (similarly for the other possible way for $\psi\mathcal{S}^-\phi$ to hold). These query rules must be universally active in order to determine truth values for the next moment. Thus we use a rule, named say $r_{g.\phi\mathcal{S}^-\psi?}$, to act as a generator (hence the "g" in its name) for a pair of (sets of) rules that determine the truth of $\phi\mathcal{S}^-\psi$ based on the previous values of its subformulas.

$$r_{\psi.\phi\mathcal{S}^-\psi?} : r_\psi \longrightarrow r_{\phi\mathcal{S}^-\psi} \qquad r_{\phi.\phi\mathcal{S}^-\psi?} : r_\phi, r_{\phi\mathcal{S}^-\psi} \longrightarrow r_{\phi\mathcal{S}^-\psi}$$
$$r_{g.\phi\mathcal{S}^-\psi?} : \longrightarrow r_{g.\phi\mathcal{S}^-\psi?}, r_{\phi.\phi\mathcal{S}^-\psi?}, r_{\psi.\phi\mathcal{S}^-\psi?}$$

Naturally, our translation must take into account the fact that the subformulas ψ and ϕ may be boolean combinations of pure past time temporal formulas (represented by rule names) and/or literals. Let WFF^- denote the set of pure past temporal formulas and WFF^{-0} the set of present and pure past time temporal formulas. We thus define a translation $\overleftarrow{T}$ that will translate a past time temporal formula (from WFF^{-0}) into an intermediate form (of a rule system) whose initial activation set, as a disjunctive set of conjunctive sets of rule names and/or literals, is to be viewed as representing the given temporal query. The difference from a proper rule system is that we use the F set to represent the initial values of rules, e.g. a formula $\phi\mathcal{S}^-\psi$ must be false initially and so the rule name $\neg r_{\phi\mathcal{S}^-\psi}$ would be included in the set F. As with the future time translation the base cases are clear, as is conjunction and disjunction. Figure 2 shows the translation for the interesting case of the strict since operator.

Separated Temporal Implicative Forms. We can now bring together the above two translations $\overrightarrow{T}$ and $\overleftarrow{T}$ to generate a rule system corresponding to the METATEM-like rule form $\phi_{\text{past}} \Rightarrow \odot\psi_{\text{future}}$ which are of universal nature,

$$\overleftarrow{T}(\phi \mathcal{S}^- \psi) =$$
$$\text{LET } \langle R_\phi, O_\phi, P_\phi, I_\phi, F_\phi \rangle = \overleftarrow{T}(\phi) \text{ AND}$$
$$\langle R_\psi, O_\psi, P_\psi, I_\psi, F_\psi \rangle = \overleftarrow{T}(\psi)$$
$$\text{IN } \langle R_\phi \cup R_\psi \cup \{r_{\phi \mathcal{S}^- \psi}, r_{g.\phi \mathcal{S}^- \psi?}\} \cup \{r_{\phi \mathcal{S}^- \psi?x} \mid x \in I_\phi\} \cup \{r_{\phi \mathcal{S}^- \psi?x} \mid x \in I_\psi\},$$
$$O_\phi \cup O_\psi,$$
$$P_\phi \cup P_\psi \cup$$
$$\{r_{g.\phi \mathcal{S}^- \psi?} : \multimap \{r_{g.\phi \mathcal{S}^- \psi?}\} \cup \{r_{\phi \mathcal{S}^- \psi?x} \mid x \in I_\phi\} \cup \{r_{\phi \mathcal{S}^- \psi?x} \mid x \in I_\psi\}\} \cup$$
$$\{r_{\phi \mathcal{S}^- \psi?x} : x \multimap r_{\phi \mathcal{S}^- \psi} \mid x \in I_\psi\} \cup$$
$$\{r_{\phi \mathcal{S}^- \psi?x} : x, r_{\phi \mathcal{S}^- \psi} \multimap r_{\phi \mathcal{S}^- \psi} \mid x \in I_\phi\},$$
$$\{\{r_{\phi \mathcal{S}^- \psi}, r_{g.\phi \mathcal{S}^- \psi?}\}\},$$
$$F_\phi \cup F_\psi \cup \{\neg r_{\phi \mathcal{S}^- \psi}\}\rangle$$

Fig. 2. Translation of $\phi \mathcal{S}^- \psi$

i.e. globally hold. Assuming both ϕ_{past} and ψ_{future} are in a negation normal form, then, in the context of

$$\langle R_{\text{past}}, O_{\text{past}}, P_{\text{past}}, I_{\text{past}}, F_{\text{past}} \rangle = \overleftarrow{T}(\phi_{\text{past}})$$

$$\langle R_{\text{future}}, O_{\text{future}}, P_{\text{future}}, I_{\text{future}}, F_{\text{future}} \rangle = \overrightarrow{T}(\psi_{\text{future}})$$

in which we assume, without loss of generality, the rule name sets are disjoint, the rule system below will represent the translation of the separated implicative form, i.e. $RS = T(\phi_{\text{past}} \Rightarrow \bigcirc \psi_{\text{future}})$.

$$RS = \langle R_{\text{past}} \cup R_{\text{future}} \cup \{r_{g.\phi_{\text{past}} \Rightarrow \psi_{\text{future}}}\} \cup \{r_{x \Rightarrow \psi_{\text{future}}} \mid x \in I_{\text{past}}\},$$
$$O_{\text{past}} \cup O_{\text{future}},$$
$$P_{\text{past}} \cup P_{\text{future}} \cup$$
$$\{r_{g.\phi_{\text{past}} \Rightarrow \psi_{\text{future}}} : \multimap \{r_{g.\phi_{\text{past}} \Rightarrow \psi_{\text{future}}}\} \cup \{r_{x \Rightarrow \psi_{\text{future}}} \mid x \in I_{\text{past}}\}\},$$
$$\{r_{x \Rightarrow \psi_{\text{future}}} : x \multimap I_{\text{future}} \mid x \in I_{\text{past}}\},$$
$$\{\{r_{g.\phi_{\text{past}} \Rightarrow \psi_{\text{future}}}, r_{x \Rightarrow \psi_{\text{future}}} \mid x \in I_{\text{past}}\} \cup F_{\text{past}}\},$$
$$F_{\text{future}} \rangle$$

Example 3. Assuming a, b, c, p and q denote propositions, we give the RULER translation of the universal separated temporal implication

$$c \wedge (b \mathcal{S}^- a) \Rightarrow \bigcirc(\Diamond p \wedge \Diamond q).$$

Recall that $\Diamond p$ will be translated as $p \vee \Diamond p$, i.e. $p \vee \text{true } \mathcal{U}^+ p$, similarly for $\Diamond q$. Using the following abbreviations

$$r_0 = r_{g.b \mathcal{S}^- a?} \qquad r_1 = r_{b \mathcal{S}^- a?b} \qquad r_2 = r_{b \mathcal{S}^- a?a} \qquad r_3 = r_{b \mathcal{S}^- a}$$
$$r_4 = r_{\text{true} \mathcal{U}^+ p} \qquad r_5 = r_{\text{true} \mathcal{U}^+ q} \qquad r_6 = r_{g.c \wedge (b \mathcal{S}^- a) \Rightarrow \bigcirc((p \vee \text{true} \mathcal{U}^+ p) \wedge (q \vee \text{true} \mathcal{U}^+ q))}$$
$$r_7 = r_{c \wedge (b \mathcal{S}^- a) \Rightarrow \bigcirc((p \vee \text{true} \mathcal{U}^+ p) \wedge (q \vee \text{true} \mathcal{U}^+ q))}$$

the rule system will thus have rules

$r_0 : \multimap r_0, r_1, r_2$	$r_1 : b, r_3 \multimap r_3$	$r_2 : a \multimap r_3$
$r_3 :$	$r_4 : \multimap p \mid r_4$	$r_5 : \multimap q \mid r_5$
$r_6 : \multimap r_6, r_7$	$r_7 : c, r_3 \multimap p, q \mid p, r_5 \mid r_4, q \mid r_4, r_5$	

with an initial rule activation set as $\{\{\neg r_3, r_0, r_1, r_2, r_6, r_7\}\}$ and the forbidden rule set as $\{r_4, r_5\}$.

The correctness of our translation scheme for propositional LTL over finite traces with respect to the given semantics for RULER follows from the correctness of separation, then an inductive proof establishing the correctness of the translation of the universal separated implicative temporal forms.

4   Parameterized RULER

The propositional RULER system corresponds to regular-based languages, which are a subclass of propositional EAGLE. Here, we extend RULER to include rule definitions parameterized by rules. The evaluation strategy used on this seemingly small extension increases the formal expressivity of RULER to be beyond context-free languages. Consider the following rule definition, indeed schema, that has been extended to include formal rule arguments.

$$r(\rho) : a \dashrightarrow b, \rho \mid c, r(\rho)$$

Suppose that the rule r is active with the propositional rule r_0 substituted for ρ, i.e. $r(r_0)$ is active. Informally, the evaluation of $r(r_0)$ will first determine the truth of the condition part a, then, assuming it holds, continue to create a set of activation states for the next step corresponding to $\{\{b, r_0\}, \{c, r(r_0)\}\}$. Let us give a few examples that show how the expressivity of rule parameterized RULER jumps into the context sensitive languages.

Example 4. Consider a rule system with the rules

$$r_b(\rho) : \dashrightarrow b, \neg a, \rho \qquad r_{ab}(\rho) : \dashrightarrow b, \neg a, \rho \mid a, \neg b, r_{ab}(r_b(\rho))$$
$$r_{end} : \dashrightarrow r_{fail} \qquad r_{fail} : \dashrightarrow r_{fail}$$

together with an initial rule activation set as $\{\{a, r_{ab}(r_{end})\}\}$ and the final forbidden rule set $\{r_b, r_{ab}, r_{fail}\}$ (meaning that no occurrence of rule r_b, r_{ab}, nor r_{fail}, may appear as an obligation in a final rule activation state). All accepted observation traces will match against a trace of $n \geq 1$ occurrences of a followed by n occurrences of b. Essentially, barring the first a, the rule r_{ab} represents the non-terminal S of the context free grammar $S = ab \mid aSb$ in which r_{ab}'s actual argument represents the continuation string for concatenation to the string of a's generated. It is straightforward to establish that the class of context free languages are a subset of parameterized RULER. We extend the above example to represent traces of the form $a^n b^n c^m$, for $n, m \geq 1$. Take the rule set

$$r_{ab}(\rho) : \dashrightarrow b, \neg a, \neg c, \rho \mid a, \neg b, \neg c, r_{ab}(r_b(\rho))$$
$$r_b(\rho) : \dashrightarrow b, \neg a, \neg c, \rho$$
$$r_c : \dashrightarrow c, \neg a, \neg b, r_{end} \mid c, \neg a, \neg b, r_c$$
$$r_{end} : \dashrightarrow r_{fail}$$
$$r_{fail} : \dashrightarrow r_{fail}$$

together with an initial activation set as $\{\{a, r_{ab}(r_c)\}\}$ and the final forbidden rule activation set $\{r_{ab}, r_b, r_c, r_{fail}\}$. This system will clearly accept traces of the form $a^n b^n$ (represented by the r_{ab} rule) followed by one or more c's (determined by the r_c argument to the initial rule activation r_{ab}). Now we can encode the intersection of the languages $a^n b^n c^m$ and $a^m b^n c^n$ $(n, m \geq 1)$, thus yielding the context sensitive language containing words of the form $a^n b^n c^n$.

$$r_{ab}(\rho) : \quad \multimap \quad b, \neg a, \neg c, \rho \mid a, \neg b, \neg c, r_{ab}(r_b(\rho))$$
$$r_b(\rho) : \quad \multimap \quad b, \neg a, \neg c, \rho$$
$$r_c : \quad \multimap \quad c, \neg a, \neg b \mid c, \neg a, \neg b, r_c$$

$$r_a(\rho) : \quad \multimap \quad b, \neg a, \neg c, \rho \mid a, \neg b, \neg c, r_a(\rho)$$
$$r_{bc}(\rho) : \quad \multimap \quad c, \neg a, \neg b, \rho \mid b, \neg a, \neg c, r_{bc}(r_{c1}(\rho))$$
$$r_{c1}(\rho) : \quad \multimap \quad c, \neg a, \neg b, \rho$$

$$r_{end} : \quad \multimap \quad r_{fail}$$
$$r_{fail} : \quad \multimap \quad r_{fail}$$

Here the rule system has an initial activation set $\{\{a, r_{ab}(r_c), r_a(r_{bc}(r_{end}))\}\}$ and final forbidden rule activation set $\{r_{ab}, r_b, r_c, r_a, r_{bc}, r_{c1}, r_{fail}\}$.

As in EAGLE, we can also parameterize RULER rules by data values, thus introducing variables and predicated atoms. It is through such means that RULER can be used for encoding/interpreting real-time and stochastic logics.

Example 5. Let us assume that each observation state is time-stamped by the unique presence of a grounded predicate $clock(t)$ for some real value t, e.g. $clock(49738.22264)$. The data parameterized rule schema

$$r(k : \mathbb{R}) : clock(?n : \mathbb{R}) \quad \multimap \quad clock(?t : \mathbb{R}), p, t - n < k \mid$$
$$clock(?t : \mathbb{R}), \neg p, t - n < k, r(k - t + n)$$

defines a constraint that the atom p must be consistent with an observation state within k time units from the observation state in which the rule $r(k)$ is required to hold. The $?n : \mathbb{R}$ appearing as argument to the $clock$ predicate name in the rule's condition means that the variable n is to be bound to some value from $\mathbb{R}$ by the current observation state. The occurrence of $clock(?t : \mathbb{R})$ in the rule consequent means that there is an obligation on the next observation state to binding t with some value. Suppose we have an observation state containing just $\{clock(1), \neg p, r(3)\}$. The rule $r(3)$, through binding n to 3, gives rise to the set $\{\{clock(?t : \mathbb{R}), p, t - 1 < 3\}, \{clock(?t : \mathbb{R}), \neg p, t - 1 < 3, r(4 - t)\}\}$. If the next actual observation state is $\{clock(3), \neg p\}$, the merge with the obligation sets yields the frontier set $\{\{clock(3), \neg p, r(1)\}\}$, which gives rise, through $r(1)$, to obligations $\{\{clock(?t : \mathbb{R}), p, t - 3 < 1\}, \{clock(?t : \mathbb{R}), p, t - 3 < 1, r(4 - t)\}\}$. If we have another observation this time with $\{clock(4), p\}$ then the merge yields the empty frontier set as $4 - 3 < 1$, which appears in both possible futures, is clearly false. Hence the actual behaviour does not conform to that required by the initial $r(3)$. On the other hand, had the observation state been, say, $\{clock(3.9), p\}$, then the rule set would be satisfied.

5   Conclusions

We have introduced a low-level rule system RULER as a kind of "byte-code" for run-time monitoring logics. A basic monitoring algorithm was described for the propositional subset of RULER. Having presented formally the semantics of the propositional subset, we demonstrated how linear time temporal logic with both past and future operators can translate to such rule systems, and then briefly, and informally, presented RULER where rules are parameterized by rule names. On the face of it, the propositional subset of RULER looks rather like a grammatical representation of the transition relation of an alternating automaton, i.e. with conjunctive and disjunctive branching, see for example [7]. However, RULER, even the propositional subset, has more to it; the rules have the capability to switch other rules on or off as an evaluation of a rule system over a trace proceeds. We are referring to such systems as reactive rule systems / grammars / Kripke structures [9]. Whilst regular grammars are closed under our notion of reactivity (including switching grammar rule sets), it can easily be shown that reactive context free grammars take us beyond context free. Some relationship with state-alternating context-free grammars [10] is clear, however, a more detailed study of reactive grammars and their place in the complexity hierarchy is work in progress, see [5] for some initial results and examples. A feature we haven't yet mentioned is rule priority in RULER. Given the ability to switch rules on and off, conflicts may occur. Sometimes the conflicts may be desired, but in other situations we may wish one rule to override another, as is the case in defeasible reasoning. Of course, this changes the nature of the logics expressible quite considerably. In addition to rule parameters, RULER has data parameters, just as in EAGLE. The semantic details are not difficult and we adopt an approach similar to that in first-order METATEM [1], but, as in EAGLE, some care needs to be taken to avoid "rule activation state set" explosion in practice.

The low-level simplicity of RULER leads to the main advantage for its potential use over EAGLE. If optimal (asymptotic) complexity bounds have been established for a particular subset logic of EAGLE, such as for the LTL subset, in general a RULER encoding will be no better asymptotically. However, we assert that smaller constants arise through the significant reduction in the symbolic processing that has to be undertaken at run-time in the interpretation of EAGLE formulas. Of course, there would be a one-off translation cost from the LTL formula to the appropriate rule systems. This a compilation versus interpretation gain.

A prototype Java implementation of the monitoring algorithm for propositional RULER has been developed, as a proof of concept. We are, however, not yet at the stage where we can properly evaluate the practical effectiveness of RULER, which requires the fully parameterized version of RULER. We hope to report on this in the near future.

References

1. Barringer, H., Fisher, M., Gabbay, D., Owens, R., Reynolds, M.: The Imperative Future: Principles of Executable Temporal Logic. Research Studies Press (1996)
2. Barringer, H., Fisher, M., Gabbay, D., Gough, G., Owens, R.: An Introduction. In: Formal Aspects of Computing, vol. 7(5), pp. 533–549. Springer, London (1995)

3. Barringer, H., Goldberg, A., Havelund, K., Sen, K.: Rule-Based Runtime Verification. In: Steffen, B., Levi, G. (eds.) VMCAI 2004. LNCS, vol. 2937, Springer, Heidelberg (2004)
4. Barringer, H., Goldberg, A., Havelund, K., Sen, K.: Run-time Monitoring in Eagle. In: Brunnstein, K., Händler, W., Haefner, K. (eds.) RGU 1974. LNCS, vol. 17, p. 264. Springer, Heidelberg (2004)
5. Barringer, H., Rydeheard, D., Gabbay, D.: Reactive Grammars: An Initial Exploration, Draft paper(2007), see http://www.cs.man.ac.uk/~david/reactive.html
6. Fisher, M.D.: A Normal Form for Temporal Logics and its Applications in Theorem-Proving and Execution. Journal of Logic and Computation 7(4), 429–456 (1997)
7. Finkbeiner, B., Sipma, H.: Checking Finite Traces Using Alternating Automata. Formal Methods in System Design 24(2), 101–127 (2004)
8. Gabbay, D.M.: Declarative Past and Imperative Future: Executable Temporal Logic for Interactive Systems. In: Banieqbal, B., Pnueli, A., Barringer, H. (eds.) Temporal Logic in Specification. LNCS, vol. 398, pp. 67–89. Springer, Heidelberg (1989)
9. Gabbay, D.M.: Introducing Reactive Kripke Semantics and Arc Accessibility. In: Gabbay, D.M. (ed.) To appear in Festschrift in Honour of Boaz Traktenbrot (2007)
10. Moriya, E., Hofbauer, D., Huber, M., Otto, F.: On State-Alternating Context-Free Grammars. Theoretical Computer Science 337(11), 183–216 (2005)

The Good, the Bad, and the Ugly, But How Ugly Is Ugly?

Andreas Bauer[1], Martin Leucker[2], and Christian Schallhart[2]

[1] National ICT Australia (NICTA)
[2] Institut für Informatik, Technische Universität München

Abstract. When monitoring a system wrt. a property defined in some temporal logic, e. g., LTL, a major concern is to settle with an adequate interpretation of observable system events; that is, models of temporal logic formulae are usually infinite streams of events, whereas at runtime only prefixes are available.

This work defines a four-valued semantics for LTL over finite traces, which extends the classical semantics, and allows to infer whether a system behaves (1) according to the monitored property, (2) violates the property, (3) will possibly violate the property in the future, or (4) will possibly conform to the property in the future, once the system has stabilised. Notably, (1) and (2) correspond to the classical semantics of LTL, whereas (3) and (4) are chosen whenever an observed system behaviour has not yet lead to a violation or acceptance of the monitored property.

Moreover, we present a monitor construction for RV-LTL properties in terms of a Moore machine signalising the semantics of the so far obtained execution trace.

1   Introduction

Runtime verification of a given correctness property φ formulated in linear temporal logic LTL [Pnu77] aims at determining the semantics of φ while executing the system under scrutiny. However, one is faced with the following obstacle: The semantics of LTL is defined over infinite (behavioural) traces whereas monitoring a running system allows an at most finite view.

While the syntax and semantics of LTL on infinite traces is well accepted in the literature, there is no consensus on defining LTL over finite strings. Several versions of a *two-valued* semantics for LTL on finite strings have been proposed [GH01a, HR01b, HR02, HR01a, SB05, dR05], see Eisner et al. for a comprehensive survey on this topic [EFH+03]. Alternatively, it has also been proposed to restrict the syntax of LTL for runtime verification, such that formulae which may contain certain future obligations cannot be specified at all [GH01b].

In monitoring a property, there can at least arise three different situations: Firstly, the property can be already satisfied for sure after a finite number of steps; secondly, the property can be shown to evaluate to false for every possible continuation, or thirdly, the finite, already observed prefix allows different continuations leading to either satisfaction or falsification. Thus, every two-valued logic must evaluate to true or false prematurely since it cannot reflect the third case properly.

O. Sokolsky and S. Tasiran (Eds.): RV 2007, LNCS 4839, pp. 126–138, 2007.

To overcome these obstacles, we propose in [ABLS05, BLS06], a three-valued semantics which extends the classical semantics over finite traces. There, a property evaluates to *true* (*false*), wrt. a finite observation, iff the observation is either a satisfying (violating) prefix. In all other cases, the observation is said to be inconclusive, and the property assigned a ?.

This scheme coincides well with the notion of *safety* (e. g., *Gp*—always *p*) and *co-safety* (e. g., *Fp*—eventually *p*) properties, since these are either finitely refutable or satisfiable. However, when monitoring a *true liveness* property, that is one that is not safety nor a co-safety property, then neither the violation nor the satisfaction of the property can be determined using a finite stream of observations, and not much is said about the possible future. Actually, in [PZ06] it is suggested to call these properties *non-monitorable*.

A typical example for a liveness property is *G*(*request* → *F grant*) saying that every request should eventually be granted. In practice, however, one is often faced with such properties and therefore it is impractical to preclude corresponding monitoring procedures.

In this work, we follow the idea that an inconclusive result of a monitor should be more detailed. To this end, we propose a four-valued semantics for LTL that not only results in either *true*, *false*, or ?, but yields *possibly true* and *possibly false* whenever the system's behaviour so far is inconclusive in the three-valued sense. We call the resulting logic *Runtime Verification Linear Temporal Logic* (RV-LTL).

Further, we have defined a translation from a formula in RV-LTL to a monitor (Moore machine) of minimal size, which then forms a suitable foundation for runtime verification, in that the output alphabet of the automaton corresponds to the four truth values sketched above.

Our logic RV-LTL seems to correspond with the semantics realised by the Temporal Rover [Dru00] and has, to the best of our knowledge, not been formally captured elsewhere.

In [dR05], a monitor construction and simplification is given. By combining two of their monitors, as briefly described in their implementation section, this approach can be used to implement the three-valued semantics as presented independently in [ABLS05, BLS06].

Outline. We briefly recall the standard infinite trace semantics of LTL in the next section. In Section 3, we first elaborate four maxims which we require to be satisfied by a temporal logic suitable for runtime verification. Then, we recall two preexisting logics for finite traces and show why they do not satisfy our maxims. However, we show how to combine the two logics towards RV-LTL and argue that RV-LTL adheres to our maxims. Finally, in Section 4, we describe a construction of a monitor procedure for RV-LTL.

2   LTL on Infinite Traces

For the remainder of this paper, let AP be a finite set of *atomic propositions* and $\Sigma = 2^{AP}$ a finite *alphabet*. We write a_i for any single element of Σ, i.e., a_i is a possibly empty set of propositions taken from AP.

Finite traces over Σ are elements of Σ^*, usually denoted by $u, u', u_1, u_2, \ldots$, whereas infinite traces are elements of Σ^ω, usually denoted by $w, w', w_1, w_2, \ldots$. For some trace $w = a_0 a_1 \ldots$, we denote by w^i the suffix $a_i a_{i+1} \ldots$.

The set of LTL formulae is inductively defined by the following grammar:

$$\varphi ::= true \mid p \mid \neg\varphi \mid \varphi \vee \varphi \mid \varphi \, U \, \varphi \mid X\varphi \quad (p \in \text{AP}) \tag{1}$$

Let $i \in \mathbb{N}$ be a *position*. The semantics of LTL formulae is defined inductively over infinite sequences $w = a_0 a_1 \ldots \in \Sigma^\omega$ as follows:

$$
\begin{aligned}
&w, i \models true \\
&w, i \models \neg\varphi &&\text{iff } w, i \not\models \varphi \\
&w, i \models p &&\text{iff } p \in a_i \\
&w, i \models \varphi_1 \vee \varphi_2 &&\text{iff } w, i \models \varphi_1 \text{ or } w, i \models \varphi_2 \\
&w, i \models \varphi_1 U \varphi_2 &&\text{iff } \text{there is a } k \geq i : w, k \models \varphi_2 \text{ and} \\
&&&\qquad \text{for all } l \text{ with } i \leq l < k : w, l \models \varphi_1 \\
&w, i \models X\varphi &&\text{iff } w, i+1 \models \varphi
\end{aligned}
$$

Further, let $w \models \varphi$ be an abbreviation for $w, 0 \models \varphi$. We call w a *model* of φ iff $w \models \varphi$. For every LTL formula φ, its set of models, denoted by $\mathcal{L}(\varphi)$, is a regular set of infinite traces and can be described by a corresponding Büchi automaton [VW86, Var96]. For $\varphi, \psi \in \text{LTL}$, we say that φ is equivalent to ψ, denoted by $\varphi \equiv \psi$, iff for all $w \in \Sigma^\omega$, we have

$$w \models \varphi \text{ iff } w \models \psi$$

For reasons to become clear in Section 3, note that, in LTL

$$\neg X\varphi \equiv X\neg\varphi \tag{2}$$

holds, which matches the intuition that something does not hold in the next position if, in the next position, it does not hold.

3   LTL on Finite Traces

While the syntax and semantics of LTL on infinite traces is well-accepted in the literature, there is no consensus on defining LTL on finite strings. Several versions of a *two-valued* semantics for LTL on finite strings have been proposed. However, as we argue below, for runtime verification, a *four-valued* semantics is preferable.

As discussed in [MP95], the difficulty for an LTL semantics on finite strings lies in the next-state operator X. Given a finite string $u = a_0, \ldots, a_{n-1}$ of length n, the question is which semantics to choose for $X\varphi$ in the last position of u:

$$u, n - 1 \overset{?}{\models} X\varphi \tag{3}$$

We follow the approach of [MP95] in understanding the next-state operator as an operator firstly assuring that there exists a next state which secondly satisfies φ. We use this assumption as the first of our four maxims, which we consider essential for a semantics for LTL on finite traces, in particular in the context of runtime verification:

$\quad$ – $X\varphi$ means there exists a next state and this state satisfies φ. $\qquad$ ($\exists$**X**)

Consequently, equation 3 yields false, as there is no next state. Our second maxim states that a negated formula indeed yields the complemented truth value of the original formula, i. e.,

$\quad$ – a formula and its negation yield complementary truth values. $\qquad$ ($\neg$=**C**)

Then, however, a negated next-state formula should be true. This, however, conflicts equation 2 ($\neg X\varphi \equiv X\neg\varphi$), which therefore can no longer hold on finite traces (unless true equals false). It is therefore helpful to distinguish a *strong* (denoted by X) and a *weak* version (denoted by $\bar{X}$) of the next-state operator.

$\quad$ We call the strong next-state operator X also *existential* next-state operator, as it requires a next-state to exist, and the weak next-state operator $\bar{X}$ also *universal* next-state operator.

$\quad$ The introduction of a strong and a weak version of a next-state operator additionally allows to cope with the intuitive meaning of LTL's finally and globally operators:

$\quad$ Intuitively, the finally operator F is of existential nature [HR02], as some property should eventually be shown, while the globally operator G is of universal character as something should hold in every position of a word. Accordingly, $F\varphi$ should evaluate to false if φ does not hold in the current state and nothing is known about the future, while $G\varphi$ should become true, if φ holds in the current state and nothing is known about the successor states.

$\quad$ In LTL, we have that $F\varphi \equiv \varphi \lor X F\varphi$, as well as, $G\varphi \equiv \varphi \land X G\varphi$. Consequently, $X F\varphi$ should be false, if no subsequent state exists, while $X G\varphi$ should be true in the same situation. This contradiction can be resolved with the addition of the universal next-state operator $\bar{X}$. Using this notation, we can rewrite the above LTL equivalences as $F\varphi \equiv \varphi \lor X F\varphi$ and as $G\varphi \equiv \varphi \land \bar{X} G\varphi$.

$\quad$ The so far developed view is meaningful in a setting which is only concerned with *completed* or *terminated* paths. In runtime verification, however, we are given a *finite prefix* of a continuously expanding trace. Therefore, it is clear that there will be a next state—this continuation is just not known yet. To reflect this situation, we postulate two further maxims for logic suitable for runtime verification. The first one says that

$\quad$ – the semantics never evaluates to true or false prematurely. $\qquad$ (**Sound**)

The string a (of length 1) clearly satisfies the proposition p iff $p \in a$. While, understanding a as a prefix of an infinite string, the value of $X\varphi$ is of less certainty, as the successor state of a is not known. Choosing either true or false (depending on whether to understand X strongly or weakly) would diminish the qualitative difference of the knowledge on p and $X\varphi$ based on the string a. Therefore, we require a semantics to yield four values: *true*, *possibly true*, *possibly false*, and *false*.

When considering $X\varphi$ in the last state of a finite string u, there is no reason to evaluate $X\varphi$ to false, possibly false, or possibly true, if every possible continuation of u satisfies φ. A trivial example would be $X\,true$. While every single letter extension of u would make $X\,true$ true in u's last position, the semantics discussed so far evaluate $X\,true$ to false or possibly false. We therefore postulate

- *the semantics is as anticipatory as possible.*   **(Precise)**

In the remainder of the section, we recall two preexisting logics for finite traces, namely FLTL and LTL$_3$, and show that they do not satisfy all our postulated maxims ($\exists$**X**), ($\neg$=**C**), **(Sound)**, and **(Precise)**. Then, we combine the two logics towards RV-LTL and argue that RV-LTL adheres to our maxims.

3.1 Existing Semantics for Finite Traces

We start by recalling two existing definitions of LTL for finite traces, namely FLTL [LPZ85] and LTL$_3$ [BLS06]. Both variants provide complementary properties for runtime verification but neither of them satisfies all four maxims as postulated above.

The set of FLTL formulae is inductively defined by the following grammar:

$$\varphi ::= true \mid p \mid \neg\varphi \mid \varphi \vee \varphi \mid \varphi \; U \; \varphi \mid X\varphi \mid \bar{X}\varphi \quad (p \in \text{AP}) \tag{4}$$

In this definition, we use two versions of the next-state operator to overcome the difficulty of deciding whether a formula $X\varphi$ holds in the last position of a finite string—thus FLTL satisfies ($\exists$**X**): The *strong* (and standard) X operator is used to express with $X\varphi$ that a next state must exist and that this next state has to satisfy property φ. In contrast, the *weak* $\bar{X}$ operator in $\bar{X}\varphi$ says that if there is a next state, then this next state has to satisfy the property φ.

The semantics function $[u, i \models \varphi]_F$ of FLTL is constructed like the one for standard LTL with one modification: If a strong next-state operator in some subformula $X\varphi$ is referring to a state beyond the known finite prefix u, then this subformula $X\varphi$ is evaluated to $\bot$, regardless of φ. Likewise, a subformula $\bar{X}\varphi$, based on the weak next-state operator, always evaluates to $\top$ if it refers to a state beyond u. This concept is explicated in the following definition:

Definition 1 (Semantics of FLTL [LPZ85]). *Let $u = a_0 \ldots a_{n-1} \in \Sigma^*$ denote a finite trace of length n. The truth value of an FLTL formula φ wrt. u*

at position $i < n$, denoted by $[u, i \models \varphi]_F$, is an element of $\mathbb{B}$ and is defined as follows:

$$[u, i \models true]_F \quad = \top$$

$$[u, i \models p]_F \quad = \begin{cases} \top & if\ p \in a_i \\ \bot & if\ p \notin a_i \end{cases}$$

$$[u, i \models \neg\varphi]_F = \overline{[u, i \models \varphi]_F}$$

$$[u, i \models \varphi \vee \psi]_F = [u, i \models \varphi]_F \sqcup [u, i \models \psi]_F$$

$$[u, i \models X\varphi]_F \quad = \begin{cases} [u, i+1 \models \varphi]_F & if\ i+1 < n \\ \bot & otherwise \end{cases}$$

$$[u, i \models \bar{X}\varphi]_F \quad = \begin{cases} [u, i+1 \models \varphi]_F & if\ i+1 < n \\ \top & otherwise \end{cases}$$

$$[u, i \models \varphi\ U\ \psi]_F = [u, i \models \psi]_F \sqcup ([u, i \models \varphi]_F \sqcap [u, i \models X\ U\ \psi]_F$$

Therefore, FLTL can satisfy the maxim ($\exists \mathbf{X}$) as well as ($\neg=\mathbf{C}$) since negated formulae always yield complementary truth values. However, FLTL does not satisfy the maxim (**Precise**) because the truth value of $[u, n-1 \models X\varphi]_F$ for $|u| = n$ does not depend on φ at all. For example, $[u, n-1 \models Xtrue]_F = \bot$ although $Xtrue$ will evaluate to $\top$ in every possible continuation. Furthermore, FLTL cannot satisfy maxim (**Sound**) since FLTL only uses a two-valued semantic domain and thus every prefix must be evaluated (possibly prematurely) to either $\top$ or $\bot$.

In[BLS06, ABLS05], we proposed LTL$_3$ as an LTL logic with a semantics for finite traces, which caters the view that a finite trace is a prefix of an so-far unknown infinite trace. More specifically, LTL$_3$ uses the standard syntax of LTL as defined in Equation (1) but employs a semantics function $[u, i \models \varphi]_3$ which evaluates for a formula φ each finite trace u of length n and each position $0 \le i < n$ to a value out of $\mathbb{B}_3 = \{\top, \bot, ?\}$. If every infinite trace with prefix u evaluates to same truth value $\top$ or $\bot$, then $[u, i \models \varphi]_3$ also evaluates to this truth value. Otherwise $[u, i \models \varphi]_3$ evaluates to ?, i.e., we have $[u, i \models \varphi]_3 =?$ if different continuations of u yield different truth values. This discussion leads to the following definition:

Definition 2 (Semantics of LTL$_3$). *Let $u = a_0 \ldots a_{n-1} \in \Sigma^*$ denote a finite trace of length n. The truth value of a LTL$_3$ formula φ wrt. u at position $i < n$, denoted by $[u, i \models \varphi]_3$, is an element of $\mathbb{B}_3$ and defined as follows:*

$$[u, i \models \varphi]_3 = \begin{cases} \top & if\ \forall \sigma \in \Sigma^\omega : u\sigma, i \models \varphi \\ \bot & if\ \forall \sigma \in \Sigma^\omega : u\sigma, i \not\models \varphi \\ ? & otherwise. \end{cases}$$

Note that LTL$_3$ satisfies three of our four maxims: A formula and its negation yield the complementary truth values ($\neg=\mathbf{C}$), the semantics never evaluates to true or false prematurely (**Sound**), and the semantics are as anticipatory as possible (**Precise**). Since LTL$_3$ uses the standard LTL syntax, it does not distinguish between a strong and weak next-state operator and consequently, the maxim ($\exists\mathbf{X}$) cannot be satisfied.

Note that ideas leading to the definition of LTL_3 have been formulated independently in [dR05]. The notion of a *(minimal) bad prefix* u is introduced and defined as a prefix that does not have any continuation satisfying a formula φ. Thus, $[u \models \varphi]_3$ would evaluate to $\bot$ for every bad prefix u for φ. By adding a dual monitor for $\neg\varphi$, as proposed in the implementation section of [dR05], the notion of a *good prefix* is obtained and the semantics of LTL_3 can be implemented.

3.2 RV-LTL

We now define RV-LTL which is a version of LTL on finite strings tailored for runtime verification. RV-LTL is designed to incorporate and resolve the requirements as stated afore. The set of RV-LTL formulae is inductively defined by the following grammar:

$$\varphi ::= true \mid p \mid \neg\varphi \mid \varphi \vee \varphi \mid \varphi \; U \; \varphi \mid X\varphi \mid \bar{X}\varphi \quad (p \in \text{AP}) \tag{5}$$

As in FLTL, we use two versions of the next-state operator to overcome the difficulty of deciding whether a formula $X\varphi$ holds in the last position of a finite string—thus RV-LTL satisfies ($\exists\mathbf{X}$). Like in FLTL, the *strong* (and standard) X operator is used to express with $X\varphi$ that a next state must exist and that his next state has to satisfy some property φ. Dually, the *weak* $\bar{X}$ operator in $\bar{X}\varphi$ says that if there is a next state, then this next state must satisfy the property φ.

To accommodate maxim (**Sound**) and in contrast to FLTL, we use a four valued semantics for RV-LTL with $\mathbb{B}_4 = \{\bot, \bot^p, \top^p, \top\}$ as the set of truth values. $\mathbb{B}_4$ can be extended to a complete lattice by ordering $\bot \leq \bot^p \leq \top^p \leq \top$. $\sqcap$ and $\sqcup$ are then defined as expected. To match maxim ($\neg=\mathbf{C}$), $\bot$ and $\top$ are defined to be complementary to each other as well as $\bot^p$ and $\top^p$, where complementation is denoted by $\bar{\ }$. Note that $\mathbb{B}_4$ is not a Boolean lattice, as, for example, $\bot^p \sqcup \overline{\bot^p} = \bot^p \sqcup \top^p \neq \top$. However, the distributive laws hold:

$$x \sqcap (y \sqcup z) = (x \sqcap y) \sqcup (x \sqcap z)$$

$$x \sqcup (y \sqcap z) = (x \sqcup y) \sqcap (x \sqcup z)$$

Definition 3 (Semantics of RV-LTL). *Let* $u = a_0 \ldots a_{n-1} \in \Sigma^*$ *denote a finite trace of length* $n = |u|$. *The* truth value *of an RV-LTL formula* φ *wrt.* u *at position* $i < n$, *denoted by* $[u, i \models \varphi]_{RV}$, *is an element of* $\mathbb{B}_4$ *and is defined as follows:*

$$[u, i \models \varphi]_{RV} = \begin{cases} \top & if \; [u, i \models \varphi']_3 = \top \\ \bot & if \; [u, i \models \varphi']_3 = \bot \\ \top^p & if \; [u, i \models \varphi']_3 = ? \; and \; [u, i \models \varphi]_F = \top \\ \bot^p & if \; [u, i \models \varphi']_3 = ? \; and \; [u, i \models \varphi]_F = \bot \end{cases}$$

where φ' *is obtained from* φ *by replacing each weak next-state operator* $\bar{X}$ *with a strong next-state operator* X.

Note that, in the last position of a word u, both $X\varphi$ and $\bar{X}\varphi$ evaluate to $\top$ ($\bot$) if the outcome is predetermined for all possible continuations. Therefore, the semantics of RV-LTL also satisfy maxim (**Precise**).

Note that the semantics of RV-LTL as given in Definition 3 directly provides an efficient way to construct a monitor procedure for RV-LTL: By running a monitor for LTL_3 and for FLTL simultaneously and by combining their respective results following Definition 3, we obtain a monitor procedure for RV-LTL. We will exploit this fact in the next section where we discuss the monitor construction for RV-LTL in detail.

For two formulae φ and ψ, we say that φ is equivalent to ψ w.r.t. RV-LTL, denoted by $\varphi \equiv_{RV} \psi$, iff for all $u \in \Sigma^*$ and $0 \le i < |u|$, we have $[u, i \models \varphi]_{RV} = [u, i \models \psi]_{RV}$.

To demonstrate the semantics of RV-LTL, we discuss in the following a number of examples. In the motivating discussion of this section, we referred to the equivalence

$$\neg X\varphi \equiv X\neg\varphi$$

which is true w.r.t. LTL. On the other hand, in RV-LTL, this equivalence does not hold, as $\neg X\varphi$ is $\top^p$ in the last position of a word u (if φ cannot be evaluated for possible continuations), while $X\neg\varphi$ is $\bot^p$. However, we have

$$\neg X\varphi \equiv_{RV} \bar{X}\neg\varphi.$$

Using the equivalence

$$\varphi \; U \; \psi \equiv_{RV} \psi \vee (\varphi \wedge X(\varphi \; U \; \psi))$$

which holds for RV-LTL as well as for standard LTL, we can define the finally operator F and globally operator G as abbreviations $F\varphi := true \; U \; \varphi$ and $G\varphi := \neg F\neg\varphi$ and evaluate them as follows:

$$
\begin{aligned}
F\varphi &\equiv_{RV} true \; U \; \varphi \\
&\equiv_{RV} \varphi \vee (true \wedge X(true \; U \; \varphi)) \\
&\equiv_{RV} \varphi \vee XF\varphi
\end{aligned}
$$

and

$$
\begin{aligned}
G\varphi &\equiv_{RV} \neg F\neg\varphi \\
&\equiv_{RV} \neg(true \; U \; \neg\varphi) \\
&\equiv_{RV} \neg(\neg\varphi \vee (true \wedge X(true \; U \; \neg\varphi))) \\
&\equiv_{RV} \neg\neg\varphi \wedge \neg(true \wedge X(true \; U \; \neg\varphi)) \\
&\equiv_{RV} \varphi \wedge \neg(X(true \; U \; \neg\varphi)) \\
&\equiv_{RV} \varphi \wedge \bar{X}\neg(true \; U \; \neg\varphi)) \\
&\equiv_{RV} \varphi \wedge \bar{X} \, G\varphi
\end{aligned}
$$

yield the two equivalences $F\varphi \equiv_{RV} \varphi \vee XF\varphi$ and $G\varphi \equiv_{RV} \varphi \wedge \bar{X} \, G\varphi$ which we discussed to motivate our four maxims. Note that in the previous calculation we used the distributive law and the equivalence $\neg X\varphi \equiv_{RV} \bar{X}\neg\varphi$.

$F\varphi \equiv_{RV} \varphi \vee XF\varphi$ reflects that φ must be satisfied in the future: If φ is not satisfied immediately, then there must be a satisfying future state. If no such future state exists, the formula evaluates to $\perp^p$. Similarly, $G\varphi \equiv \varphi \wedge \bar{X}\, G\varphi$ shows that φ must be satisfied in the current state and in all observable future states. If we do not know the future, the formula evaluates to $\top^p$.

As a final example, we evaluate the property that some request must be answered by a corresponding answer:

$$G(p \rightarrow Fq) \equiv_{RV} (p \rightarrow Fq) \wedge \bar{X}(G(p \rightarrow Fq))$$
$$\equiv_{RV} (\neg p \vee q \vee XFq) \wedge \bar{X}(G(p \rightarrow Fq))$$

This formula evaluates to $\perp^p$ under RV-LTL if the trace contains a p but ends before q occurs and evaluates to $\top^p$ in all other cases. This behaviour is intuitive, since the first case corresponds to a request which has not been answered yet, while the second case means that all requests so far have been answered properly.

Let us close this section by recalling that RV-LTL's semantics can be understood as refinement of LTL_3's semantics. Consequently, we can obtain the semantics of LTL_3 by mapping a $\top^p/\perp^p$ value to ?:

Remark 1. Let $u = a_0 \ldots a_{n-1} \in \Sigma^*$ denote a finite trace of length n and let φ be an LTL_3 formula. Then the following holds

$$[u, i \models \varphi]_3 = \begin{cases} \top & \text{if } [u, i \models \varphi]_{RV} = \top \\ \perp & \text{if } [u, i \models \varphi]_{RV} = \perp \\ ? & \text{if } [u, i \models \varphi]_{RV} \in \{\top^p, \perp^p\} \end{cases}$$

where the X of LTL_3 is interpreted as strong next-state operator in RV-LTL.

4   Monitors for RV-LTL

A monitor is a device that consumes the input letter by letter and outputs the semantics of the string read so far with respect to the formula the monitor was built for.

In our setting, we use a *Moore machine*, also called *finite-state machine* (FSM), which is a finite state automaton enriched with output. Formally, an FSM is a tuple $\mathcal{A} = (\Sigma, Q, Q_0, \delta, \Delta, \lambda)$, where

- Σ is a *finite alphabet*,
- Q is a finite non-empty set of *states*,
- $q_0 \in Q$ is the *initial state*,
- $\delta : Q \times \Sigma \rightarrow Q$ is the *transition function*,
- Δ is the *output alphabet*, and
- $\lambda : Q \rightarrow \Delta$ is the *output function*.

The output of a Moore machine, defined by the function λ, is thus determined by the current state $q \in Q$ alone, rather than by input symbols.

We extend the transition function $\delta : Q \times \Sigma \rightarrow Q$, as usual, to $\delta' : Q \times \Sigma^* \rightarrow Q$ by $\delta'(q, \epsilon) = q$ where $q \in Q$ and $\delta'(q, ua) = \delta(\delta'(q, u), a)$. To simplify notation, we use δ for both δ and δ'. Similarly, we extend the output function $\lambda : Q \rightarrow \Delta$

to $\lambda' : Q \times \Sigma^* \rightarrow \Delta$ by $\lambda'(q, u) = \lambda(\delta(q, u))$, for $q \in Q$ and $u \in \Sigma^*$. Thus, function λ' yields for a given word u the output in the state reached by u rather than the sequence of outputs. To simplify notation, we use λ for both λ and λ'. We also say that $\mathcal{A}$ *computes* the function $\lambda : \Sigma^* \rightarrow \Delta$.

Following the characterisation of RV-LTL in terms of LTL$_3$ and FLTL developed in the previous section, we base the monitor construction for RV-LTL on the monitor constructions for the respective logics.

Monitors for LTL$_3$. In [BLS06], a monitor construction for a given formula φ with respect to the three-valued semantics was elaborated:

Theorem 1 ([BLS06]). *Let φ be an LTL$_3$ formula. Then there is an effective procedure constructing an FSM $\mathcal{A}_3^\varphi = (\Sigma, Q, q_0, \delta, \mathbb{B}_3, \lambda)$ such that for all $u \in \Sigma^*$ the following holds:*

$$[u \models \varphi]_3 = \lambda(\delta(q_0, u)).$$

Moreover, the size of $\mathcal{A}_3^\varphi$ is at most double exponential in the size of φ.

Monitors for FLTL. Following [MP95], it is easy to come up with a non-deterministic automaton accepting precisely the words satisfying a given LTL formula φ with respect to the FLTL semantics. Such an automaton can be made deterministic as usual. Moreover, a deterministic automaton can be understood as an FSM by outputting $\top$ in each accepting state and $\bot$ in the remaining states. This gives:

Theorem 2 ([MP95]). *Let φ be an FLTL formula. Then there is an effective procedure constructing an FSM $\mathcal{A}_F^\varphi = (\Sigma, Q, q_0, \delta, \mathbb{B}, \lambda)$ such that for all $u \in \Sigma^*$ the following holds:*

$$[u \models \varphi]_F = \lambda(\delta(q_0, u)).$$

Moreover, the size of $\mathcal{A}_F^\varphi$ is at most double exponential in the size of φ.

Monitors for RV-LTL. We are now ready to define a monitor computing the RV-LTL semantics.

Definition 4 (Monitor $\bar{\mathcal{A}}_{RV}^\varphi$ for a RV-LTL-formula φ). *Let φ be an RV-LTL formula. Let $\mathcal{A}_3^\varphi = (\Sigma, Q, q_0, \delta, \mathbb{B}_3, \lambda)$ be the monitor that computes the 3-valued semantics for φ (cf. Theorem 1) where weak next has been replaced with the standard next-state operator.*

Moreover, let $\mathcal{A}_F^\varphi = (\Sigma, Q', q_0', \delta', \mathbb{B}, \lambda')$ be the monitor that computes the (two-valued) FLTL semantics of φ (cf. Theorem 2). Then we define the monitor $\bar{\mathcal{A}}_{RV}^\varphi$ as the FSM $(\Sigma, \bar{Q}, \bar{q}_0, \bar{\delta}, \mathbb{B}_4, \bar{\lambda})$, where

- $\bar{Q} = Q \times Q'$,
- $\bar{q}_0 = (q_0, q_0')$,

- $\bar{\delta}((q, q'), a) = (\delta(q, a), \delta'(q', a))$, and
- $\bar{\lambda} : \bar{Q} \to \mathbb{B}_4$ is defined by

$$\bar{\lambda}((q, q')) = \begin{cases} \top & \text{if } \lambda(q) = \top \\ \bot & \text{if } \lambda(q) = \bot \\ \top^p & \text{if } \lambda(q) = ? \text{ and } \lambda'(q') = \top \\ \bot^p & \text{if } \lambda(q) = ? \text{ and } \lambda'(q') = \bot \end{cases}$$

Thus, we simultaneously compute the three-valued as well as the FLTL semantics by taking the Cartesian product of the corresponding monitors. However, we keep $\top$ and $\bot$ from the three-valued semantics and go for possibly true ($\top^p$) or possibly false ($\bot^p$) whenever the three-valued semantics gives don't know (?) and FLTL semantics yields $\top$ or $\bot$, respectively. This gives:

Theorem 3. *Let φ be an RV-LTL formula and let $\bar{\mathcal{A}}_{RV}^\varphi = (\Sigma, \bar{Q}, \bar{q}_0, \bar{\delta}, \mathbb{B}_4, \bar{\lambda})$ be the monitor according to Definition 4. Then for all $u \in \Sigma^*$ the following holds:*

$$[u \models \varphi]_{RV} = \bar{\lambda}(\bar{\delta}(\bar{q}_0, u)).$$

Moreover, the size of $\bar{\mathcal{A}}_{RV}^\varphi$ is at most double exponential in the size of φ.

While the size of the final FSM is in $O(2^{2^n})$ which sounds a lot, standard minimisation algorithms for FSMs can be used to derive an *optimal* deterministic monitor wrt. the number of states. Optimality implies that any other method, in the worst case, has the same complexity. Better complexity results in other approaches are either due to using a restricted fragment of LTL or otherwise imply that the chosen temporal operators might not limit the expressive power of LTL but sometimes impose long formulas for encoding the desired behaviour.

In practice, however, one might trade a precomputed deterministic monitor towards an on-the-fly determinisation on a non-deterministic monitor as described in [BLS06].

5   Conclusion

In this paper we introduced RV-LTL which is a new variant of LTL defined over finite traces. We developed RV-LTL in order to match four maxims which are motivated by runtime verification applications: A suitable semantics for runtime verification should evaluate each formula and its negation to complementary truth values ($\neg = \mathbf{C}$), the semantics should never evaluate to true or false prematurely (**Sound**), the semantics should be as anticipatory as possible (**Precise**), and finally, the logic should provide a strong and weak next-state operator ($\exists \mathbf{X}$). While preexisting logics can satisfy these maxims partially, none of them does satisfy all four properties simultaneously.

This gap is closed by RV-LTL which matches all four maxims. To turn RV-LTL in a practically applicable device for runtime verification, we first showed how to define the semantics of RV-LTL in terms of two other variants of LTL, namely LTL$_3$ and FLTL, and second we translated this relationship into an efficient monitor construction.

Acknowledgement. We thank the anonymous reviewers for their valuable and detailed comments.

References

[ABLS05] Arafat, O., Bauer, A., Leucker, M., Schallhart, C.: Runtime verification revisited. Technical Report TUM-I0518, Technische Universität München (2005)

[BLS06]   Bauer, A., Leucker, M., Schallhart, C.: Monitoring of real-time properties. In: Arun-Kumar, S., Garg, N. (eds.) FSTTCS 2006. LNCS, vol. 4337, Springer, Heidelberg (2006)

[dR05]   d'Amorim, M., Rosu, G.: Efficient monitoring of omega-languages. In: Etessami, K., Rajamani, S.K. (eds.) CAV 2005. LNCS, vol. 3576, pp. 364–378. Springer, Heidelberg (2005)

[Dru00]   Drusinsky, D.: The temporal rover and the atg rover. In: Havelund, K., Penix, J., Visser, W. (eds.) SPIN. LNCS, vol. 1885, pp. 323–330. Springer, Heidelberg (2000)

[EFH+03] Eisner, C., Fisman, D., Havlicek, J., Lustig, Y., McIsaac, A., Campenhout, D.: Reasoning with temporal logic on truncated paths. In: Hunt Jr., W.A., Somenzi, F. (eds.) CAV 2003. LNCS, vol. 2725, pp. 27–39. Springer, Heidelberg (2003)

[GH01a]   Giannakopoulou, D., Havelund, K.: Automata-based verification of temporal properties on running programs. In: ASE, pp. 412–416. IEEE Computer Society, Los Alamitos (2001)

[GH01b]   Giannakopoulou, D., Havelund, K.: Runtime analysis of linear temporal logic specifications. Technical Report 01.21, RIACS/USRA (2001)

[HR01a]   Havelund, K., Rosu, G.: Monitoring Java Programs with Java PathExplorer. Electr. Notes Theor. Comp. Sci. 55(2) (2001)

[HR01b]   Havelund, K., Rosu, G.: Monitoring programs using rewriting. In: ASE 2001. Proceedings of the 16th IEEE International Conference on Automated Software Engineering, Washington, DC, USA, p. 135. IEEE Computer Society, Los Alamitos (2001)

[HR02]   Havelund, K., Rosu, G.: Synthesizing Monitors for Safety Properties. Tools and Algorithms for Construction and Analysis of Systems, 342–356 (2002)

[LPZ85]   Lichtenstein, O., Pnueli, A., Zuck, L.: The Glory of the Past. In: Proceedings of the Conference on Logic of Programs, pp. 196–218 (1985)

[MP95]   Manna, Z., Pnueli, A.: Temporal Verification of Reactive Systems: Safety. Springer, Heidelberg (1995)

[Pnu77]   Pnueli, A.: The temporal logic of programs. In: Proceedings of the 18th IEEE Symposium on the Foundations of Computer Science (FOCS-77), pp. 46–57. IEEE, Los Alamitos (1977)

[PZ06]   Pnueli, A., Zaks, A.: Psl model checking and run-time verification via testers. In: Misra, J., Nipkow, T., Sekerinski, E. (eds.) FM 2006. LNCS, vol. 4085, pp. 573–586. Springer, Heidelberg (2006)

[SB05]   Stolz, V., Bodden, E.: Temporal Assertions using AspectJ. In: Fifth Workshop on Runtime Verification (RV 2005). To be published in ENTCS, Elsevier, Amsterdam (2005)

[Var96]   Vardi, M.Y.: An Automata-Theoretic Approach to Linear Temporal Logic. In: Moller, F., Birtwistle, G. (eds.) Logics for Concurrency. LNCS, vol. 1043, pp. 238–266. Springer, Heidelberg (1996)

[VW86]   Vardi, M.Y., Wolper, P.: An automata-theoretic approach to automatic program verification. In: Symposium on Logic in Computer Science LICS 1986, pp. 332–345. IEEE Computer Society Press, Washington (1986)

Translation Validation of System Abstractions*

Jan Olaf Blech, Ina Schaefer, and Arnd Poetzsch-Heffter

Software Technology Group
University of Kaiserslautern
Germany

Abstract. Abstraction is intensively used in the verification of large, complex or infinite-state systems. With abstractions getting more complex it is often difficult to see whether they are valid. However, for using abstraction in model checking it has to be ensured that properties are preserved. In this paper, we use a translation validation approach to verify property preservation of system abstractions. We formulate a correctness criterion based on simulation between concrete and abstract system for a property to be verified. For each distinct run of the abstraction procedure the correctness is verified in the theorem prover Isabelle/HOL. This technique is applied in the verification of adaptive embedded systems.

1 Introduction

Recently, a large amount of research has addressed the verification of large, complex or infinite-state systems using model checking. Due to inherent limitations model checkers are unable to deal with such systems directly. So research concentrated on finding abstractions reducing the state space sufficiently while preserving necessary precision. However, since abstraction procedures are getting more complex it is not always clear if they are valid, i.e. that properties verified for the abstract system also hold in the concrete system. In principle, there are two approaches to guarantee correctness of abstractions: Abstraction algorithms (and their implementations!) are verified once and for all. Alternatively, abstraction results of each distinct run of the abstraction procedure are proved correct. In this work, we will propose a technique for guaranteeing abstraction correctness using the second approach.

The overall structure of our approach is depicted in Figure 1. For verifying a system abstraction, the abstraction procedure is given a concrete system comprising a property to be checked. As output an abstract system with a corresponding abstract property is produced. Furthermore, a proof script is generated doing the actual proof that the abstraction preserves the considered property. A correctness criterion based on simulation between abstract and concrete system is formalized. Using the proof script, this criterion is checked for the considered concrete and abstract systems and properties in the theorem prover Isabelle/HOL [14]. Thus the correctness of an abstraction is verified for each run

---

* Supported by the Rheinland-Pfalz Cluster of Excellence 'Dependable Adaptive Systems and Mathematical Modelling' (DASMOD).

O. Sokolsky and S. Tasiran (Eds.): RV 2007, LNCS 4839, pp. 139–150, 2007.

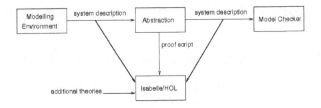

Fig. 1. Our Translation Validation Infrastructure

of the abstraction procedure. Note that the correctness of the technique does not depend on the proof script provided. An incorrect proof script may never lead to an incorrect proof but rather to no proof at all.

Our work towards runtime verification of system abstractions is inspired by a translation validation [15] based approach for compilers [4, 12, 18]. In the area of compiler verification, it has turned out that runtime verification of compilers is often the method of choice for achieving guaranteed correct compilation results. As for compilers, correctness proofs for distinct abstractions are usually less complex and easier to establish than proofs for a general abstraction procedure. An additional advantage is that the abstraction procedure can be tailored to a particular system and property under consideration and thus match the requirements of the concrete problem very closely while still being proved correct. Also note, that in our approach the correctness of abstractions is proved formally using a theorem prover instead of a paper-and-pencil-proof.

The proposed technique is applied in verification of adaptive embedded systems [1]. Beside potentially unbounded data domains the size of the considered systems is huge. For efficient verification by model checking, these systems have to be abstracted in a property-preserving way. We have successfully applied runtime verification of the necessary abstractions in this domain.

This paper is structured as follows: Section 2 describes the application domain of our work. In Section 3, we present a theorem on property preservation. This is used in the implementation and proving strategies in Section 4. A short evaluation is given in Section 5. We discuss related work in Section 6 before concluding in Section 7.

2   Adaptive System Verification

In the EVAS project [1], the application domain is the verification of adaptive embedded systems. The considered adaptive systems consist of a set of synchronously operating modules. Each module is equipped with a set of different predetermined behavioral variants it can adapt to depending on the status of the environment. This enhances system reliability and dependability but also increases design complexity making support for formal verification highly necessary. The systems are developed in a modeling environment also used for other purposes such as code generation. Hence, they contain a level of detail not amenable for automatic verification making system abstractions indispensable.

Module = (var, init, configurations, adaptation) with var $\subseteq$ Var and init : var $\rightarrow$ Val
configurations = {(guard$_j$, next_state$_j$, next_out$_j$)} for i = 1, ..., n
guard$_j$: a Boolean constraint on adapt_var
next_state$_j$, next_out$_j$: (var $\rightarrow$ Val) $\rightarrow$ (var $\rightarrow$ Val)
adaptation = (adapt_var, adapt_init, adapt_next_state, adapt_next_out)
adapt_var $\subseteq$ Var and adapt_init : adapt_var $\rightarrow$ Val
adapt_next_state, adapt_next_out : (adapt_var $\rightarrow$ Val) $\rightarrow$ (adapt_var $\rightarrow$ Val)

System = ({Module$_1$, ..., Module$_n$}, var, adapt_var, conn$_a$, conn$_d$)

Fig. 2. SAS Module and System Description

Figure 2 shows a part of our representation for synchronous adaptive systems (SAS). A full formal account can be found in [1]. A SAS module consists of a set of variables var (divided into state and output variables) together with their initial values, a set of configurations modeling the functional behavior and an adaptation aspect representing the adaptive behavior. Each configuration consists of a guard determining when this configuration is enabled and the attached state transition functions for the state and output variables. The adaptation aspect comprises a distinct set of adaptation specific variables, their initial values and state transition functions for the adaptive state and output variables. This explicit account of adaptive and functional behaviour allows to reason about functional and adaptive aspects in isolation as well as in combination. The semantics of SAS modules is similar to ordinary transition systems with the difference that a transition between two module states evolves in two stages: First, the adaptation aspect computes the new valuation of adaptive state and output variables. Then, the configuration with valid guard is selected and the respective state and output transition functions are executed. A SAS system is composed from a set of modules by connecting their functional and adaptive variables and the system's functional and adaptive variables by functional and adaptive connection functions, conn$_a$ and conn$_d$ resp.

As an example of how abstraction facilitates verification of synchronous adaptive systems, consider a system that consists of one module with two different configurations. Every time the input is bigger than a certain threshold, say 50, the module switches to its first configuration. This configuration uses a specific algorithm for computing the output. If the input is smaller than 50, the module uses configuration 2 computing the output in a different way. An important property of this example system is that every time the input exceeds 50 configuration 1 is used in order to make sure that the appropriate algorithm is employed. This property can be stated in a variant of the temporal logic CTL*[11] as $\varphi \equiv AG(input \geq 50 \rightarrow useconf = 1)$ modeling the used configuration by a variable $useconf$. For φ, the actual functionality of the system is irrelevant.

Because the input domain in the example system is unbounded φ cannot be model checked directly. However, we can abstract the system by mapping the infinite domain of input values to a finite abstract domain while preserving the property under consideration. We choose the abstract domain $\widehat{Val} = \{low, high\}$.

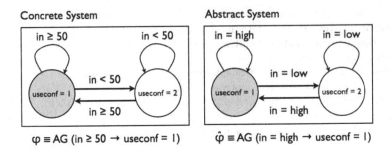

Fig. 3. Illustration of the example system

The abstraction function $h : Val \rightarrow \widehat{Val}$ is defined as $h(v) = low$ if $v < 50$ and $h(v) = high$ if $v \geq 50$. Then the abstract system will use configuration 1 if the input is *high* and configuration 2 if it is *low*. Figure 3 depicts the concrete and abstract system as automata. The property φ is abstracted to $\hat{\varphi} \equiv \text{AG}(input = high \rightarrow useconf = 1)$. With the approach presented in this paper we will be able to verify at runtime of the abstraction procedure that the abstraction preserves φ. This means that if we are able to verify $\hat{\varphi}$ for the abstract system φ also holds for the concrete.

We apply our approach to adaptive systems in the automotive sector. An adaptive system implementing the ABS (antilock braking system) consists of a large number of different modules and hundreds of different variables ranging over unbounded domains. While in the simple example, the correctness of the abstraction can be easily seen, in real-world examples abstractions become very complex and require support for automatically verifying their correctness.

3 Property Preservation by Simulation

In this section, we present the basis for the correctness criterion used in our translation validation approach. It uses the fact that a property is preserved under abstraction if there is a consistent simulation between abstract and concrete system. In this presentation, we will use general transition systems as SAS semantics are defined in this way. Futhermore, this allows to extend the approach to a broader range of systems expressible as transition systems. For a more detailed formal account and proofs, see the extended version of this paper [5].

Definition 1 (Transition System). *A transition system $\mathcal{T} = (\Sigma, Init, \rightsquigarrow)$ is defined by Σ, the set of states $\sigma : Var \rightarrow Val$ for a set of variables Var and a set of values Val, $Init \subseteq \Sigma$, the set of initial states and $\rightsquigarrow \subseteq \Sigma \times \Sigma$, the transition relation. A path of $\mathcal{T}$ is defined as a sequence of states $\pi = \sigma_0 \sigma_1 \ldots$ where $\sigma_0 \in Init$ and $\sigma_i \rightsquigarrow \sigma_{i+1}$ for all $i \geq 0$. The set $Paths(\mathcal{T})$ denotes the set of possible paths of $\mathcal{T}$.*

We use a variant of the temporal logic CTL*[11] to express properties over computation paths of $\mathcal{T}$. The atomic propositions are constraints on variables, e.g.

$x = y$ or *input* ≤ 50. Besides Boolean negation, conjunction and disjunction we have temporal operators, e.g. $\mathsf{X}\varphi$ ("next") denoting that φ holds in the next state or $\mathsf{G}\varphi$ ("globally") denoting that φ holds on all states of a path. Additionally, we have path quantifiers $\mathsf{E}\varphi$ and $\mathsf{A}\varphi$. $\mathsf{E}\varphi$ denotes that there exists a computation path on which φ holds. $\mathsf{A}\varphi$ denotes that for all computation paths φ holds. Atomic propositions are interpreted over a state σ by evaluating the variable assignments, e.g. $(\mathcal{T}, \sigma) \models (x = y)$ iff $\sigma(x) = \sigma(y)$. Boolean and CTL* operators are interpreted standardly. $\mathcal{T} \models \varphi$ denotes that φ holds on paths starting in the initial states. $Atoms(\varphi)$ returns the set of atomic propositions used in a CTL* formula φ. ACTL* denotes the fragment of CTL* where only the universal path quantifier A is used.

In order to be able to formulate a criterion when a property is preserved we need the notion of simulation between two transition systems. A transition system $\mathcal{T}$ is simulated by an abstract transition system $\widehat{\mathcal{T}}$ if we can find a simulation relation $\mathcal{R}$ between the two sets of states such that firstly for all initial states of $\mathcal{T}$ there exists a related initial state in $\widehat{\mathcal{T}}$ and secondly that for any pair of related states with a transition in $\mathcal{T}$ there is also a transition in $\widehat{\mathcal{T}}$ such that the resulting states are related.

Definition 2 (Simulation of transition systems). *Let $\mathcal{T}$ and $\widehat{\mathcal{T}}$ be two transition systems. We say that $\widehat{\mathcal{T}}$ simulates $\mathcal{T}$, denoted $\mathcal{T} \preceq \widehat{\mathcal{T}}$, iff there exists a simulation relation $\mathcal{R} \subseteq \Sigma \times \widehat{\Sigma}$ such that*

1. *for all $\sigma_0 \in Init$ there exists $\hat{\sigma}_0 \in \widehat{Init}$ such that $\mathcal{R}(\sigma_0, \hat{\sigma}_0)$*
2. *for $0 \leq i$ and $\sigma_i, \sigma_{i+1} \in \Sigma$ and $\hat{\sigma}_i \in \widehat{\Sigma}$ with $\mathcal{R}(\sigma_i, \hat{\sigma}_i)$ and $\sigma_i \rightsquigarrow \sigma_{i+1}$ there exists $\hat{\sigma}_{i+1} \in \widehat{\Sigma}$ such that $\hat{\sigma}_i \rightsquigarrow \hat{\sigma}_{i+1}$ and $\mathcal{R}(\sigma_{i+1}, \hat{\sigma}_{i+1})$.*

If a transition system $\mathcal{T}$ is simulated by $\widehat{\mathcal{T}}$ we can show that for each path in $\mathcal{T}$ there is a corresponding path in $\widehat{\mathcal{T}}$. This result is important for the preservation of temporal operators in a CTL* formula. The proof proceeds by induction on the length of a path.

Lemma 1 (Corresponding paths in $\mathcal{T}$ and $\widehat{\mathcal{T}}$). *Let $\mathcal{T}$ and $\widehat{\mathcal{T}}$ be two transition systems such that $\mathcal{T} \preceq \widehat{\mathcal{T}}$ with simulation relation $\mathcal{R}$. Then for every path $\pi = \sigma_0\sigma_1 \ldots \in Paths(\mathcal{T})$ there exists a corresponding path $\hat{\pi} = \hat{\sigma}_0\hat{\sigma}_1 \ldots \in Paths(\widehat{\mathcal{T}})$ such that $\mathcal{R}(\sigma_i, \hat{\sigma}_i)$ for all $i \geq 0$.*

Now we are in the position to justify the criterion that allows to conclude $\mathcal{T} \models \varphi$ from $\widehat{\mathcal{T}} \models \hat{\varphi}$ for φ and $\hat{\varphi}$ in ACTL*. Existential properties are typically lost under abstraction. The result is based on simulation between the concrete and the abstract system and an additional consistency condition between concrete and abstract property. The consistency criterion intuitively expresses that the atomic propositions must be preserved under abstraction. In order to state the consistency condition we need a concretization function $\mathcal{C}$ that maps an abstract property $\hat{\varphi}$ to an corresponding property φ over the concrete system $\mathcal{T}$. It is defined on atomic propositions and compatibly lifted to ACTL* formulas. This reflects the potentially different interpretations of variables in concrete and abstract system. The concrete choice of simulation relation and concretization mapping depends on the abstraction procedure used.

Theorem 1 (Property-Preservation of ACTL*). *Let* $T = (\Sigma, Init, \rightsquigarrow)$ *and* $\widehat{T} = (\widehat{\Sigma}, \widehat{Init}, \hat{\rightsquigarrow})$ *be two transition systems,* φ *a* $ACTL^*$ *formula over* T *and* $\hat{\varphi}$ *an* $ACTL^*$ *formula over* $\widehat{T}$. *Then it holds that*

$$\widehat{T} \models \hat{\varphi} \text{ implies } T \models \varphi$$

iff there exists a simulation relation $\mathcal{R} \subseteq \Sigma \times \widehat{\Sigma}$ *and a concretization function* $\mathcal{C} : ACTL^*[\widehat{T}] \rightarrow ACTL^*[T]$ *such that the following conditions hold:*

1. *Initial Simulation: for all* $\sigma_0 \in Init$ *there exists* $\hat{\sigma}_0 \in \widehat{Init}$ *such that* $\mathcal{R}(\sigma_0, \hat{\sigma}_0)$
2. *Step Simulation: for all* $i \geq 0$, $\sigma_i, \sigma_{i+1} \in \Sigma$ *and* $\hat{\sigma}_i \in \widehat{\Sigma}$ *with* $\mathcal{R}(\sigma_i, \hat{\sigma}_i)$ *and* $\sigma_i \rightsquigarrow \sigma_{i+1}$ *there exists* $\hat{\sigma}_{i+1} \in \widehat{\Sigma}$ *such that* $\hat{\sigma}_i \hat{\rightsquigarrow} \hat{\sigma}_{i+1}$ *and* $\mathcal{R}(\sigma_{i+1}, \hat{\sigma}_{i+1})$.
3. *Consistency: for all* $\hat{a} \in Atoms(\hat{\varphi})$ *if* $\mathcal{R}(\sigma, \hat{\sigma})$ *and* $(\widehat{T}, \hat{\sigma}) \models \hat{a}$ *then* $(T, \sigma) \models \mathcal{C}(\hat{a})$
4. *Implication:* $T \models \mathcal{C}(\hat{\varphi}) \rightarrow \varphi$.

The proof is by induction of the structure of the formula $\hat{\varphi}$. The base case uses the consistency condition. The induction step for temporal operators and path quantifiers uses the path lemma. This theorem constitutes the necessary conditions for the correctness criterion in our translation validation approach. It differs from other approaches using property-preservation by simulation [2, 7, 10] therein that states of the underlying system model are characterized by variable assignments and that atomic propositions in the applied logic are constraints over these assignments. This requires a concretization function but eases to work with systems where states are described by valuations of variables such as in SAS.

Furthermore, Theorem 1 is formulated in a very general fashion that allows to instantiate it with a number of different kinds of abstractions. In this direction, it can be used to justify the domain abstraction approach proposed in [6]. The concrete transition system is defined over a concrete data domain D, either very large or infinite. Thus, the system can only be model checked very inefficiently if at all. So the concrete domain is mapped to an abstract domain $\widehat{D}$ by an homomorphic abstraction function $h : D \rightarrow \widehat{D}$. In order to prove that a property φ is preserved under this form of domain abstraction we have to establish a simulation relation between Σ and $\widehat{\Sigma}$ satisfying the conditions of Theorem 1. This is the relation defined by $(\sigma, \hat{\sigma}) \in \mathcal{R}$ if $\hat{\sigma}(x) = h(\sigma(x))$ for all $x \in Var$. The concretization function $\mathcal{C}$ for an atomic proposition maps the formula $x = \hat{v}$ for $x \in Var$ and $\hat{v} \in \widehat{D}$ to the disjunction over all concrete values that are mapped to the abstract value $\hat{v}$, i.e

$$\mathcal{C}(x = \hat{v}) = \bigvee_{h(v) = \hat{v}} (x = v)$$

The concretization function is compatibly lifted to ACTL* formulas. This form of abstraction is also applied in the example of Section 2.

Another abstraction procedure that can be mapped to this theorem is omitting variables that are irrelevant for the considered property, similar to dead code elimination in compiler optimization. Here, the abstract system $\widehat{\mathcal{T}}$ only contains a subset of the variables of $\mathcal{T}$, i.e. $\widehat{Var} \subseteq Var$ while the rest of the system remains the same. The simulation relation between two states can be defined as $\mathcal{R}(\sigma, \hat{\sigma})$ iff $\sigma(x) = \hat{\sigma}(x)$ for all $x \in \widehat{Var}$. The concretization function is simply the identity function since the interpretation of the atomic propositions does not change if the abstraction is carried out correctly. Besides these two abstraction procedures we aim at extending our work to more complicated and powerful abstractions (see Future Work in Section 7).

4   The Translation Validation Infrastructure

In this section, we describe the different steps for verifying a system abstraction correct in Isabelle/HOL[14]. Firstly, we have to generate an Isabelle/HOL description of both the concrete and the abstract system. Secondly, we have to formalize a criterion stating the correctness of an abstraction in Isabelle corresponding to the conditions of Theorem 1. Finally, we need a proof script that proves that the concrete and abstract system description fulfill the correctness criterion. Note that instead of the more general transition relation in Theorem 1 we use explicit state transition functions in the Isabelle formalization corresponding to the SAS system specification (cf. Figure 2). We chose the higher order theorem prover Isabelle/HOL for its greater degrees of freedom in specification allowing shorter and more elegant formalizations.

4.1   Representing Systems in Isabelle

In our implementation, Isabelle representations of concrete and abstract system are generated right before and after a run of the abstraction procedure. Concrete and abstract systems are represented using the same datatypes. We use a shallow embedding of our system description language into the Isabelle/HOL theorem prover. This means that we formalize the semantics of a system directly within Isabelle's Higher Order Logic constructs. Since the semantics is basically defined via state transition functions we use Isabelle syntax to directly encode these functions. In contrast to a shallow embedding, a deep embedding would require to formalize the syntax of the system description language in Isabelle[1] and define a semantics on top of the syntactical elements. Some of the SAS specifications are not entirely formulated as executable programs. Instead they are only characterized via pre- and postconditions. Due to the more abstract nature of shallow embeddings such issues are much easier to deal with in our approach. We also believe that we can adopt to changes in the underlying datatypes faster if we do not formalize them in Isabelle directly.

---

[1] See e.g. [18] for a comparison between deep and shallow embedding in an Isabelle/HOL environment.

Thus, to generate Isabelle system semantics representations we need to convert a system description directly into Isabelle (state transition) functions. Furthermore, we generate datatypes representing system states to serve as arguments for these functions. Due to the finite number of variables in each system we encode states as tuples of values rather than in a mapping function. This simplifies conducting the proofs. Variable references are encoded as selectors to such tuples. We do not distinguish between different kinds of variables (adapt_var, var cp. Fig 2) in the state encoding. Input is implicitly regarded as a stream of input elements. One element after the other is consumed during system execution. Initial states are encoded as functions assigning initial values to an arbitrary state.

A SAS module is divided into an adaptation aspect for adaptive behavior and functional configurations. Before evaluating the functionality of a configuration the adaptive part (adapt_next_state and adapt_next_out) is evaluated. The actual functionality of a configuration (next_state$_j$ and next_out$_j$) is selected using a guard formula. In our semantics framework we encode this behavior by evaluating the Isabelle representation for adapt_next_state and adapt_next_out first. Then we make a case distinction on the guard formulas (several if-clauses) selecting the appropriate Isabelle representation for the configuration functions next_state$_j$ and next_out$_j$ to be evaluated. The generation of the system state transition function is done using a visitor pattern on the datatypes representing the input systems. While visiting parts of the system description corresponding parts for the state transition function are emitted in Isabelle/HOL syntax. These parts are composed to a large state transition function representing a system's semantics within Isabelle/HOL.

In systems with more than one module, we generate Isabelle representations for each module. Since we deal with synchronous systems, modules do not affect each other during a single transition. Hence, we can evaluate the modules' state transition functions one after the other. Evaluation order does not matter. An addition to this, we generate Isabelle representations for the connections between modules which are functions themselves. All these functions are composed into a single state transition function representing a system's semantics. This technique works for concrete and abstract systems equally well.

4.2 Formalizing Abstraction Correctness in Isabelle

For proving that an abstraction is valid we need a formalization of property preservation in Isabelle/HOL. Such a formalized correctness criterion (Figure 4) has to fulfill the conditions stated in Theorem 1. The first two conditions (in both the theorem and the figure) correspond to the simulation between the two systems. These first two conditions are formalized once for all systems. With a slight generalization they can also be applied for the verification of compiler optimization phases (cf. [4, 12]).

The third condition in Theorem 1 requires that the simulation relation preserves consistency. We are free to chose the notion of consistency by instantiating the concretization function C. However, we have to ensure that the fourth condition of Theorem 1 still holds. In order to establish condition 4 in Theorem 1, one

```
constdefs systemequivalence ::
   (state => state) => (state' => state') => state => state' =>
    (state => state' => bool) => concprop => absprop => concfun => bool
  "systemequivalence nextstate nextstate' s0 s0' R c a C ==
  R s0 s0' &
  ALL s s'. R s s' --> R (next s) (next s') &
  consistency(R,C) & implies(C (a),c)"
```

Fig. 4. Correctness Criterion

can formulate properties to be checked in terms of the abstractions in the first place. In our case studies, however, properties are usually formulated in terms of the concrete system. Hence, one has to verify that the concretization of the abstract property implies the concrete property.

Figure 5 shows a small extract from a typical simulation relation for a domain abstraction. It takes two states A and B of concrete and abstract system and ensures that whenever the variable in1 in the concrete system has a value less than 50 then the value of in1 in the simulating abstract system must be low. In the complete simulation relation for a system, we encode a condition for every variable abstraction being performed. In contrast to this fragment of a simulation relation designed for domain abstractions the simulation relation for omission of variables is even simpler. Here, no condition is put on an omitted variable in the relation.

```
constdefs inputequivalence :: "S1 => S2 => bool"
"inputequiv A B == ( ( (in1 A = low) = (in1 B <= 50) ) & ..."
```

Fig. 5. Simulation Relation

The simulation relation for a concrete system can be generated by the abstraction procedure or adjusted by hand. It reflects the performed abstractions. Note that the concretization function C in Theorem 1 directly corresponds to the simulation relation. In our example simulation relation, the abstract value on the left side of the equation is the argument of C whereas the concrete value on the right side refers to the result of the concretization.

4.3   Proving Abstractions Correct

To conduct the correctness proof we still need a proof script. In our current implementation we first prove additional lemmata implying the actual correctness criterion. The simu_step_helper lemma is a generic part for proving abstraction of variable domains and omission of variables correct. The lemma as well as its proof is depicted in Figure 6. The formalization of the lemma is shown in the first line. The rest is the proof script computing the proof for this lemma. A proof script can be considered as a kind of program that tells the theorem prover how to conduct a proof. It comprises the application of several tactics

```
lemma simu_step_helper:
   "(funequiv A B) & (inputequiv A B) & (funequiv' A B) --> (funequiv (M1' A A) (M1 B B))"
apply (clarify, unfold funequiv_def inputequiv_def, clarify  )
apply (unfold M1_def, unfold M1'_def)
apply (erule subst)+
apply (unfold funequiv'_def funequiv_def inputequiv_def )
apply clarify
apply (rule conjI, simp) +
apply simp
done
```

Fig. 6. Proof Script

(apply) which can be regarded as subprograms in the proving process. In the proving process the theorem prover symbolically evaluates state transition functions (M1,M1') on symbolic states. These symbolic states are specified by their relation to each other. The theorem prover checks that the relation between the states still holds after the evaluation of the transition functions. The predicates funequiv and inputequiv together imply system equivalence and in general do highly depend on the chosen simulation relation. For the case studies examined so far, we have developed a single highly generic proof script (which the lemma simu_step_helper is a part of) that proves the correctness in all scenarios containing domain abstractions and omission of variables. For more complicated scenarios the proof script might need adaptation. This was the case in the original compiler scenario where adaptations could be done fully automatically [4].

5   Evaluation of Our Framework

The AMOR (Abstract and MOdular verifieR) tool prototypically implements the technique proposed in this paper for domain abstractions and omitting variables. We have successfully applied it in several case studies in the context of the EVAS project [1] and proved that interesting system properties were preserved by abstractions. Our largest example with domain abstractions contained amongst others 39 variables with infinite domains. Examined system representations had up to 2600 lines of Isabelle code. In some of these scenarios, model checking was not possible without abstractions. Thus, our technique bridges a gap in the verification process between a system model representation in a modeling environment (used e.g. for code generation) and an input representation for verification tools. The time to conduct the proofs did not turn out to be a problem contrary to our translation validation work on compilers [4].

6   Related Work

While previously correctness of abstractions was established by showing soundness for all possible systems, for instance in abstract interpretation based approaches [8, 9], our technique proves an abstraction correct for a specific system and property to be verified. In this direction, we adopted the notion of translation validation [15, 19] to correctness of system abstractions. Translation validation focuses on guaranteeing correctness of compiler runs. After a compiler has translated a source into a target program a checker compares the two programs and decides whether they are equivalent. In our setting, we replace the compiler by the abstraction mechanism, the source program by the original system and the target program by the abstract system. Isabelle/HOL[14] serves as checker in our case. In the original translation validation approach[15] the checker derives the equivalence of source and target via static analysis while the compiler is regarded as a black box. In subsequent works, the compiler was extended to generate hints for the checker, e.g. proof scripts or a simulation relation as in our case, in order to simplify the derivation of equivalence of source and target programs. This approach is known as credible compilation [17] or certifying compilation [12]. Translation validation in general is not limited to simulation based correctness criteria. However, also for compiler and transformation algorithm verification simulation based correctness criteria can be used (see e.g. [3] for work with a similar Isabelle formalization of simulation).

Simulation for program correctness was originally introduced by [13]. Since, property preservation by simulation has been studied for different fragments of CTL* and the μ-calculus. The authors in [2, 7, 10] use Kripke structures as their underlying system model where either states are labeled with atomic propositions or atomic propositions are labeled with states. This reduces the consistency condition to checking that the labeling of two states in simulation is the same. However, this complicates the treatment of systems defined by valuations of variables such as SAS. In [6], the authors use a system model similar to ours, but this work is restricted to data domain abstraction while our technique can be applied for different abstraction mechanisms. Abstract interpretation based simulations as used in [2, 10] are also less general than generic simulation relations considered here.

7   Conclusion

In this paper, we presented a technique for proving correctness of system abstractions using a translation validation approach. Based on property-preservation by simulation we formalized a correctness criterion in Isabelle/HOL. With the help of generic proof scripts we are able to verify abstractions correct at runtime of the abstraction procedure. Our technique was successfully applied in various case studies verifying data domain abstractions and omission of variables.

For future work, we want to apply our technique to further and more complex abstraction procedures. In particular, we want to focus on abstractions of hierarchical systems where simple stepwise simulation relations will no longer be sufficient. Additionally, we are planning to investigate the interplay between modularization and abstraction in order to further reduce verification effort.

References

1. Adler, R., Schaefer, I., Schuele, T., Vecchie, E.: From Model-Based Design to Formal Verification of Adaptive Embedded Systems. In: Proc. of ICFEM 2007, (November 2007)
2. Bensalem, S., Bouajjani, A., Loiseaux, C., Sifakis, J.: Property preserving simulations. In: Probst, D.K., von Bochmann, G. (eds.) CAV 1992. LNCS, vol. 663, pp. 260–273. Springer, Heidelberg (1993)
3. Blech, J.O., Gesellensetter, L., Glesner, S.: Formal Verification of Dead Code Elimination in Isabelle/HOL. In: Proc. of SEFM, pp. 200–209 (2005)
4. Blech, J.O., Poetzsch-Heffter, A.: A certifying code generation phase. In: Proc. of COCV 2007 ENTCS, Braga, Portugal, (March 2007)
5. Blech, J.O., Schaefer, I., Poetzsch-Heffter, A.: On Translation Validation for System Abstractions. Technical Report 361-07, TU Kaiserslautern, (July 2007)
6. Clarke, E.M., Grumberg, O., Long, D.E.: Model checking and abstraction. ACM TOPLAS 16(5), 1512–1542 (1994)
7. Clarke, E.M., Grumberg, O., Peled, D.A.: Model Checking. MIT Press, Cambridge (1999)
8. Cousot, P., Cousot, R.: Abstract interpretation: A unified lattice model for static analysis of programs by construction or approximation of fixpoints. In: Proc. of POPL, pp. 238–252. ACM Press, New York (January 1977)
9. Cousot, P., Cousot, R.: Systematic design of program analysis frameworks. In: Proc. of POPL, pp. 269–282. ACM Press, New York (January 1979)
10. Dams, D., Gerth, R., Grumberg, O.: Abstract interpretation of reactive systems. ACM Trans. Program. Lang. Syst. 19(2), 253–291 (1997)
11. Emerson, E.A.: Temporal and modal logic. In: van Leeuwen, J. (ed.) Handbook of Theoretical Computer Science, Elsevier, Amsterdam (1990)
12. Gawkowski, M.J., Blech, J.O., Poetzsch-Heffter, A.: Certifying Compilers based on Formal Translation Contracts. Technical Report 355-06, TU Kaiserslautern (November 2006)
13. Milner, R.: An algebraic definition of simulation between programs. In: Proc. of IJCAI, pp. 481–489 (1971)
14. Nipkow, T., Paulson, L.C., Wenzel, M. (eds.): Isabelle/HOL. LNCS, vol. 2283. Springer, Heidelberg (2002)
15. Pnueli, A., Siegel, M., Singerman, E.: Translation validation. In: Steffen, B. (ed.) ETAPS 1998 and TACAS 1998. LNCS, vol. 1384, Springer, Heidelberg (1998)
16. Poetzsch-Heffter, A., Gawkowski, M.J.: Towards proof generating compilers. Electronics Notes in Theoritical Computer Science 132(1), 37–51 (2005)
17. Rinard, M., Marinov, D.: Credible compilation with pointers. In: Proc. of the FLoC Workshop on Run-Time Result Verification, Trento, Italy, (July 1999)
18. Wildmoser, M., Nipkow, T.: Certifying machine code safety: Shallow versus deep embedding. In: Theorem Proving in Higher Order Logics, Springer, Heidelberg (2004)
19. Zuck, L., Pnueli, A., Fang, Y., Goldberg, B.: VOC: A methodology for the translation validation of optimizing compilers. Journal of Universal Computer Science 9(3), 223–247 (2003)

Instrumentation of Open-Source Software for Intrusion Detection

William Mahoney and William Sousan

University of Nebraska at Omaha 282F PKI 6001 Dodge Street, Omaha Nebraska 68182-0500
wmahoney@mail.unomaha.edu, wsousan@mail.unomanha.edu

Abstract. A significant number of cyber assaults and intrusion attempts are made against open source software written in C, C++, or Java. Detecting all flaws in a large system is still a daunting, unrealistic task. The information assurance area known as "intrusion detection" (ID) senses unauthorized access attempts by monitoring key pieces of system data. There is a desire to at least detect intrusion attempts in order to stop them while in progress, or repair the damage at a later date. Most ID systems examine system log files, or monitor network traffic. This research presents a new approach to generating records for intrusion detection by means of instrumentation. Open source code such as a web server can be compiled and the execution path of the server can be observed externally in near real-time. This method thus creates a new data source for ID which can be incorporated into a discovery system.

Keywords: Intrusion Detection, Instrumentation, Domain Specific Language.

1 Introduction

Intrusion detection is an area of information assurance which deals with monitoring the events occurring in a computer system or network, analyzing them for signs of security problems [1]. These systems are typically one of two types: Anomaly Detection, and Misuse Detection. Misuse Detection can be thought of as similar to virus detection software, where one searches for known patterns of attack. Anomaly Detection uses statistical methods to determine "typical" behavior, and then monitors various data sources for "atypical" behavior. Both methods, though, often utilize two sources of input data. These sources are system logs, which track files accessed, user activity, and so on, and network traffic.

This research paper describes a new data source which we are using to perform intrusion detection; this data source is a running executable program, typically a recompiled open-source package, which has been instrumented in order to generate tracing data. We outline our intrusion detection scheme and include contributions to intrusion detection in two main foci.

First, we discuss the techniques used to modify the internal representations used by the GCC compilers to allow this instrumentation. The compiler uses

O. Sokolsky and S. Tasiran (Eds.): RV 2007, LNCS 4839, pp. 151–163, 2007.
© Springer-Verlag Berlin Heidelberg 2007

an internal representation called RTX. Additional calls to the instrumentation functions are automatically generated in RTX by our modified compiler just prior to emitting assembly language output. The research paper addresses the techniques for locating the instrumentation points and avoiding problems when software is compiled with optimization. We also present figures addressing the slowdown due to the instrumentation overhead that results by including our monitoring code. The slowdown in compute-bound programs is significant, but our focus is typified by heavily I/O bound processes such as web servers. This work is completed and the modifications to GCC have been successfully tested on several large open source projects.

Secondly, we have designed and describe a simple a priori domain specific language which we are implementing as a proof of concept system to determine the feasibility of this method for intrusion detection. Our system does not currently encompass any learning modes; instead we manually enter rules based on the past known good observed behavior of the software we are compiling for instrumentation. This portion of our research is partially completed and currently ongoing; the paper outlines the direction in which we are headed in order to support our ID system.

Section two of this paper contains a short review of typical methods used for intrusion detection for those that may not be familiar with the concepts. Section three includes details of the first focus of our research, instrumentation within open-source software. This is followed by an overview of the intrusion detection domain language in section four. Section five contains early experimental results. Finally, we conclude by outlining some areas in which our research is currently headed, and our motivations for future work.

2   Intrusion Detection Overview

There are several traditional methods used for intrusion detection, which can be categorized into two broad classes: Anomaly Detection, and Misuse Detection.

Anomaly Detection uses statistical approaches and pattern prediction techniques to generate profiles of "typical" user interaction with a system. For example, a certain percentage of the page accesses on a web site may be to a log-in page, and a certain percentage may refer to a page showing the users "shopping cart". Occasionally the user will mistype their password and the login will fail; for this and other reasons, one might suppose that it is likely that more references are be made to the login page than the shopping cart page. If certain pages such as the shopping cart page are suddenly referenced far more frequently, the system would view this as unusual activity which may indicate an intrusion attempt. Anomaly detection has advantages and disadvantages, and this method is often used in conjunction with others. The advantages of this technique include the capability to detect intrusions which other methods miss, and the fact that the systems are generally adaptable to change over time. But anomaly detection via statistical approaches suffers from an obvious few drawbacks. For example, a nefarious user who knows that the system is adaptable can gradually change the probability for future events until the system behavior is considered to be normal. At that point the attacker can penetrate the system without triggering any of the detection alarms. As a counter to these approaches, many anomaly intrusion detection systems also incorporate some form of neural network, which may also be based on statistics but not adaptable, which predicts a user's next activity and signals an alarm when this prediction is not met.

Misuse Detection systems are typified by expert system software which has knowledge of many known attack scenarios and can monitor user behavior searching for these patterns. A misuse detection system can be thought of as more similar to anti-virus software, which continually searches files and memory for known attack patterns, and alerts the user if any are matched. Misuse systems include a state-based component called an "anticipator", which tries to predict the next activity that will occur on a system. A knowledge base contains the scenarios which the expert system uses to make this prediction, and the audit trail in the system is examined by the expert system to locate partial matches to these patterns. A wildly differing "next event" in a pattern could be an indicator that an intrusion attempt is in progress.

Both types of intrusion detection systems can rely on a variety of data sources in order to build an accurate picture of the normal versus abnormal system activity. However these data sources are almost exclusively comprised of two types: network traffic, and audit logs [2]. Our research introduces a third component which is monitoring an actively executing process.

3   Basic Block Instrumentation in GCC

A region of code that has only a single entry point and a single exit point (everything from a label up to a jump or return instruction) is called a basic block. The start of a basic block might be jumped to from multiple locations and the end of a basic block might be a jump to a different basic block. The basic blocks thus form a directed graph in the compiled code, called the control flow graph. A typical small program may easily contain hundreds of these basic blocks; in fact there could be hundreds in a single function within a larger software system. Basic blocks are the fundamental "straight line" sections of code within the larger framework of the program. A single line of executable code may contain several basic blocks, or a basic block may span several lines. As an example consider the following snippet of code in Fig. 1, which has the basic blocks identified:

The first step in generating execution trace data from a program is to instrument the basic blocks within the program as it is being compiled. These instrumentation points will insert calls to an instrumentation function, which can be inserted into the program when the object files are linked. Alternatively it can be added as a dynamic library, although we currently do not do this in order to simplify our design.

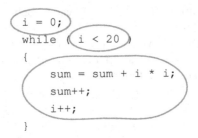

Fig. 1. Basic Blocks within Sample Code

In the process of converting source code into machine code, the GCC compilers perform several steps:

- The front end language is converted into a parse tree.
- The parse tree is converted into a more simplistic format called "gimple".
- The gimple format may be optimized.
- The gimple format is converted into a register transfer level representation called RTL, also called RTX.
- The RTX code may optionally be optimized. Whether or not optimization is performed has an impact on the slowdown due to instrumentation, as we will describe below.
- The RTX is converted to assembly language, which is then assembled by a separate program.

Within the GCC internal RTX format, the basic blocks appear on a linked list. Each basic block structure delimits the beginning and ending of the RTX code which corresponds to that block. The entire RTX for a function is contained on a doubly linked list, with the basic blocks as pointers into this list.

In order to instrument a function, the list of basic blocks in that function is traversed, and for each basic block, additional RTX is inserted into the beginning of the block. The inserted RTX consists of a call to an external function, with appropriate parameters passed as arguments. Included in the RTX are both executable code instructions, and information nodes. Information nodes are a form of commentary and include the name and line number of the original source code. Our arguments to the instrumentation function include the address of the function (which will be resolved at link time), the basic block number, and the line number in the source code that this block is associated with. This additional RTX will yield an assembly language call to our instrumentation function. Included in the basic block structures is a list of the "live" registers at the beginning of that block, as well as the block number which is unique within the compiled function's linked list. We desire to have the line number and block number information. This requires that our compiler modifications search the RTX sequence to locate information nodes containing the line numbers and consult the basic block structures for the block numbers. A search proceeds backwards from the end of the basic blocks RTX until the proper type of information node entry is located. The line number is then inserted into the parameters as a constant that will be passed to the function via a normal value parameter. The block number is obtained from the basic block structure corresponding to this section of RTX.

Since the source code is compiled function by function, there must be an assembly language target label generated for the function. This is the location that a "call" instruction will aim for when the program is executing, and the assembler and linker are responsible for converting the symbolic name over to an address. For these reasons, one of the first RTX nodes in a linked list belonging to a function must be the symbolic name of that function. The RTX is scanned until this data is located, and thus the name of the function can be inserted directly as one of the parameters on the instrumentation call. Note that one can simply place the name (i.e. "main") in the RTX and the assembler and linker that is "down stream" will handle converting this to an address at assembly and link time.

Thus the instrumentation function will be called with an integer argument containing the source line from the original code, the address of the compiled function, and the basic block number within that function. The C-style prototype for the destination of this call appears as:

void _ _cyg_block_enter(void *func, unsigned int line, unsigned int block);

Once the compilation is complete it is necessary to supply this function to the linker so that there are no unresolved references. Note, though, that this function can perform just about any desired aim - sending the execution trace information to an external intrusion detection module is the aim in our case.

If optimization is enabled for the compiled code, the situation is somewhat more complex. A basic block is considered to be (and is) a straight line section of code. Adding a function call in the middle of a basic block makes this, theoretically, no longer a basic block. GCC version 4.1 contains 170 different passes that might be made through the RTX once it is initially created. Some of these are relatively simple, warning if a function does not return, for example, while some are heavily involved in optimization; among these are various loop optimizations, tail recursion handling, checking for possible aliases, and many others.

Since the optimization is complete before the instrumentation is inserted, there are registers which, due to global common sub-expression elimination, a type of optimization, are "live" on the entry to the block. Live registers contain values which are carried in from predecessor blocks, and it is assumed that they contain valid variable contents. There are also "live" registers at the end of each basic block which are then live into another successor block. Since we are inserting the instrumentation code at the top of the block, we are concerned with the incoming live registers and not the outgoing live registers. In order to insert our instrumentation without having an impact on the executable code, it is necessary to save and restore these registers around the instrumentation function call. Initially we accomplished this by saving these in a static array;

this prevents one from instrumenting code which is multi-threaded, and many of the target software packages we wish to test with (e.g. Apache) can be compiled as threaded code. Our current system pushes these incoming live registers on the stack prior to the instrumentation call, and restores them after the call. Since each thread contains a separate stack area, this local storage of registers solves the multiple thread issue. One result of this is that there is a larger slowdown when instrumentation is added to an optimized program, because of the added work in saving and restoring these registers.

Lastly, we note that our modified compiler appears to share some common features with the Linux utility "gcov", and similar software engineering programs which are used for verifying that each line of code has been executed and tested. However "gcov" operates in a batch mode where it first collects statistics, and then later displays the program coverage. Our modifications create trace information as each block of the original code is executed at run time. Our data could obviously be saved to a file for later analysis, similar to "gcov". But the data is readily available as the program executes and thus can serve as an immediate data feed to our misuse detection system. Utilizing the "gcov" data at a later time would require one to stop the process that is being used for ID, save the logged data, and then restart the process. In addition, our system has the capability to change the coverage dynamically during runtime. We can enable and disable the instrumentation on a function by function basis, without restarting the program. For our ID system this is not utilized, but if one wished to add additional ID methodologies on the fly it would not be necessary to stop the instrumented process.

4   The Intrusion Detection Domain Language

Once the data from an executing process is available, the subsequent problem is to utilize this data for instruction detection. Here the method we are employing is to use this data as a source for a set of deterministic finite automatons (DFAs) which monitor the program. DFAs are a popular logical choice, although other current research in this area includes a trinary tree based approach [3].

Our instrumentation compiler is first used for software which is run in a controlled environment in order to gather typical usage patterns. These patterns are ideal for an "anticipator" module in a misuse detection system, as they are made up of the actual execution path of the software under typical usage scenarios. But currently this data is used solely for the manual creation of the intrusion detection rules. The data included in the instrumentation tracks each procedure entry and exit point in the software as well as the entry to each basic block in the compiled code.

Prior to examining the syntax for the language it is useful to consider the data being emitted from the monitored program. One such program which we test with is called "thttpd" - the tiny HTTP daemon [4]. Since our current system is in a prototype mode we have a separate program as "middleware" that converts the raw function address sent out of the process over to the process name. Of course this is just a convenience, and everything could be accomplished, albeit in a format not as easy to read, with the "raw" addresses passed to the instrumentation function as described above. Recall that each call to the instrumentation has three items: the function address, the line number, and the basic block number used during the compilation. In our test environment these are converted back to the function name for simplicity and to make the testing more human readable. For example the "thttpd" server periodically times out and does housekeeping chores:

```
tmr_run entry
tmr_run 261 14
tmr_run 262 2
tmr_run 261 14
tmr_run 262 2
tmr_run 261 14
tmr_run 262 2
(etc.)
tmr_run exit
```

In order to construct the DFAs we have designed an implemented a domain specific language (DSL) which is used to create the intrusion detection module. Our domain language is a way in which we can specify possible sequences of events which are expected from the instrumentation output, along with the successor to that event. In this way, potential state transitions create a DFA. Since there may be more than one possible path through the software, and since we can choose to instrument from the beginning of a certain function through the end of that function, we allow the language user to create multiple DFAs corresponding to these alternatives. There is one automaton structure for each possible sequence, and these automatons are combined by "or-ing" them together at the starting state. The DFAs then are traversed in parallel according to the instrumentation output of the program being observed. It is simpler, and the description which follows uses this method, to consider the DFAs as being traversed "in parallel".

Unlike a typical pattern-based intrusion detection system, where reaching a complete pattern indicates a possible attack, a final state in our DFA represents exactly the opposite - a normal sequence of events that should generate no alerts at all. Thus, final states in the DFA correspond to acceptable sequences of events, while a sufficient number of invalid transitions may be an indicator of an intrusion attempt. Reaching a final state causes all automatons to reset to their initial state. Our language is thus compiled from a human readable format into this set of automatons, which the intrusion detection system then matches against the instrumentation coming from the server program in near real-time.

Since there is naturally a correspondence between the languages accepted by a DFA and the set of regular languages, we have selected syntax not unlike operations normally seen in regular expressions. Specifically, alternation, catenation, and Kleene ("star") closure are included. Also included as shortcuts are the usual usage of "+" for positive closure and "?" as an optional element. There is also a time component in the grammar, which will be explained shortly. The grammar for our DSL is as follows in Fig. 2:

```
program -> program rule | ε
rule -> 'within' INT 'max' INT func
func -> '(' identifier not_empty ')'
elist -> expression { '|' expression } | ε
expression -> '(' not_empty ')' optmod
not_empty -> item { item }
item -> elist | identifier | INT
optmod -> '+' | '*' | '?' | ε
```

Fig. 2. Domain Specific Intrusion Detection Language

In the usual EBNF notation, braces '{' '}' surround zero or more repeated items, a vertical bar '|' indicates alternates, and ε represents the empty string.

Informally, the semantics of the language are as follows: a program is a collection of rules, and each rule has timing requirements specific to that rule. The expression portion of a rule consists of a not empty list of function names and block numbers. Lists can contain sub-lists with the same syntax, and all lists may contain modifiers such as "*" which apply to the entire preceding list. Rules must start at the highest level with a function name; that is, the outer-most list within a rule must begin at a function entry point.

Using this syntax and the above sample data, a pattern the user might write to represent the previous execution path might be:

```
within 30 max 10
(tmr_run
     (14 2 (3)? )+ )
```

The normal course of events is starts with an entry to the function "tmr_run". This is followed by block 14, then block 2, and occasionally block 3 (not shown in the sample data). Note that the line numbers are not used in the description - only the block numbers are considered. This path is often executed in the code, (and in fact the original example data has it repeating for 140 lines). Since the function "tmr_run" is a timeout function for housekeeping purposes, we see this repeat approximately every 10-15 seconds. The initial specification of the rule indicates that we must see this within 30 seconds, and it must not take longer than 10 seconds to match this rule. Of course we have selected a very simple example with a correspondingly simple pattern to match. A portion of the pattern used when a page is served to the user, is:

```
within 0 max 10
(handle_newconnect
     22 4 7 (8 10)? 11
     (httpd_get_conn
       (2
             (httpd_realloc_str
                  2 6)+
       )?
       3 7
       (sockaddr_check
            2 5)
       9
       (sockaddr_len
            2 5)
   ))
```

Since we do not know when to "expect" a page to be served, the "within" section contains zero. This indicates that there is no timeout associated with how frequently we need to see this function execute in the process.

Currently we are constructing these patterns by hand; an obvious area listed under our future research is a system which will automate this process to a certain extent. Also note that we are only using the block numbers and not the line number data, as either one or the other is redundant.

Our current implementation generates a DFA corresponding to the DSL given by the user. There is no attempt to minimize or optimize this DFA in any way - there may very well be duplicated states which would normally be removed when the DFA is minimized. Most automata text books, such as Linz [5], contain standard DFA minimization algorithms, and we will no doubt take advantage of these in the future. The rationale behind deferring this DFA minimization is that it allows us to further the research by investigating "approximate automata" [6] . An "approximate automaton" allows the language accepted by the user specification to be a subset of the language accepted by the automaton: L(USER) $\subseteq$ L(DFA). Very large automata tend to be unwieldy, and a great deal of effort has been invested in tuning DFA algorithms for large pattern matching applications; in the case of pattern matching, approximate automata are sometimes referred to as "factor oracles" [7] .

When searching for viruses or other patterns using traditional intrusion detection, the final state in a DFA indicates a virus or other nefarious item. Thus an approximate DFA is sufficient because if a pattern is matched, it can be vetted separately using a longer algorithm or more accurate DFA and corresponding language. If the pattern does not match L(DFA) then it certainly does not match L(USER), and therefore it can be ignored. This creates the possibility for a fast rejection of most data, with the possible signatures falling through for further examination. Approximate automata used in this way are often based on Brzozowski's construction algorithm [8].

In our intrusion detection scheme, though, the final states in the DFA indicate a successful transition from the starting point of the trace data to the ending point of the trace data; in other words, there is no detected intrusion; "a positive result is a negative result". Either transitioning to an "error state" in the DFA or exceeding the time limits set forth in the rule indicates a potential intrusion.

The technique we are utilizing for the DFA construction is based on the standard construction algorithm by Thompson [9], also covered in most introductory automata texts. In this case the algorithm first constructs a nondeterministic finite automata (NFA), and then merges sets of NFA states to create the DFA. Using this method and our short example rule, we might generate the DFA shown in Fig. 3.

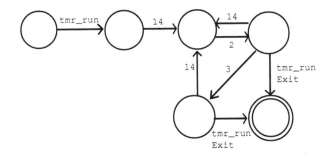

Fig. 3. DFA Prior to Similarity Test

Each DFA state corresponds to the set of NFA states that the non-deterministic machine would have been in, given a certain previous set of states and an input symbol. Once the DFA is constructed, the list of these corresponding NFA states is easily maintained within the DFA state data structure as a set:

N(i) = { s | DFA state i was created from NFA state s }

Thus, we can use this data to determine some measure of the "similarity" of any two DFA states. If the states are greater than a certain similarity, they can potentially be merged into one state in the resulting DFA. The entry point to a function in the DSL specification and the exit point for the function in the DSL specification will never be merged. At the top-level of one of the parallel DFAs these correspond to the start and final states of the DFA handling that DSL statement. Currently we are experimenting with this method and we consider the similarity as:

S(i,j)=|N(i) ∩ N(j)| / (|N(i)|+|N(j)|),

the ratio of the original NFA states which are in common between two DFA states. If the ratio exceeds an experimental parameter, the DFA states will be merged; an example is shown in Fig. 4.

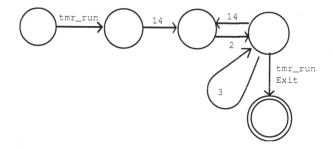

Fig. 4. DFA After Similarity Test

Lastly we note that speed is an issue. We utilize DFAs in the intrusion detection matching specifically because of their faster implementation relative to NFAs. Although there is a certain amount of buffering between the instrumented program which is generating the data and the intrusion detection program which is monitoring it, we wish to execute the original software as quickly as possible and not have it blocked when calling "write" with data! An interesting comparison between various NFA and DFA algorithms is made by Cox [10], who states that "Today, regular expressions have also become a shining example of how ignoring good theory leads to bad programs". His comparison between an implementation of DFAs using C versus NFAs using Perl is insightful.

5   Experimental Results

One issue to deal with is the slowdown due to the instrumentation of the application. Calculating the performance impact of instrumented code is difficult because the time penalty depends almost entirely on the actions performed by the supplied user functions. That is, writing the execution records into a file or a pipe has a much greater impact on the execution time than would updating counters in a memory mapped shared data segment. For these reasons we tested the performance impact by measuring the effect of the instrumentation calls, with the actual called functions performing no action. The programs we have utilized to measure the slowdown due to instrumentation represents a "worst case" scenario - heavily compute bound and containing many small, tight looping constructs. Two test programs were run, one which we obtained and one which we authored. Our test program approximates the value of π using an iterative method by John Wallis (1616-1703). The program also calculates an approximation of ϕ (the golden ratio) using the Fibonacci sequence. For π, one million double floating point factors are taken into account and the calculation is repeated 100 times. For ϕ, one million loop iterations are executed, or up to a Fibonacci number which overflows a 64-bit integer, whichever comes first. For the public domain benchmark we utilized the Fhourstones Benchmark version 3.1 [11]. The tests were run on a 1.4 GHz AMD Opteron dual-CPU machine running Linux; however since the programs are not threaded, only one processor is loaded. The averages of the slowdown due to instrumentation are shown in Fig. 5 (times are in seconds):

Description	Time	Slowdown
Pi Test, no instrumentation, no opt.	2.50	1.81
Pi Test, instrumentation, no opt.	4.54	
Pi Test, no instrumentation, O2	1.20	2.70
Pi Test, instrumentation, O2	3.24	
Pi Test, no instrumentation, O3	1.21	2.69
Pi Test, instrumentation, O3	3.25	
Fhourstones, no instrumentation, no opt.	712	1.93
Fhourstones, instrumentation, no opt.	1375	
Fhourstones, no instrumentation, O2	428	2.83
Fhourstones, instrumentation, O2	1210	
Fhourstones, no instrumentation, O3	353	2.76
Fhourstones, instrumentation, O3	973	

Fig. 5. Slowdown

The need to save and restore live registers, as outlined in section three, accounts for the greater slowdown factor on optimized code versus un-optimized code. Notice that the process with optimization still outperforms the same process without optimization, but that the slowdown due to the inserted instrumentation is greater due to the necessity of saving the live registers.

Our target for intrusion detection, though, is software such as web servers, DHCP servers, etc. which are typified by small bursty CPU requirements, followed by extended periods of inactivity. Thus we believe that the slowdown figures shown should not deter us from using this technique for intrusion detection. So currently our intrusion detection laboratory consists of several instrumented web servers: "Apache" [12], "Fizmez"[13], "monkey" [14], and "thttpd"[4]. The patterns we have shown as examples in this paper correspond to execution traces from "thttpd"; however the selection of software was made based on several factors.

6   Conclusions Thus Far and Future Research

Much, but not all, of our experimentation software is complete. Thus, there are several areas which we would like to complete and further explore, including the following:

- A comparison of the actual DFA sizes versus the patterns used in typical instrumented code remains to be seen. We are not sure to what extent the approximate automata might be necessary.

- It also remains to be seen what impact the approximate automata have on detecting actual intrusions in open source code.
- Is our domain specific language sufficient for all patterns which we might want to construct for our intrusion detection efforts?
- We've been unable to determine any slowdown in our instrumented web servers, due to the short bursts of activity. We must next generate sufficient network request traffic so that the effects of the instrumentation can be measured easily.

We feel, though, that this method represents an exciting new method for monitoring applications and providing an additional data source for intrusion detection. Given the quantity and questionable quality of open-source software this method could be a very useful tool.

References

1. Gurley, R.: Intrusion detection (2000)
2. DARPA: Darpa intrusion detection evaluation data sets 2007, http://www.ll.mit.edu/IST/ideval/index.html
3. Huang, J.-c., et al.: Research of pattern matching in intrusion detection. In: Proceedings of the Second International Conference on Machine Learning and Cybernetics, pp. 2–5 (November 2003)
4. Poskanzer, J.: thttpd - tiny/turbo/throttling http server (2007), http://www.acme.com/software/thttpd/
5. Linz, P.: An introduction to formal languages and automata (2006)
6. Watson, B., et al.: Efficient automata constructions and approximate automata. In: Prague Stringology Conference proceedings (2006)
7. Cleophas, L., et al.: Constructing factor oracles. In: Prague Stringology Conference proceedings (2003)
8. Brzozowski, J.A.: Derivations of regular expressions. JACM 11(4), 481–494 (1964)
9. Thompson, K.: Regular expression search algorithm. In: CACM, pp. 419–422 (June 1968)
10. Cox, R.: Regular expression matching can be simple and fast (but is slow in java, perl, php, python, ruby (2007), http://swtch.com/rsc/regexp/regexp1.html
11. Tromp, J.: The fhourstones benchmark version 3 (2007), http://homepages.cwi.nl/tromp/c4/fhour.html
12. Apache: Apache http server project, http://httpd.apache.org/ (2007)
13. Bond, D.: Fizmez web server (2007), http://freeware.fizmez.com/
14. Silva, E.: Monkey http daemon (2007), http://monkeyd.sourceforge.net/

Statistical Runtime Checking of Probabilistic Properties

Usa Sammapun[1], Insup Lee[1], Oleg Sokolsky[1], and John Regehr[2]

[1] University of Pennsylvania
{usa,lee,sokolsky}@cis.upenn.edu
[2] University of Utah
regehr@cs.utah.edu

Abstract. Probabilistic correctness is an important aspect of reliable systems. A soft real-time system, for instance, may be designed to tolerate some degree of deadline misses under a threshold. Since probabilistic systems may behave differently from their probabilistic models depending on their current environments, checking the systems at runtime can provide another level of assurance for their probabilistic correctness. This paper presents a statistical runtime verification for probabilistic properties using statistical analysis. However, while this statistical analysis collects a number of execution paths as samples to check probabilistic properties within some certain error bounds, runtime verification can only produce one single sample. This paper provides a technique to produce such a number of samples and applies this methodology to check probabilistic properties in wireless sensor network applications.

Keywords: Runtime verification, statistical monitoring, probabilistic properties.

1 Introduction

Probabilistic correctness is an important aspect of reliable systems, which could tolerate some undesirable behaviors such as deadline misses or data loss. For example, unlike hard real-time systems that strictly require computation to complete within its deadline, soft real-time systems can tolerate some degree of deadline misses. We can characterize this degree in terms of the acceptable probability of a deadline miss. Another example is a wireless sensor network application with probabilistic constraints on its behaviors to tolerate some degree of data loss. Since probabilistic systems may deviate from their probabilistic requirements due to unexpected environments or incorrect implementation, checking the systems at runtime in addition to a static probabilistic check can provide additional level of assurance for their probabilistic correctness.

Runtime verification is a technique for checking correctness of a system at runtime by observing a system execution and checking it against its property specification. One runtime verification framework is called MaC or Monitoring and Checking [9,12]. MaC provides expressive specification languages based on Linear Temporal Logic [11] to specify system properties. Once the properties

O. Sokolsky and S. Tasiran (Eds.): RV 2007, LNCS 4839, pp. 164–175, 2007.

are specified, MaC observes the system by retrieving system information from probes instrumented into the system prior to the execution. MaC then checks the execution against the system properties and reports any violations.

To check probabilistic properties, runtime verification can adopt the statistical technique [16] used in model checking to verify probabilistic properties. The statistical technique simulates, samples many execution paths, and estimates probabilities by counting successful samples against all samples. After the probabilities are estimated, statistical analysis such as hypothesis testing is used to determine statistically whether a system satisfies a probabilistic property with a given level of confidence.

One particular difficulty in using this technique in runtime verification, however, is that a runtime checker follows only one execution path and cannot easily collect many different executione paths as in probabilistic model checking. Therefore, this one execution path, usually in a form of a trace of states or events, needs to be decomposed into different individual samples, which can be done only if a probabilistic system being observed has repeated or periodic behaviors. Such behaviors are typically exhibited by the systems in our target domain. Soft real-time schedulers repeatedly schedule tasks; network protocols repeatedly transmit or receive messages. This paper describes how MaC can break down one execution into different individual samples and how MaC adopts the statistical technique to check probabilistic properties at runtime. This technique has been applied to check probabilistic properties in wireless sensor network applications.

Our contributions are: 1) we provide a general statistical technique for checking probabilistic properties at runtime, 2) the technique is described to and implemented in an existing runtime verification framework called MaC, and 3) a case study is presented for checking probabilistic properties in wireless sensor network application.

Related Work. Runtime verification frameworks based on Linear Temporal Logic, such as Java PathExplorer [7], work by Kristoffersen *et al.* [10], and work by Stolz and Bodden [13], typically cannot be used to check probabilistic properties. Those that provide probabilistic properties such as EAGLE [1], Temporal Rover [4], and a framework by Jayaputera et al. [8] do not prescribe statistical analysis to support the estimated probabilities. Finkbeiner *et al.* [5] discussed collection of statistics over execution traces, yet their work was not concerned with probability estimation.

2   Background: MaC

Monitoring and Checking or MaC [9,12] is an established runtime verification framework that can be used to check whether that a program is executing correctly with respect to its formal requirement specification. Before execution, specification is written, and a program is instrumented with probes to extract observation. During runtime, a program execution is observed and checked against the formal specification. An *event recognizer* detects low-level observation specific to program implementation and transforms it into high-level information, which is forwarded to a *checker*. A *checker* determines whether the high-level information satisfies the formal specification. If violations are detected, the checker reports to the user.

The main aspect of MaC is the formal requirement specification. MaC provides two specification languages. The low-level monitoring specification or Primitive Event Definition Language (PEDL), defines which low-level application-dependent observation is extracted, and how the observation is transformed into high-level information. The high-level requirement specification or Meta-Event Definition Language (MEDL), based on Linear Temporal Logic (LTL) [11], allows one to specify safety properties in terms of high-level information. PEDL is tied to a particular implementation while MEDL is independent of any implementation. Only MEDL is presented in this paper. See MaC [9] for PEDL.

High-level information in MEDL can be distinguished into events or conditions. Events occur instantaneously during execution, whereas conditions represent system states that hold for a duration of time and can be *true*, *false*, or *undefined*. For example, an event denoting a call to a method *init* occurs at the instant the control is passed to the method, and a condition $v < 5$ holds as long as the value v is less than 5. Events and conditions can be composed using boolean operators such as negation !, conjunction &&, disjunction ||, and other operators, as shown in Fig. 1.

$$E ::= e \mid E||E \mid E\&\&E \mid start(C) \mid end(C) \mid E \text{ when } C$$
$$C ::= c \mid !C \mid C||C \mid C\&\&C \mid C \rightarrow C \mid defined(C) \mid [E, E)$$

Fig. 1. Syntax of events and conditions

There are some natural events associated with conditions, namely, an instant when a condition C becomes *true* and *false*, denoted as $start(C)$ and $end(C)$, respectively. An event $(E \text{ when } C)$ is present if E occurs at a time when a condition C is *true*. A condition $defined(C)$ is true whenever a condition C has a well-defined value, namely, *true* or *false*. Any pair of events define an interval forming a condition $[E_1, E_2)$ that is *true* from an event E_1 *until* an event E_2.

MEDL distinguishes special events and conditions that denote system specification. Safety properties are conditions that must *always* be true during an execution. Alarms, on the other hand, are events that must *never* be raised. From the viewpoint of expressiveness, both safety properties and alarms correspond to the safety properties [11].

3   Probabilistic Properties

MaC offers additional syntax and semantics for specifying probabilistic properties. To check these probabilistic properties, MaC adopts a statistical technique used in model checking [16]. The statistical technique simulates, samples many execution paths, and estimates probabilities by counting successful samples against all samples. MaC and other runtime verification frameworks operate on the current execution path and are not typically designed to accumulate data from many different execution paths. Because of this, the current execution path, usually in a form of a trace of states or events, needs to be decomposed into non-overlapping individual samples, which can be done only if a probabilistic system being observed has repeated or periodic behaviors such as soft real-time schedulers or network protocols.

To decompose an execution, MaC distinguishes one repetitive behavior from another by using conditional probabilities. Written in terms of probabilistic properties, one can specify as given a condition A, does the probability that an outcome B occurs fall within a given range? In terms of MaC events, one can specify as given that an event e_0 occurs, does the probability that an event e will occur fall within a given threshold? This way, a sample space is reduced from events of the entire system to only those events relevant to a given probabilistic property. A set of e_0 and e can be collected as one individual sample, and a sequence of these sets can be collected as many different individual samples.

The probability observed from the system can be estimated by counting the outcome event e that occurs in response to the given event e_0 against all the outcome event e. After probabilities are estimated, MaC uses statistical analysis to determine statistically whether a system satisfies a probabilistic property using hypothesis testing. Hypothesis testing provides a systematic procedure with an adequate level of confidence to determine the satisfiability of probabilistic properties.

3.1 Syntax

To specify probabilistic constraints, we extend MaC with a probabilistic event operator. The operator expresses the property that an event e occurs within a certain probability threshold given that an event e_0 occurs. The syntax for the new operator is $e\ pr(\odot p_0, e_0)$ where $\odot \in \{<, >\}$ and p_0 is a probability constant. The event $e\ pr(\odot p_0, e_0)$ can be used in any context where ordinary MaC event operators (listed in Fig. 1) can. This event is raised when the checker has accumulated enough confidence to reject the hypothesis that the above property does not hold.

3.2 Semantics

To give semantics for the probabilistic properties, we describe how samples can be collected from an execution and then show how to use hypothesis testing over this set of samples to determine statistically the satisfaction of probabilistic properties.

Recall that we have to answer the following question: given that an event e_0 occurs, does the probability that an event e will occur fall within a given threshold? Such probabilistic properties can be defined directly using conditional probabilities as

$$Pr(e|e_0) = \frac{Pr(e \text{ and } e_0)}{Pr(e_0)}$$

To estimate $Pr(e$ and $e_0)$, let m be the number of occurrences of all MaC events in the trace. Let's call these MaC events *experiments*. Let $X = X_1 + X_2 + ... + X_m$ be the random variable representing the number of successful experiments. Here, X_i is the random variable representing the result of the ith experiment. Then, $X_i = 1$ when the ith experiment is successful, and $X_i = 0$ otherwise. The experiment is successful when e occurs in response to e_0. By this we mean that either e occurs at the same time as e_0, or e follows an occurrence of e_0, without a prior occurrence of e in between. Formally, $X_i = 1$ when the event $e' = e$ && $(e_0 \; || \; end([e_0, e)))$ occurs at time t_i, and $X_i = 0$ otherwise. Note that our notion of "occurs in response" does not necessarily imply a causal dependency between the most recent occurrence of e_0 and the current occurrence of e, but reflects the fact that there is an occurrence of e_0 that has not been matched to an earlier occurrence of e.

Therefore, each X_i has a Bernoulli distribution with an unknown parameter $q \in [0, 1]$ where $Pr(X_i = 1) = q$, meaning that the probability that e' will occur is equal to q. X, therefore, has a Binomial distribution with parameters m and q. Finally, let $\bar{q}$ be an observed probability obtained from the samples we collect where $\bar{q} = \frac{X}{m} = \frac{\Sigma X_i}{m}$.

Using similar reasoning, let $Y = Y_1 + Y_2 + ... + Y_m$ be a random variable representing the number of e_0 occurrences, where m is the number of all MaC events or *experiments*. $Y_i = 1$ when e_0 occurs at in the ith experiment, and $Y_i = 0$ otherwise. Each Y_i has a Bernoulli distribution with an unknown parameter $q' \in [0, 1]$ where $Pr(Y_i = 1) = q'$. Thus, Y has a Binomial distribution with parameters m and q'. Let $\bar{q}'$ be an observed probability obtained from the samples where $\bar{q}' = \frac{Y}{m} = \frac{\Sigma Y_i}{m}$.

Let $p = Pr(e|e_0)$, and let $\bar{p}$ be an observed probability of p. Since

$$p = Pr(e|e_0) = \frac{Pr(e \text{ and } e_0)}{Pr(e_0)} = \frac{Pr(X_i = 1)}{Pr(Y_i = 1)},$$

then,

$$\bar{p} = \frac{\bar{q}}{\bar{q}'} = \frac{\frac{\Sigma X_i}{m}}{\frac{\Sigma Y_i}{m}} = \frac{\Sigma X_i}{\Sigma Y_i}.$$

Hence, the observed probability $\bar{p}$ is a ratio of the number of occurrences of the event e' over the number of e_0 occurrences:

$$\bar{p} = \frac{|\text{occurrences of } e'|}{|\text{occurrences of } e_0|}$$

e' also ensures that the number of occurrences of e_0 is always greater or equal to the number of occurrences of e && $(e_0 \; || \; end([e_0, e)))$, and thus $\bar{p}$ will always be less than or equal to 1. For the rest of this paper, let n be the number of occurrences of e_0.

Hypothesis Testing. Assume one needs to check a probabilistic property $e \; pr(\odot p_0, e_0)$ where $\odot \in \{<, >\}$, and p_0 is a probability bound. It means given that an event e_0 occurs, does the probability that an event e will occur fall within p_0? The observed probability $\bar{p}$ needs to be tested against p_0. This is done by using $\bar{p}$ to approximate the true Binomial probability p based on a statistical procedure of hypothesis testing. The first step, done before running experiments, is to set up two hypotheses H_0 and H_A. H_0, called null hypothesis, is what we have previously believed and what we want to use the hypothesis testing to *disprove*. H_A, called alternative hypothesis, is an alternative to H_0; we will believe H_A only if the data supports it strongly. In our case, we previously believe that the probabilistic event does not occur, and we would trigger the probabilistic event only when we have strong evidence. For example, if the probabilistic event is $e\ pr(< p_0, e_0)$, then H_0 is $p \geq p_0$ and H_A is $p < p_0$. Hence, the acceptance of H_0 means $M, t \not\models e\ pr(< p_0, e_0)$, and the acceptance of H_A means $M, t \models e\ pr(< p_0, e_0)$.

To perform hypothesis testing, we first define our test procedure. A test procedure is the rule for making a decision on whether to accept or reject hypothesis. It has two components: a test statistic and a rejection region. A test statistic is a function of the sample data that is used to decide hypothesis acceptance or rejection. A rejection region is a set of values in which a null hypothesis H_0 would be rejected. Our test statistic is based on the *z-score*, which represents how far a normally distributed sample data is from the population mean. The *z*-score allows us to tell whether the difference is statistically significant.

From the Central Limit Theorem, a large number of samples from any distribution approximates Normal distribution. For the Binomial distribution, the sample is considered large enough when it satisfies both $np \geq 10$ and $n(1-p) \geq 10$ [3]. Our implementation ensures that these constraints are satisfied before a decision on the property satisfaction is made. Once the necessary sample size is reached, the *z-score* can be used as our test statistic. The following equation is used to calculate the *z-score* for $\bar{p}$ [3]:

$$Z = \frac{\bar{p} - p_0}{\sqrt{p_0(1 - p_0)/n}} \tag{1}$$

Since $\bar{p} = \frac{X}{Y}$ where X and Y are random variables with Binomial distribution, then Z is a random variable with an approximately standard normal distribution. z is defined as the expected value of Z. Positive values of z mean that $\bar{p}$ is greater than p_0, while negative values mean that it is less than p_0. When z is close to zero, $\bar{p}$ is close to p_0. These simple observation will help us define the rejection region.

To find the rejection region, we utilize the notion of error bounds. There are two kinds of error bounds, known as Type I (α) and Type II (β). Type I error is the probability of incorrectly verifying a property satisfaction and Type II error is the probability of incorrectly verifying a property violation. Formally, $\alpha = Pr\{\text{reject } H_0 | H_0 \text{ is true}\}$ and $\beta = Pr\{\text{accept } H_0 | H_A \text{ is true}\}$. We bound the acceptable Type I error by the *significance level* z_α, and use this bound as the rejection region. For example, if $H_0 : p \leq p_0$ and $H_A : p > p_0$, then

$$\alpha = Pr\{Z \geq z_\alpha \text{ when } Z \text{ has approximately a standard Normal distribution}\}$$

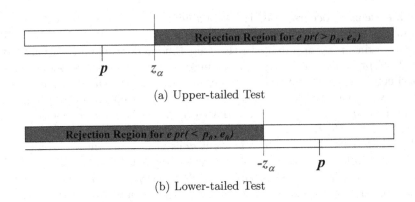

(a) Upper-tailed Test

(b) Lower-tailed Test

Fig. 2. Upper- and Lower-tailed Tests

Since the value of the test statistic can be calculated using (1), hypotheses and rejection regions can be set up, and a decision can be made. Consider $e\, pr(< p_0, e_0)$ and $e\, pr(> p_0, e_0)$.

(a) **Upper-tailed test: $e\, pr(> p_0, e_0)$.** A hypothesis is set up as $H_0 : p \leq p_0$ and $H_A : p > p_0$. The rejection region is $z \geq z_\alpha$, shown in Fig. 2 (a). Thus, reject H_0 if $z \geq z_\alpha$, meaning there is strong evidence supporting that $\bar{p}$ is greater than p_0. Accept H_0 otherwise. Hence, an event $e\, pr(> p_0, e_0)$ is raised or $M, t \models e\, pr(> p_0, e_0)$ when H_0 is rejected because of the strong evidence supporting that the probability of e occurring given e_0 is greater than p_0.

(b) **Lower-tailed test: $e\, pr(< p_0, e_0)$.** A hypothesis is set up as $H_0 : p \geq p_0$ and $H_A : p < p_0$. The rejection region is $z \leq -z_\alpha$, shown in Fig. 2 (b). Thus, reject H_0 if $z \leq -z_\alpha$, meaning there is strong evidence supporting that $\bar{p}$ is less than p_0. Accept H_0 otherwise. Hence, an event $e\, pr(< p_0, e_0)$ is triggered or $M, t \models e\, pr(< p_0, e_0)$ when H_0 is rejected because of the strong evidence supporting that the probability of e occurring given e_0 is less than p_0.

The two error types have an inverse effect on each other: decreasing the value of α will increase the value of β. The value of β depends on the true value of a system's probability p. Assuming that $p = p'$, for the upper-tailed test β is the following function of p': $\beta(p') = Pr\{Z < z_\alpha \text{when } p = p'\}$, and can be estimated as

$$\beta(p') = \Phi\left(\frac{p_0 - p' + z_\alpha\sqrt{p_0(1 - p_0)/n}}{\sqrt{p'(1 - p')/n}}\right).$$

Similarly, for the lower-tailed test, $\beta(p')$ is $Pr\{Z > -z_\alpha \text{when } p = p'\}$. Thus,

$$\beta(p') = 1 - \Phi\left(\frac{p_0 - p' + z_\alpha\sqrt{p_0(1 - p_0)/n}}{\sqrt{p'(1 - p')/n}}\right).$$

3.3 Discussion

The implemention for checking probabilistic properties is done through a sliding window technique. When the number of experiments is small, both Type I and Type II errors can be large. When Type I error or α is fixed and as the number of experiments increase, Type II error or β decreases providing more reliable results. Thus, more samples or more experiments can increase the confidence in the results. However, in our first implementation of hypothesis testing [12], we noticed that considering too many experiments leads to false alarms.

Recall from the semantics that the z value depends directly on the number of experiments n. When p_0 and the observed probability $\bar{p}$ are fixed, if n increases, z also increases and can become very sensitive to p_0. It means that when $\bar{p}$ only differs slightly from p_0, an alarm can be triggered. In practice, the observed probability that is only slightly different from p_0 has little practical significance while the observed probability that differs from p_0 by a large magnitude would be worth being detected. Thus, our goal is to detect only those behaviors that greatly differ from the desired probabilistic behaviors.

Consider the miss deadline example specified as $missDeadline\ pr(> 0.2,$ $startT)$. If $|missDeadline\ \&\&\ (startT\ ||\ end([startT, missDeadline)|$ is 21 and $|startT|$ events is 100, then the observed $\bar{p} = \frac{21}{100} = 0.21$ and its z-score is $z = 0.25$. With $\alpha = 97.5\%$ and $z_\alpha = 1.96$, then $z < z_\alpha$, which provides no strong evidence that the observed probability $\bar{p} = 0.21$ is greater than $p_0 = 0.2$. Therefore, an alarm is not raised. However, with the same observed probability $\bar{p} = 0.21$ where $n = 10000$ and $|missDeadline\ \&\&\ (startT\ ||$ $end([startT, missDeadline)| = 2100$, its z-score is $z = 2.50$. Assuming the same $\alpha = 97.5\%$ and $z_\alpha = 1.96$, then $z \geq z_\alpha$, meaning that there is strong evidence that the observed probability $\bar{p} = 0.21$ is greater than $p_0 = 0.2$, and thus, an alarm is raised. This example shows that the same observed probability and error bounds can produce different hypothesis testing decisions depending on the number of experiments considered. It follows that although a higher number of experiments can provide higher confidence of detecting violations, it also generates false alarms.

This effect is studied in the area of statistics known as sequential analysis [15]. The proposed solution is to adjust z_α when more samples become available. Here, we provide an alternative solution that keeps the significance level constant but instead removed older samples from the set. We maintain the sliding window of samples that keeps the number of experiments used in checking constant. When the number of observed experiments exceeds the window size, we discard the earliest experiments. In MaC, the default window size is chosen to satisfy the constraints $np \geq 10$ and $n(1-p) \geq 10$. This way, we can ensure that the sample size is large enough to approximate Normal distribution and reduce Type II errors but still not too large to affect the sensitivity of the z-score to large sample size. We believe that the size of the window should also depend on the chosen significance level. This relation is the subject of our on-going research.

Sliding windows also help deal with unobservable mode switches in the system. For example, a soft real-time task may miss its deadline more often in an emergency situation, when a machine is more heavily loaded with extra tasks to handle the emergency, than in the nominal case, when the machine is more lightly loaded. Without the sliding window, experiments that occurred before the mode switch would affect the statistics long after the mode switch happens and delay — or even prevent — the detection of the probabilistic property violation in the new mode. The underlying assumption here, of course, is that mode changes are infrequent relative to the experiments. Precise characterization of the relationship between mode switching behavior and window size also requires further research.

4   Case Study: Checking Wireless Sensor Network Applications

A wireless sensor network (WSN) usually comprises of a collection of tiny devices with built-in processors that gather physical information such as temperature, light, or sound, and communicate with one another over radio. WSN applications sit on top of an operating system called TinyOS [2]. TinyOS provides component-based architecture with tasks and event-based concurrency allowing applications to connect different components that coordinate concurrency via tasks and events. TinyOS has a small scheduler and many reusable system components such as timers, LEDs, and sensors. These components are either software modules or thin wrappers around hardware components.

TinyOS itself and WSN applications are written in nesC [6], an extension of C that provides a component-based programming paradigm. Before applications can be run on hardware, TinyOS itself and applications are compiled into C programs, which are then compiled again into specific hardware instructions. These hardward instructions can be downloaded directly onto the physical devices or a simulator. Most WSN applications are developed and tested on a simulator before they are deployed in the environment because on-chip testing and debugging are very difficult since it cannot tell a developer what causes the perceived errors. A simulator usually produces detailed execution steps taken in a program and allows a developer to examine his or her program to find bugs or errors.

However, the data returned by a simulator may be too detailed and overwhelming making the process of finding errors difficult. This case study takes a higher level approach by using MaC to aggregate the simulator data and allows developers to formally specify specific patterns of bugs or properties that an application must hold in an aggregate fashion. Properties of WSN applications may be specified to examine periodic behaviors, identify a faulty node, and analyze send and forward behaviors. MaC then monitors the application's data produced by a simulator and checks the data against the application's specification. In this case study, we use Avrora [14], a widely used simulator for WSN applications. Avrora provides an instrumentation capability for MaC to retrieve information about each sensor node running on the network environment within Avrora. It allows MaC to use this information to monitor and check applications run on Avrora against their specification requirements.

The result of the monitoring and checking allows us to gain some understanding of relevant behaviors of wireless sensor devices and can narrow the gap between the high-level requirement and the implementation of an application.

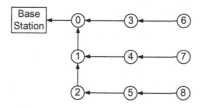

Fig. 3. Possible routes discovered by Surge

For the case study, we chose Surge application [6]. Surge periodically samples a sensor to obtain environment information such as light or temperature and reports its readings to a base station. Before sampling, each node discovers a multi-hop route to a base station in terms of a spanning tree by sending messages to its neighbor and then establishing an appropriate node as its *parent*. After the route is discovered, each node samples environment and sends data to its parent, which then forwards to its parent until the data arrives at the base station. When Surge is run on Avrora, node locations must be supplied to the simulator. In this paper, nine nodes are formed in a 3×3 grid. Figure 3 presents possible multi-hop routes that can be discovered by Surge. Surge consists of different TinyOS components such as a timer, a multi-hop router, and a sensor, among others. Surge wires these TinyOS components appropriately and implements operations such as a task **SendData** that reads a sensor and sends data. Tasks from Surge and TinyOS are logged and sent to MaC to be checked against Surge's specification.

4.1   Identifying a Faulty Node

One property in the Surge application is to identify a faulty node using probabilistic properties. A node can be identified as faulty if it often fails to send data periodically or stops sending data where *often* means with probability of 0.15. It can be written in terms of a MaC alarm as $failSend\ pr(> 0.15, sendData)$. It states an alarm should be raised when a task misses its deadline with a probability > 0.15 given that an event $sendData$ has occurred. Thus, the observed probability $\bar{p}$ can be calculated as follows.

$$\bar{p} = \frac{|\ failSend\ \&\&\ (sendData\ ||\ end([sendData, failSend)))\ |}{|\ sendData\ |}$$

Once the properties are specified, MaC can check Surge via Avrora against these properties. The faulty node error is a physical error rather than a software error. Because the environment simulated by Avrora is perfect, it is impossible to detect this error on Avrora unless an artificial bug is introduced into Avrora to simulate the unpredictable environment of sensor nodes. In this paper, using the java class `Random`, an artificial bug is introduced into nodes 1, 4, and 8, shown in Figure 3. The faulty nodes would fail to send a message with probabilities indicated in Table 1. Given the window size of 80 and a 97.5% significance level (which yields $z_\alpha = 1.96$), an alarm is raised only for Node 4. Note that the alarm is not raised for Node 8, which barely exceeds the threshold. The absence of an alarm means that the difference is not statistically significant for the given confidence level.

Table 1. Probabilistic send in nodes 1, 4, and 8

Node	Number of Sends	Number of Failss	$\bar{p}$	z	Alarm
0,2,3,5,6,7	80	0	0.0	-3.757	No
1	80	5	0.0625	-2.192	No
4	80	19	0.2375	2.192	Yes
8	80	13	0.1625	0.313	No

5   Conclusions

Probabilistic property specifications for runtime verification are needed because system behaviors are often unpredictable due to ever-changing environments and cannot be checked statically. Unlike model checking, which can sample multiple execution paths, runtime verification operates on a single execution path, which needs to be decomposed into non-overlapping samples. We present a technique to decompose a trace into several samples based on specification of two kinds of events: one that starts an experiment and the other that denotes its successful completion. Once samples are collected, the probability of success is estimated, and the probabilistic property is checked using hypothesis testing. This paper extends our earlier work [12] by presenting a cleaner semantics based on conditional probabilities and discusses a new implementation approach that is based on a sliding window of samples considered in the hypothesis testing. We present case study, in which we monitor executions of wireless sensor network applications via a simulator. Future work includes a more thorough analysis of the sliding window technique and a more complete case study of the WSN application, directly via their physical devices instead of a simulator.

References

1. Barringer, H., Goldberg, A., Havelund, K., Sen, K.: Rule-based runtime verification. In: Proceedings of 5th International Conference on Verification, Model Checking and Abstract Interpretation, Vanice, Italy, pp. 44–57 (2004)
2. Culler, D.E., Hill, J., Buonadonna, P., Szewczyk, R., Woo, A.: A network-centric approach to embedded software for tiny devices. In: Henzinger, T.A., Kirsch, C.M. (eds.) EMSOFT 2001. LNCS, vol. 2211, Springer, Heidelberg (2001)

3. Devore, J.L.: Probability and Statistics for Engineering and the Sciences. Duxbury Thomson Learning (2000)
4. Drusinsky, D.: Monitoring temporal rules combined with Time Series. In: Hunt Jr., W.A., Somenzi, F. (eds.) CAV 2003. LNCS, vol. 2725, Springer, Heidelberg (2003)
5. Finkbeiner, B., Sankaranarayanan, S., Sipma, H.B.: Collecting statistics about runtime executions. Formal Methods in System Design 27(3), 253–274 (2005)
6. Gay, D., Levis, P., von Behren, R., Welsh, M., Brewer, E., Culler, D.: The nesC language: A holistic approach to networked embedded systems. In: Proceedings of the ACM SIGPLAN Conference on Programming Language Design and Implementation (2003)
7. Havelund, K., Roşu, G.: Java PathExplorer – A runtime verification tool. In: Proceedings of the 6th International Symposium on Artificial Intelligence, Robotics and Automation in Space (2001)
8. Jayaputera, J., Poernomo, I., Schmidt, H.: Runtime verification of timing and probabilistic properties using WMI and .NET. In: Proceedings of the 30th EUROMICRO Conference (2004)
9. Kim, M., Kannan, S., Lee, I., Sokolsky, O., Viswanathan, M.: Java-MaC: a runtime assurance approach for Java programs. Formal Methods in Systems Design 24(2), 129–155 (2004)
10. Kristoffersen, K.J., Pedersen, C., Anderson, H.R.: Runtime verification of Timed LTL using disjunctive normalized equation systems. In: Proceedings of the 3rd International Workshop on Runtime Verification (2003)
11. Manna, Z., Pnueli, A.: The Temporal Logic of Reactive and Concurrent Systems. Springer, Heidelberg (1992)
12. Sammapun, U., Lee, I., Sokolsky, O.: RT-MaC: Runtime monitoring and checking of quantitative and probabilistic properties. In: Proceedings of the 11th IEEE International Conference of Embedded and Real-Time Computing Systems and Applications (2005)
13. Stolz, V., Bodden, E.: Temporal assertions using AspectJ. In: Proceedings of the 5th International Workshop on Runtime Verification (July 2005)
14. Titzer, B.L.: Avrora: The AVR simulation and analysis framework. Master's thesis, University of California, Los Angeles, June (2004)
15. Wald, A.: Sequential Analysis. In: Dover Phoenix Editions (2004)
16. Younes, H.L.S., Kwiatkowska, M., Norman, G., Parker, D.: Numerical vs. statistical probabilistic model checking: An empirical study. In: Proceedings of the 10th International Conference on Tools and Algorithms for the Construction and Analysis of Systems (2004)

Temporal Assertions with Parametrised Propositions*

Volker Stolz

United Nations University
Institute for Software Technology (UNU-IIST)

Abstract. We extend our previous approach to runtime verification of a single finite path against a formula in Next-free Linear-Time Logic (LTL) *with free variables and quantification*. The existing approach is extended from event-based to set-based states, and the design-space of quantification is discussed. By introducing a binary operator that *binds* values based on the current state, we can dispense with the static analysis of a formula. The binding semantics of propositions containing quantified variables is simplified by a pure top-down evaluation. The *alternating binding automaton* corresponding to a formula is evaluated in a breadth-first manner, allowing us to instantly detect refuted formulae during execution.

1 Introduction

In earlier work [15,6], we introduced a framework for runtime verification based on LTL with parametrised propositions for the Java programming language. AspectJ [10] pointcuts served as propositions of the logic and call into a runtime checker implementing an alternating automaton for the desired LTL property.

In this article, we discuss the formal semantics of an alternative way of specifying formulae with parametrised propositions that differentiates between *binding* and *using* variables. A specific operator that binds parameters in propositions simplifies the semantic check for well-formed formulae: a static analysis had to assure that parameters would be indeed always bound in specific locations. Additionally, we extend the system from event-based systems to set-based states and discuss the meaning of quantification.

Many programs can benefit from runtime verification: *semantic interfaces* [6] validate proper interaction in an object-based system, or trace properties trigger some behaviour, as an extension to Aspect-oriented Programming techniques where usually only single events are instrumented.

Events in program execution (method calls, specific instructions) can be used as *propositions* in the runtime verification framework. Interesting properties over *traces* usually relate resources, like processes, locks, or objects/object references

---

* Extended version published in [14]. Partially supported by the projects HighQSoftD and HTTSS funded by the Macao Science and Technology Development Fund.

O. Sokolsky and S. Tasiran (Eds.): RV 2007, LNCS 4839, pp. 176–187, 2007.

with each other, which ties together different propositions in the property specification. It proves problematic to specify the resources some property should be checked on in dynamic systems: identifiers of newly created objects vary from run to run of a program and can only be difficultly statically specified.

A different approach is specifying the *behaviour* (events) that makes some resource "interesting" to the verifier, in the sense that it should check some temporal property on its execution. Once such an event occurs, the pertinent data, e.g. in the case of a method call, caller, callee and arguments are noted and can be referred to by events occurring later on the trace. We have to encode the following together with the property: which events we are interested in, what values from the environment are relevant to the event, and whether we compare those values with previously bound values or if they should be used for future comparisons. Also, it proved practical to have a means of reasoning about any bound values through predicates, e.g., comparing attributes of bound objects.

Another interesting feature for the specification language was a short-hand notation to specify what should happen in the *absence* of an event, which implies not having any variable bindings for evaluation of the remaining formula. In the tool JLO [15], we used implicit quantification depending on the "parent" temporal operator shadowing a proposition. Propositions inside a Finally were existentially quantified, while those inside a Globally were universal. This semantics short-cuts evaluation if the corresponding event was missing, which is exactly the behaviour desired on finite traces: on the end of a trace, a Globally formula should be satisfied, while a Finally should cause a refutation.

Most practically focused approaches only treat event-based system, where at most one proposition holds in each state. Explicit quantification becomes important when there is more than one, e.g., when actions occur truly concurrent and are not serialised. A proposition $p(x_1, \ldots, x_n)$ is used to enumerate the matching instances of this pattern on the current state. Quantifiers attached to the variables indicate whether all or any generated instances must also fulfill the remainder of the formula. The *domain* for each variable should be based on the *current state*. Alternative interpretations, like declaring the domain beforehand or accumulating all seen values for a variable are possible, but impractical: we would have to track many instances, or need the complete trace beforehand [14].

We introduce the operator $\rightarrow$, as in the presence of temporal operators it is important to control instantiation. We found it hard to assign a meaning to the benign looking $\mathbf{G}\,(open(x) \rightarrow \mathbf{F}\,close(x))$, ("every file opened must be closed"), that expands into $\mathbf{G}\,(\neg open(x) \vee \mathbf{F}\,close(x))$ which seemingly enumerates *all files which are not being opened*; $\mathbf{G}\,(open(x) \wedge \mathbf{F}\,close(x))$ has similar drawbacks.

Outline. Firstly, we introduce the finite path semantics for next-free LTL with parametrised propositions. Then, we discuss the on-the-fly evaluation of a trace through an alternating automaton, augmented by bindings. This is illustrated through an example. We conclude with a summary and related work.

2   Parametrised LTL

Parametrised propositions in a formula consist of a constructor with a given arity and the corresponding number of variables as arguments. In a *state*, the arguments to the constructor are values from some fixed object domain. A state defines a mapping of a parametrised proposition to a set of valuations for the variables in a formula. When matching against a parametrised proposition which contains quantified and bound variables, each unbound variable in the proposition may get a value from the underlying domain. This mechanism is closely related to unification in the Prolog system [12], although we only handle constants, and not arbitrary terms.

Syntactically, we will enforce by construction that a quantifier is tied to the proposition that *binds* valuations. In the remainder of the formula, the quantified variables are only *used* but do not generate any new bindings.

The operators of pLTL formulae are virtually the same as in well-known LTL. As propositions may contain variables, we must introduce quantification. We permit quantifiers also inside subformulae shadowed by temporal operators and limit ourselves to *sentences*, where every variable is quantified. Syntactically, we restrict formulae to the form where quantifiers occur only together with a *positive* proposition.

The introduction of a special operator makes it easier for us to specify and enforce semantic constraints already on a syntactical level: a quantified *existence predicate* is the left-hand side of a special non-commutative implication denoted by $\dotrightarrow$, where the right-hand side is another temporal formula.

As an example, consider the formula $\mathbf{G} \; \exists x : p(x) \dotrightarrow \psi(x)$, applied to the state $\{p(1), p(2), q(3)\}$. We have to verify the formulae $\mathbf{G} \; p(1) \dotrightarrow \psi(1)$, $\mathbf{G} \; p(2) \dotrightarrow \psi(2)$ starting from the *current* state, and the recurrent $\mathbf{G} \; \exists x : p(x) \dotrightarrow \psi(x)$ again from the *next* state.

Definition 1. *Let $\mathcal{PN}$ be a set of* proposition names, *where $p \in \mathcal{PN}^{(n)}$ denotes a constructor of arity $n \in \mathbb{N}$. The set of all propositions $\mathcal{P}$, given a fixed value domain $\mathcal{D}$ and a set of variables $\mathcal{V}$, is defined as:*

$$\mathcal{P} := \bigcup_{n \in \mathbb{N}} \bigcup_{p \in \mathcal{PN}^{(n)}} \{p(v_1, \ldots, v_n) \mid v_k \in \mathcal{D} \cup \mathcal{V}, 1 \leq k \leq n\}$$

The set of ground propositions *$\mathcal{P}_\perp$ is the subset of all propositions where each position is instantiated with an element of $\mathcal{D}$, i.e., no position contains a variable:*

$$\mathcal{P}_\perp := \{p(d_1, \ldots, d_n) \in \mathcal{P} \mid \forall i : d_i \in \mathcal{D}, n \in \mathbb{N}\}$$

Definition 2. *The set pLTL of parametrised LTL formulae over a set of variables $\mathcal{V}$, a set of terms $T_{\Sigma(\mathcal{V})}$ composed of function symbols and variables, and* *a set of* predicates $\mathcal{P}r\mathcal{N}$ *over terms, is defined by the following grammar where quantified variables are propagated top-down:*

$$
\begin{aligned}
\text{PLTL} \qquad &::= pLTL(\emptyset) \\
pLTL(V \subseteq \mathcal{V}) &::= \textbf{tt} \mid \textbf{ff} \\
&\mid\; p(u_1, \ldots, u_n) \in \mathcal{P}^{(n)},\ u_1, \ldots, u_n \in V \cup \mathcal{D} &\text{(propositions)} \\
&\mid\; q(t_1, \ldots, t_n),\ q \in \mathcal{P}r\mathcal{N}^{(n)},\ t_1, \ldots, t_n \in T_{\Sigma(V)} &\text{(predicates)} \\
&\mid\; pLTL(V) \oplus pLTL(V),\ \oplus \in \{\, \boldsymbol{U}, \boldsymbol{R}, \vee, \wedge \,\} &\text{(binary operators)} \\
&\mid\; \neg pLTL(V) &\text{(negation)} \\
&\mid\; Q_1 x_1 \ldots Q_m x_m : p(u_1, \ldots, u_n) \overset{.}{\to} pLTL(V'), \\
&\quad\ \forall i : x_i \in \mathcal{V},\ \exists j : x_i = u_j,\ Q_i \in \{\forall, \exists\}, &\text{(quantification)} \\
&\quad\ V' := V \uplus \{x_1, \ldots, x_m\},\ \forall k : u_k \in V' \cup \mathcal{D}
\end{aligned}
$$

For clarity, quantifiers always use fresh variables, i.e., variables which are not yet contained in V. We omit the implication and the right-hand side in the leaf of a formula if it implies **tt**. Each quantified variable *must occur at least once* in the existence predicate (left-hand side).

A formula $Q_1 x_1 \ldots Q_m x_m : p(u_1, \ldots, u_n) \overset{.}{\to} \psi$ can be understood as:

> *There exists a set of valuations derived from the current state (depending on the quantifiers) satisfying both $p(u_1, \ldots, u_n)$ and ψ. If no such valuations exist, the outermost quantifier Q_1 indicates whether evaluation succeeds (universal quantification over empty domain) or fails (existential quantification).*

We define the finite paths semantics for a PLTL formula over a set of variables with respect to a given (partial) *valuation (binding)* $\beta : \mathcal{V} \mapsto \mathcal{D}$ and a path $w = w[0] \ldots w[n-1] \in (2^{\mathcal{P}_\perp})^n$.

Definition 3. *Let $\hat{\beta}$ be the natural extension of $\beta : U \to \mathcal{D}$ over PLTL propositions and formulae $\varphi \in pLTL(V)$, $U, V \subset \mathcal{V}$, $\mathrm{bound}(\varphi) \cap U = \emptyset$:*

$$
\begin{aligned}
&\hat{\beta} : pLTL(V) \to pLTL(V) \\
&\hat{\beta}(p(v_1, \ldots, v_m)) := p(u_1, \ldots, u_m),\ \text{where} \\
&u_i := \begin{cases} \beta(v_i), & \text{if } v_i \in \mathcal{V} \text{ and } \beta(v_i) \text{ defined} \\ v_i, & \text{otherwise} \end{cases}
\end{aligned}
$$

$$
\begin{aligned}
&\hat{\beta}(\textbf{tt}) := \textbf{tt},\ \hat{\beta}(\textbf{ff}) = \textbf{ff} \\
&\hat{\beta}(\neg \varphi) := \neg \hat{\beta}(\varphi) \\
&\hat{\beta}(Q_1 x_1 \ldots Q_m x_m : p(u_1, \ldots, u_n) \overset{.}{\to} \psi) := Q_1 x_1 \ldots Q_m x_m : \hat{\beta}(p(u_1, \ldots, u_n)) \overset{.}{\to} \hat{\beta}(\psi) \\
&\hat{\beta}(\boldsymbol{F}\, \varphi) := \boldsymbol{F}\, \hat{\beta}(\varphi),\ \hat{\beta}(\boldsymbol{G}\, \varphi) := \boldsymbol{G}\, \hat{\beta}(\varphi) \\
&\hat{\beta}(\varphi \oplus \psi) := \hat{\beta}(\varphi) \oplus \hat{\beta}(\psi),\ \oplus \in \{\boldsymbol{R}, \boldsymbol{U}, \wedge, \vee\}\ \text{(binary operators)}
\end{aligned}
$$

We use $\beta_\emptyset$ to denote the empty valuation which does not assign a value to any variable. When representing valuations in the text, we will use a set of tuples consisting of variable/value pairs, for example, $\{x/3, y/4\}$, resembling the function that maps x to 3 and y to 4.

Definition 4. *The $\odot$ operator specialises a valuation. We use it in an environment where the two bindings are disjoint and one binding* extends *another.*

$$\odot \; : \; (\mathcal{V} \mapsto \mathcal{D}) \times (\mathcal{V} \mapsto \mathcal{D}) \to (\mathcal{V} \mapsto \mathcal{D})$$

$$\beta_2 \odot \beta_1 := \lambda x. \begin{cases} \beta_1(x), & \text{if } x \in \mathcal{V} \text{ bound in } \beta_1 \\ \beta_2(x), & \text{otherwise} \end{cases}$$

Definition 5. *Given a parametrised proposition $p(u_1, \ldots, u_n) \in \mathcal{P}$ and a state $a \in 2^{\mathcal{P}_\perp}$, we obtain all* possible *valuations for a variable $x \in \{u_1, \ldots, u_n\}$:*

$$vals : \mathcal{P} \times 2^{\mathcal{P}_\perp} \times \mathcal{V} \to 2^{\mathcal{D}}$$
$$vals(p(u_1, \ldots, u_n), a, x) := \{d \in \mathcal{D} \mid \exists p(d_1, \ldots, d_n) \in a :$$
$$(\widehat{\{x/d\}})(p(u_1, \ldots, u_n)) \downarrow p(d_1, \ldots, d_n)\}$$

where $\downarrow : \mathcal{P} \times \mathcal{P} \to \mathbb{B}$ indicates whether two parametrised propositions are unifiable, *i.e., there exist substitutions for all variables occurring in them such that both propositions are identical under these substitutions.*

Definition 6 (Finite path semantics). *We define the* finite path satisfaction *relation $(w[j], \beta) \models \varphi$ for a non-empty path $w = w[0] \ldots w[n-1] \in (2^{\mathcal{P}_\perp})^n$, $0 \leq j < n$, $\beta : \mathcal{V} \mapsto \mathcal{D}$, an interpretation for predicates with $free(q(\beta(t_1), \ldots, \beta(t_n))) = \emptyset$, a formula $\varphi \in pLTL(V)$, $V \subset \mathcal{V}$ by induction on the structure of φ.*

$$
\begin{aligned}
(w[j], \beta) &\models \mathbf{tt}, \qquad (w[j], \beta) \not\models \mathbf{ff}, \\
&\models p(u_1, \ldots, u_m) \quad \text{iff } \hat{\beta}(p(u_1, \ldots, u_m)) \in w[j], \\
&\models q(t_1, \ldots, t_n) \quad \text{iff } [\![q(\beta(t_1), \ldots, \beta(t_n))]\!] = \mathbf{tt} \\
&\models \neg\varphi \qquad\qquad \text{iff } w[j] \not\models \varphi \\
&\models \varphi \mathbf{\,U\,} \psi \qquad \text{iff } \exists k \; (j \leq k < n) \text{ s.th. } (w[k], \beta) \models \psi \\
&\qquad\qquad\qquad\quad \wedge \; \forall l \; (j \leq l < k) \to (w[l], \beta) \models \varphi \\
&\models \varphi \mathbf{\,R\,} \psi \qquad \text{iff } \forall k \; (j \leq k < n) \to (w[k], \beta) \models \psi \\
&\qquad\qquad\qquad\quad \vee \; \exists l \; (j \leq l < k) \text{ s.th. } (w[l], \beta) \models \varphi \\
&\models \varphi \oplus \psi \qquad \text{iff } (w[j], \beta) \models \varphi \oplus (w[j], \beta) \models \psi, \oplus \in \{\vee, \wedge\}
\end{aligned}
$$

In the presence of existence predicates with quantifiers, we first derive the set of all possible valuations for each variable and are obliged to prove the remaining formula with respect to these bindings. We need to be aware that quantification over an empty set D' results in either **ff** or **tt**, depending on the quantifier. This is achieved through the disjunctive normal form (DNF), where we calculate the *set of sets of valuations*, where for at least one item in the outer set, all valuations of the inner set must satisfy the formula on the remaining path:

$$(w[j], \beta) \models Q_1 x_1 \ldots Q_k x_k : p(u_1, \ldots, u_m) \dot{\to} \psi, \text{ iff}$$

$$\bigvee_{\theta \in \Theta} \bigwedge_{\sigma \in \theta} (w[j], \sigma \odot \beta) \models (w[j], \sigma \odot \beta) \models \psi, \text{with}$$
$$\Theta = spec(\beta, w[j], Q_1 x_1 \ldots Q_k x_k : p(u_1, \ldots, u_m)), \text{where}$$
$$spec : (\mathcal{V} \mapsto \mathcal{D}) \times 2^{\mathcal{P}_\perp} \times pLTL(V) \to 2^{2^{\mathcal{V} \mapsto \mathcal{D}}}$$
$$spec(\beta, w[j], Q_1 x_1 \ldots Q_k x_k : p(u_1, \ldots, u_m))$$

$$:= valid(vals_{x_1} \otimes_1 (\ldots (vals_{x_k} \otimes_k \{\{\beta_{\emptyset}\}\}) \ldots)),$$
$$\text{or } \{\{\beta_{\emptyset}\}\} \text{ if } k = 0 \text{ (no quantifiers)}$$
$$vals_{x_i} := vals(\hat{\beta}(p(u_1, \ldots, u_m)), w[j], x_i)$$

$$\otimes_i \ : \ 2^{\mathcal{D}} \times 2^{2^{\mathcal{V} \mapsto \mathcal{D}}} \to 2^{2^{\mathcal{V} \mapsto \mathcal{D}}}$$

$$D \otimes_i \Theta' := \begin{cases} \displaystyle\bigcup_{\theta' \in \Theta'} \left\{ \bigcup_{\sigma' \in \theta'} \{\ \{x_i/d\} \odot \sigma'\} \,\middle|\, d \in D \right\}, \text{ if } Q_i = \exists \\ \displaystyle\bigotimes_{d \in D} \{\{\{\ \{x_i/d\} \odot \sigma' \mid \sigma' \in \theta'\} \mid \theta' \in \Theta'\}\}, \text{ if } Q_i = \forall \end{cases}$$

with $\displaystyle\bigotimes\{\Theta_1, \ldots, \Theta_n\} := \Theta_1 \otimes \ldots \otimes \Theta_n$, where
$$S \otimes T := \{s \cup t \mid s \in S, \ t \in T\}, \text{and}$$
$$valid(\Omega) := \left\{ \{\sigma \mid \sigma \in \theta, (\widehat{\sigma \odot \beta})(p(d_1, \ldots, d_m)) \in w[j]\} \,\middle|\, \theta \in \Omega \right\}$$

The above calculation of *spec* is thus the extension of the *vals* function (Def. 5) to multiple quantifiers. Observe that although β is passed in to the function, the resulting valuations are calculated modulo the pre-existing binding. Old and new bindings are composed through the expression $\sigma \odot \beta$ in the consumer. The right-hand side of the existence-predicate passed into the evaluation of *spec* takes no part in the result and is therefore omitted where convenient.

An existentially quantified variable x will create $|vals_x|$ times the number of disjoint valuations new outer sets, while universal quantification has the same effect on each inner (conjoined) valuation, leaving the number of disjoint sets unmodified. We define two shorthands for convenience:

$$(w, \beta) \models \varphi :\Longleftrightarrow (w[0], \beta) \models \varphi.$$

A path is a model for a PLTL formula, if the formula can be proved for the initially empty valuation $\beta_{\emptyset}$:

$$w \models \varphi :\Longleftrightarrow (w, \beta_{\emptyset}) \models \varphi.$$

The following theorem allows us to either accumulate substitutions during evaluation or apply them to a formula.

Theorem 1. *For all non-empty paths* $w \in (2^{\mathcal{P}_{\perp}})^+$, $\varphi \in$ PLTL, *and valuations* $\beta : \mathcal{V} \mapsto \mathcal{D}$ *it holds that:*

$$(w, \beta) \models \varphi \iff (w, \beta_{\emptyset}) \models \hat{\beta}(\varphi) \iff w \models \hat{\beta}(\varphi).$$

From the declarative semantics it follows that partially instantiated propositions never satisfy any state.

3   Parametrised Automaton

In the spirit of the well-known alternating automaton construction that accepts the same language as its respective LTL formula [16], we give an on-the-fly construction of the *parametrised automaton*, where each instantiation of quantified variables specialises the sub-automaton corresponding to the right-hand side of the newly introduced binding expressions.

Definition 7. *Let* $cl : \text{PLTL} \to 2^{\text{PLTL}(V)}$ *for* $V = bound(\phi)$ *denote the closure of a normalized formula, where negation is pushed down into the leaves through recursive application of the* $()^+$ *operation following DeMorgan and the respective rules for temporal operators, using the following rewriting rule for quantification:*

$$\neg\, Q_1 x_1 \ldots Q_n x_n : p(y_1, \ldots, y_m) \overset{\cdot}{\to} \psi$$
$$\longrightarrow\quad \overline{Q}_1 x_1 \ldots \overline{Q}_n x_n : p(y_1, \ldots, y_m) \overset{\cdot}{\to} (\neg\,\psi)^+ \ . \ Then:$$

- $\phi \in cl(\phi)$, $\mathbf{tt}, \mathbf{ff} \in cl(\phi)$
- *if* $\varphi \oplus \psi \in cl(\phi)$ *then* $\varphi, \psi \in cl(\phi)$, $\oplus \in \{\vee, \wedge, \boldsymbol{R}, \boldsymbol{U}\}$
- *if* $Q_1 x_1 \ldots Q_n x_n : p(u_1, \ldots, u_m) \overset{\cdot}{\to} \psi \in cl(\phi)$ *then* $\psi \in cl(\phi)$

Contrary to fully instantiated propositions, the quantified left-hand side of a binding expression is not an explicit state in the construction since it is not a syntactically valid sub-formula.

Definition 8 (Parametrised automaton). *The* parametrised automaton *of a* PLTL *formula* ϕ *in positive form is a quintuple* $A(\phi) := \langle 2^{\mathcal{P}_\perp}, Q, q_0, \delta, F \rangle$ *which behaves like a normal alternating finite automaton, but additionally, it passes bindings along through the transition function and is able to augment them when taking a transition from a state whose label is prefixed with an existence predicate:*

$$\delta : (Q \times [\mathcal{V} \mapsto \mathcal{D}]) \times \Sigma \to 2^{2^{(Q \times [\mathcal{V} \mapsto \mathcal{D}])}}$$

The states of the automaton are the elements of the closure of the corresponding PLTL *formula* ϕ *in positive form augmented by the binding function; the final states are the* $\mathbf{tt}$ *state and all Release nodes:*

$$Q := cl(\phi) \times [\mathcal{V} \mapsto \mathcal{D}], \quad q_0 := (\phi, \beta_\emptyset)$$
$$F := (\{\mathbf{tt}\} \cup \{q \in cl(\phi) \mid q = \varphi \ \boldsymbol{R} \ \psi\}) \times [\mathcal{V} \mapsto \mathcal{D}]$$

We statically determine the parametrised, static structure, and explore it through instantiation on the fly. The binding function now carries the burden of dynamically tracking the valuations. The transition function is defined through:

$$\delta((\mathbf{tt}, \beta), a) := \{\emptyset\}, \ \ \delta((\mathbf{ff}, \beta), a) := \emptyset$$

Propositions:

$$\delta((p(\boldsymbol{u}), \beta), a) \ := \begin{cases} \{\{(\mathbf{tt}, \beta)\}\}, & \textit{iff } \hat{\beta}(p(\boldsymbol{u})) \in a \\ \{\{(\mathbf{ff}, \beta)\}\}, & \textit{otherwise} \end{cases}$$

$$\delta((\neg p(\boldsymbol{u}), \beta), a) := \begin{cases} \{\{(\mathbf{tt}, \beta)\}\}, & \textit{iff } \hat{\beta}(p(\boldsymbol{u})) \notin a, \textit{free}(\hat{\beta}(p(\boldsymbol{u}))) = \emptyset \\ \{\{(\mathbf{ff}, \beta)\}\}, & \textit{otherwise} \end{cases}$$

Predicates:

$$\delta((q(\boldsymbol{u}), \beta), a) \ := \begin{cases} \{\emptyset\}, & \textit{iff } [\![\hat{\beta}(q(\boldsymbol{u}))]\!] = \mathbf{tt} \\ \emptyset, & \textit{otherwise} \end{cases}$$

$$\delta((\neg q(\boldsymbol{u}), \beta), a) := \begin{cases} \{\emptyset\}, & \textit{iff } [\![\hat{\beta}(q(\boldsymbol{u}))]\!] = \mathbf{ff} \\ \emptyset, & \textit{otherwise} \end{cases}$$

$$\delta((\varphi \vee \psi, \beta), a) \ := \delta((\varphi, \beta), a) \cup \delta((\psi, \beta), a)$$
$$\delta((\varphi \wedge \psi, \beta), a) \ := \delta((\varphi, \beta), a) \otimes \delta((\psi, \beta), a)$$
$$\delta((\varphi \ \boldsymbol{U} \ \psi, \beta), a) := \delta((\psi, \beta), a) \cup (\{\{(\varphi \ \boldsymbol{U} \ \psi, \beta)\}\} \otimes \delta((\varphi, \beta), a))$$
$$\delta((\varphi \ \boldsymbol{R} \ \psi, \beta), a) := (\delta((\varphi, \beta), a) \otimes \delta((\psi, \beta), a)) \cup (\{\{(\varphi \ \boldsymbol{R} \ \psi, \beta)\}\} \otimes \delta((\psi, \beta), a))$$

We only modify the bindings on states prefixed with an existence predicate. For correct behaviour with respect to universal quantification over an empty domain we introduce a separate short-cut rules. We only have to consider the first quantifier, as due to the definition of spec, it is not possible to have valuations for some of the quantified variables in the same parametrised proposition but not for others. Existential quantification coincides with the general case as Θ will be empty, thus producing no successor states.

$$\delta((Q_1 x_1 \ldots Q_n x_n : p(u_1, \ldots, u_m) \xrightarrow{\cdot} \psi, \beta), a)$$

$$:= \begin{cases} \{\emptyset\}, & \text{iff } Q_1 = \forall \text{ and } \Theta = \emptyset \\ \bigcup_{\theta \in \Theta} \left\{ \bigotimes \{\delta((\psi, \sigma \odot \beta), a) \mid \sigma \in \theta\} \right\}, \end{cases}$$

$$\Theta := spec(\beta, a, Q_1 x_1 \ldots Q_n x_n : p(u_1, \ldots, u_m))$$

A run of the parametrised automaton *is a tree where nodes are labelled with tuples from* $(Q \times [\mathcal{V} \mapsto \mathcal{D}])$. *The run is* accepting, *if all leaves are labelled with tuples where the state component is in* F. *Note that each leaf may be labelled with a different binding function. The incremental nature of the bindings is still visible in the tree: the valuation of a child node is always* at least as specific *(in the sense that it binds at least as many variables) as its parent.*

Theorem 2. *For a path* w, *a* PLTL *formula* ϕ *and the corresponding parametrised automaton* $A(\phi)$ *it holds that:* $\phi \equiv A(\phi)$.

Again, we refer the interested reader to [14] for the proof.

Size of the Construction. The static size of the automaton which abstracts from a concrete binding is *linear* in the size of the formula. At runtime, in the worst case we observe $|cl(\phi)| \times |\mathcal{D}|^{|V|}$ states (exponential in the number of variables, since each state can be replicated once for each instantiation of its free variables). In practice, this places the burden on the user to keep the number of expected/possible instantiations in mind when devising a formula. For example, although she could match on object creation through `new()` and later match on a specific event with the bound value, there is no added value in that: a matching directly on the event for instantiating any parameters should produce exactly the necessary bindings (unless of course it is essential for the behaviour to be observed to have a `new`-event). Evaluating a run of an instantiated alternating automaton has an additional double-exponential overhead (from alternating automaton to non-deterministic, and then to deterministic automaton).

However, we found in [15] that non-discriminate instrumentation is the most limiting factor. For improvements on instrumenting, e.g., Java, applications for runtime verification, we refer the reader to [5].

3.1   Example: Lock-Order Reversal

As an example for a refutation, we shall consider an actual concurrent programming problem we reported in [13]: to avoid the problem of Lock-order Reversal

```
class Main
                                   method take(11,12)
method main
    var lockA lockB                L1: lock 11
                                        lock 12
    lockA := (Lock) new ()              /* critical section */
    lockB := (Lock) new ()              unlock 12
    thread this.take(lockA,lockB)       unlock 11
    this.take(lockB,lockA)              jmp L1
```

Fig. 1. Sample code exhibiting potential Lock-order Reversal

(LOR) (see also [9,4]), we would like to assert through an LTL formula that if two locks are taken in a given order (with no unlocking in between), the system should warn the user if he also uses these locks in swapped order because in concurrent programs this would mean that two threads could deadlock when their execution is scheduled in an unfortunate order.

The trace data we are interested in are the **lock** and **unlock** operations. We need both the information as to *which lock* is affected and *which thread* is taking the action and assume a trace of the corresponding propositions.

The pseudo-program in Fig. 1 generates a trace containing the above propositions, possibly in the order indicating the erroneous behaviour. We can detect this and warn the developer that his application has the potential to enter a deadlock under certain conditions.

Thus, if we consider a class **Lock** with explicit **lock** and **unlock** methods like we might find them in any programming language, we obtain for two threads t_i, t_j and two locks l_x, l_y the following formula, where we assign names to the different subformulae and push down negation (the Globally operator is just a short-hand for **ff R** ϕ):

$$\Psi \quad := \mathbf{G} \ [\forall t_i \forall l_x : \mathtt{lock}(t_i, l_x) \dotrightarrow (\varphi^{\mathbf{R}}(t_i, l_x) \vee \varphi^{\mathbf{U}}(t_i, l_x))]$$

$$\varphi^{\mathbf{R}}(t_i, l_x) \quad := \mathtt{unlock}(t_i, l_x) \ \mathbf{R} \ \forall l_{z'} : \mathtt{lock}(t_i, l_{z'}) \dotrightarrow \neg(l_{z'} \neq l_x)$$

$$\varphi^{\mathbf{U}}(t_i, l_x) \quad := \neg \mathtt{unlock}(t_i, l_x) \ \mathbf{U} \ \exists l_z : \mathtt{lock}(t_i, l_z) \dotrightarrow [l_z \neq l_x$$
$$\wedge \ \forall l_y : \mathtt{lock}(t_i, l_y) \dotrightarrow (l_y \neq l_x \wedge \varphi'(t_i, l_x, l_y))]$$

$$\varphi'(t_i, l_x, l_y) \quad := \mathbf{G} \ \forall t_j : \mathtt{lock}(t_j, l_y) \dotrightarrow [\neg(t_i \neq t_j) \vee \varphi''(t_i, t_j, l_x, l_y)]$$

$$\varphi''(t_i, t_j, l_x, l_y) := \mathtt{unlock}(t_j, l_y) \ \mathbf{R} \ \neg\mathtt{lock}(t_j, l_x)$$

The variable l_z is necessary because there cannot be any information transfer from the right-hand side of an Until to any "subsequent" formula in PLTL. This is also a main difference from J-LO where valuations can spill over from one side to the other of a binary operator, making evaluation more problematic. We use an implication to rebind the same event, but now to the proposition with the variable l_y. For this formula, $\exists l_z : \mathtt{lock}(t_i, l_z)$ and $\forall l_y : \mathtt{lock}(t_i, l_y)$ will always coincide.

The constraints on the identifiers are *predicates*, which are moved immediately after the respective event which will cause the variables mentioned in the constraint to become fully instantiated. Ψ, $\varphi^{\mathbf{R}}$, φ', and φ'' are accepting states of the automaton at the end of the trace, while $\varphi^{\mathbf{U}}$ is not. Fig. 2 gives the schematic

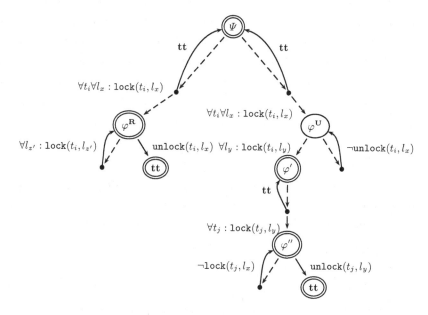

Fig. 2. Schematic automaton for Lock-order Reversal

structure of the corresponding automaton. Multiple edges leaving a single proper node are disjuncts, while conjuncts are indicated using the intermediate small nodes. Labels on edges indicate input symbols or instantiation of parametrised propositions for the corresponding sub-automaton. **tt** indicates an edge that is taken under any input. Dashed edges are used during intermediate construction and indicate that the current input symbol is re-used in the sub-automaton: the right-hand side of a parametrised expression must be evaluated under the current input, using the instantiations obtained by the left-hand side. The sequence of events that we assume is:

Step	1	2	3	4	5
Thread 1:	$\texttt{lock}(t_1, l_A)$;	$\texttt{lock}(t_1, l_B)$;	$\texttt{unlock}(t_1, l_B)$;		
Thread 2:				$\texttt{lock}(t_2, l_B)$;	$\texttt{lock}(t_2, l_A)$

We obtain the following intermediate configurations in DNF, starting from the initial configuration s_0:

$s_0 = \{\{(\Psi, \beta_\emptyset)\}\}$

$s_1 = \{\{(\Psi, \beta_\emptyset), (\varphi^{\mathbf{R}}, \{t_i/1, l_x/A\})\},$
$\qquad \{(\Psi, \beta_\emptyset), (\varphi^{\mathbf{U}}, \{t_i/1, l_x/A\})\}\}$

$s_2 = \{\{(\Psi, \beta_\emptyset), (\varphi^{\mathbf{R}}, \{t_i/1, l_x/B\}), (\varphi', \{t_i/1, l_x/A, l_y/B\})\},$
$\qquad \{(\Psi, \beta_\emptyset), (\varphi^{\mathbf{U}}, \{t_i/1, l_x/B\}), (\varphi', \{t_i/1, l_x/A, l_y/B\})\}\}$

$s_3 = \{\{(\Psi, \beta_\emptyset), (\varphi', \{t_i/1, l_x/A, l_y/B\})\}\}$

$s_4 = \{\{(\Psi, \beta_\emptyset), (\varphi^{\mathbf{R}}, \{t_i/2, l_x/B\}), (\varphi', \{t_i/1, l_x/A, l_y/B\}), (\varphi'', \{t_i/1, t_j/2, l_x/A, l_y/B\})\}\}$
$\qquad \{(\Psi, \beta_\emptyset), (\varphi^{\mathbf{U}}, \{t_i/2, l_x/B\}), (\varphi', \{t_i/1, l_x/A, l_y/B\}), (\varphi'', \{t_i/1, t_j/2, l_x/A, l_y/B\})\}\}$

$s_5 = \emptyset$

The last state refutes the formula, as an empty set of disjunctions is unsatisfiable, i.e., the trace does not satisfy the formula. We note that each prefix of this trace would be accepted, as in each configuration, there is always at least one disjunct consisting only of accepting states.

4   Conclusion

In this article we have presented an extension of well-known finite path LTL and extended the semantics with an explicit binding operator for parametrised propositions. This makes the decision on when exactly to derive valuations from the trace explicit. We also illustrated how to translate PLTL formulae into a variant of alternating automata which gives us a means of checking a path. A short example illustrates the application, although it is certainly arguable whether LTL is an appropriate language for specifying real-world properties. A short comparison with related work is provided.

Related Work. The rule-based frameworks EAGLE [3] and RULER [2] are very similar, but more flexible: our $\rightarrow$ operator resembles a rule. Temporal logics can be encoded through rules. EAGLE also allows data parametrization.

Walker and Viggers [17] proposed a language extension to ASPECTJ, *tracecuts*. Tracecuts match on sequences of events in the execution flow and are specified by means of context-free expressions over Java pointcut, but do not provide automatic tracking of state through parametrization. Allan *et al.* [1] extended the *abc* compiler with *tracematches* which allow to bind free variables in pointcut expressions. Free variables are only available in the symbol declaration, so the trace match itself is not parametrised and may require duplicate symbol definitions under renaming (e.g. `lockA1,lockA2,lockB1,lockB2` instead of `lock(x,y)`). Douence *et al.* [7] discussed regular trace-based aspects with variables. The *Program Query Language* [11] allows for both static and dynamic analysis of Java programs and permits matching context-free patterns.

Finkbeiner *et al.* proposed *algebraic alternating automata* [8] which collect statistics over runtime executions. It allows to evaluate queries over finite traces like "what is the average number of retransmissions" or "what is the maximum packet delay". Basic observations on the trace constitute experiments, which are then aggregated with the help of algebraic alternating automata. Each symbol in a formula gets an additional function corresponding to its arity, that is, propositions and the **X** operator carry a unary function, Boolean functions $\vee$, $\wedge$, and **U** a binary function. These functions are used to combine results from both branches. Similarly, for aggregate statistics *interval* and *unconditional collection* can be used to compute, for example, the maximum number of times that a predicate holds in a specific interval. The collection mechanism of this framework could surely be used to "accumulate" the variable bindings used in our approach instead of some statistics, but the overall result does not influence the acceptance condition of the automaton, as our mechanism does.

Acknowledgement. The author thanks Eric Bodden for his work in [15,6].

References

1. Allan, C., Avgustinov, P., Simon, A.S., Hendren, L., Kuzins, S., Lhoták, O., de Moor, O., Sereni, D., Sittamplan, G., Tibble, J.: Adding Trace Matching with Free Variables to AspectJ. In: OOPSLA 2005 (2005)
2. Barrigner, H., Rydeheard, D., Havelund, K.: Rule systems for run-time monitoring: from EAGLE to RULER. In: Sokolsky, O., Tasiran, S. (eds.) RV 2007. LNCS, vol. 4128, pp. 188–201. Springer, Heidelberg (2007)
3. Barringer, H., Goldberg, A., Havelund, K., Sen, K.: Rule-based runtime verification. In: Steffen, B., Levi, G. (eds.) VMCAI 2004. LNCS, vol. 2937, Springer, Heidelberg (2004)
4. Bensalem, S., Havelund, K.: Dynamic deadlock analysis of multi-threaded programs. In: Ur, S., Bin, E., Wolfsthal, Y. (eds.) Hardware and Software, Verification and Testing. LNCS, vol. 3875, Springer, Heidelberg (2006)
5. Bodden, E., Hendren, L., Lhoták, O.: A staged static program analysis to improve the performance of runtime monitoring. In: Ernst, E. (ed.) ECOOP 2007. LNCS, vol. 4609, Springer, Heidelberg (2007)
6. Bodden, E., Stolz, V.: Tracechecks: Defining semantic interfaces with temporal logic. In: Löwe, W., Südholt, M. (eds.) SC 2006. LNCS, vol. 4089, Springer, Heidelberg (2006)
7. Douence, R., Fradet, P., Südholt, M.: Composition, reuse and interaction analysis of stateful aspects. In: Murphy, G.C., Lieberherr, K.J. (eds.) Proc. of the 3rd Intl. Conf. on Aspect-oriented software development (AOSD 2004). ACM (2004)
8. Finkbeiner, B., Sankaranarayanan, S., Sipma, H.: Collecting statistics over runtime executions. In: Havelund, K., Roşu, G. (eds.) Semantics of Concurrent Computation. ENTCS, vol. 70, Elsevier, Amsterdam (2002)
9. Havelund, K.: Using Runtime Analysis to Guide Model Checking of Java Programs. In: Havelund, K., Penix, J., Visser, W. (eds.) SPIN Model Checking and Software Verification. LNCS, vol. 1885, Springer, Heidelberg (2000)
10. Laddad, R.: AspectJ in Action: Practical Aspect-Oriented Programming. Manning Publications Co. (2003)
11. Martin, M., Livshits, B., Lam, M.S.: Finding application errors and security flaws using PQL: a program query language. In: OOPSLA 2005 (2005)
12. Sterling, L., Shapiro, E.: The Art of Prolog. MIT Press, Cambridge (1986)
13. Stolz, V., Huch, F.: Runtime Verification of Concurrent Haskell Programms. In: Havelund, K., Roşu, G. (eds.) Stochastic Automata: Stability, Nondeterminism and Prediction, vol. 113, Elsevier, Amsterdam (2005)
14. Stolz, V.: Temporal assertions for sequential and concurrent programs. Technical Report AIB-2007-15, RWTH Aachen University, August 2007. PhD thesis(2007), http://aib.informatik.rwth-aachen.de/2007/2007-15.pdf
15. Stolz, V., Bodden, E.: Temporal Assertions using AspectJ. In: Barringer, H., Finkbeiner, B., Gurevich, Y., Sipma, H. (eds.) ISSAC 1982 and EUROCAM 1982. ENTCS, vol. 144, Elsevier, Amsterdam (2005)
16. Vardi, M.Y.: An automata-theoretic approach to linear temporal logic. In: Moller, F., Birtwistle, G. (eds.) Logics for Concurrency: Structure versus Automata. LNCS, vol. 1043, Springer, Heidelberg (1996)
17. Walker, R.J., Viggers, K.: Implementing protocols via declarative event patterns. In: Taylor, R.N., Dwyer, M.B. (eds.) Proc. of the 12th ACM SIGSOFT Intl. Symp. on Foundations of Software Engineering, ACM Press, New York (2004)

Rollback Atomicity

Serdar Tasiran and Tayfun Elmas

Koc University, Istanbul, Turkey

Abstract. We introduce a new non-interference criterion for concurrent programs: rollback atomicity. Similarly to other definitions of atomicity, rollback atomicity of a given concurrent execution requires that there be a matching serial execution. Rollback atomicity differs from other definitions of atomicity in two key regards. First, it is formulated as a special case of view refinement. As such, it requires a correspondence between the states of a concurrent and a serial execution for each atomic block rather than only at quiescent states. Second, it designates a subset of shared variables as peripheral and has more relaxed requirements for peripheral variables than previous non-interference criteria.

In this paper, we provide the motivation for rollback atomicity. We formally define it and compare it with other notions of atomicity and non-interference criteria. We built a runtime checker for rollback atomicity integrated into the refinement checking tool, VYRD. This implementation was able to verify that concurrent executions of our motivating example are rollback atomic.

1 Introduction

Shared-memory multi-threaded programs are prone to concurrency-related bugs. In addition to program-specific correctness properties, several generic correctness and non-interference criteria have been studied for such programs, including freedom from race conditions and deadlocks. Such generic criteria provide a separation of concerns. By first verifying or trying to ensure that his program does not violate a generic correctness criterion, a programmer can then make certain assumptions and simplify his reasoning while ensuring other properties of the program. For instance, for Java programs, ensuring race freedom allows the programmer to assume sequential consistency for his program [9].

A higher-level correctness criterion that is frequently used is atomicity. Programmers designate blocks of their code *atomic* and would like to have certain mutual-exclusion and non-interference guarantees about such blocks. A programmer may ensure the atomicity of code blocks himself using synchronization constructs provided by the platform he is working on, or he may use a transactional memory implementation to ensure atomicity [8]. Several different variations of atomicity have been defined and investigated in the literature. In this study, we propose and investigate a new notion of atomicity called *rollback atomicity* that addresses certain limitations of existing definitions of atomicity.

O. Sokolsky and S. Tasiran (Eds.): RV 2007, LNCS 4839, pp. 188–201, 2007.
© Springer-Verlag Berlin Heidelberg 2007

Definitions of atomicity have the following general form:

Definition 1 (Atomicity). *A concurrent execution σ^{conc} of a program is atomic iff there exists an equivalent, serial execution σ^{ser} in which actions of each atomic block are executed consecutively.*

Rollback atomicity follows this template as well. Rollback atomicity requires a particular kind of match between the states of σ^{conc} and the witness execution σ^{ser} at certain points in each execution. These points approximately correspond to completion points of atomic blocks. A subset F of the shared data variables is designated by the user as the set of *focus variables*. The rest of the shared variables (the set P) are called *peripheral* variables. The valuation of focus variables in σ^{ser} right after an atomic block **A** completes is required to match a valuation obtained from σ^{conc} by (i) considering the program state at the point where **A** completes in σ^{conc} and (ii) by "rolling back" the effects of other atomic blocks **B** that commit later, i.e. appear later than **A** in σ^{ser}. Rollback atomicity is defined precisely in Section 3.

Different notions of atomicity in the literature differ in their formalization of the equivalence of executions that they use to interpret the Definition 1. Reduction and its variants [2,12] are defined based on actions that are left-, right- and both-movers and actions that are non-movers. Reduction requires that it be possible to obtain σ^{ser} from σ^{conc} by swapping actions that commute for σ^{ser} and σ^{conc} to be equivalent. Conflict serializability (See e.g. [10,12]) requires σ^{ser} to consist of the same accesses as in σ^{conc} and for the order of accesses to each variable to be the same in the two executions. View serializability [10,12] is a more relaxed notion for atomicity. It requires that σ^{ser} consist of the same accesses as in σ^{conc}, that the final write to each variable in both executions be the same and that the write seen by each read be the same in both executions. Commit atomicity [4] requires that the order of the atomic blocks in σ^{ser} be the same as the order of occurrence of their commit points in σ^{conc}. All quiescent states, i.e., states in which no atomic block is in progress, including the final state of σ^{conc} are then required to match corresponding states of σ^{ser}. Rollback atomicity is a weaker requirement than reduction and conflict serializability, but is incomparable with view serializability and commit-atomicity. It provides more observability at more points along the execution and is therefore more stringent than the latter two criteria, but is more permissive and abstract than them in other regards.

In Section 2.1, we provide an example which we use to motivate and illustrate various aspects of rollback atomicity. In Section 2.2, we review existing non-interference criteria for concurrent programs and provide examples where they produce counterintuitive results. In some of these examples, existing criteria are too restrictive. In others, they miss errors when applied in the context of runtime verification because they only pose a requirement about the end states of executions. We propose the novel criterion of rollback atomicity to address some of these issues. In Section 3, we define rollback atomicity formally. Section 4 describes our runtime algorithm for checking whether a concurrent execution of a Java program is rollback atomic. Section 5 describes our implementation and presents preliminary results.

2   Motivation

2.1   Rollback Atomicity Example

In this example, several concurrent threads can each run the **send** method of a different **Msg** object (See Figures 1 and 2). The **Msg** objects that are to be sent wait in a queue called **toSendQueue**, thus, **toSendQueue** is shared among different threads. The static field **Msg.KBSentThisSec** and the pool of bytes to be sent, **SendPool** are also shared among threads. Each **Msg** object has a boolean field **sent** that indicates whether or not it has been copied into **SendPool**. The **send** method copies the contents of the message (a byte array) to **SendPool** byte by byte. In **SendPool**, each byte has a message identifier (shown by **msg1**, etc. in the leftmost box representing each message in Figure 1) and a sequence number. The programmer wants the modifications of the **sent** fields and the **toSendQueue** to be atomic. While the **sentPool** data structure is also a shared variable, since the network can already re-order messages, it is not necessary for the sequence of updates to **sentPool** by each **send** method to be atomic. The **KBytesSentThisSec** static field is shared (read and written to) by all threads. It is used for rate control and occasionally causes a **send** method to abort, but otherwise, in non-exceptionally-terminating executions of **send**, it does not affect the functionality of the method. This field is reset every second, and is incremented by all threads manipulating **Msg** objects. The user does not need the complete sequence of updates to the **KBytesSentThisSec** field within a single execution of **send** to be atomic. Also, the fact that, of two concurrent executions of **send**, one writes to **KBytesSentThisSec** while the other one reads the written value does not point to a true data dependency between the two executions of **send**. **KBytesSentThisSec** is simply there for rate control.

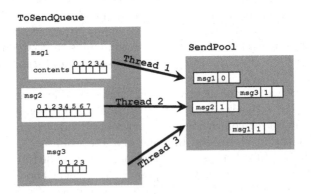

Fig. 1. Concurrent threads and objects in Example 1

```
 0: class Msg {
 1:   long msgId;                    /* @Focus */
 2:   static long KBSentThisSec = 0; /* @Peripheral */
 3:   boolean sent = false;          /* @Focus  */
 4:   byte[] contents;               /* @Focus  */
 5:
 6:   static synchronized long getKBSentThisSecIncr() {
 7:     return ++KBSentThisSec;
 8:   }
 9:
10:   static synchronized long getKBSentThisSec() {
11:     return KBSentThisSec;
12:   }
13:
14:   synchronized atomic void send() {
15:
16:     if ( sent  || !toSendQueue.isIn(this))
17:       abort;  // Caller must retry
18:
19:     if (Msg.getKBSentThisSec() > MAX_RATE)
20:       abort;  // Caller must retry
21:
22:     int i = 0;
23:     while (i < contents.length) {
24:
25:       sendPool.insert(msgId, i, content[i]);
26:       if ( (++i % 1000) == 0 )
27:         if (Msg.getKBSentThisSecIncr() > MAX_RATE)
28:           abort; // Caller must retry
29:     }
30:
31:     sent = true;
32:     toSendQueue.remove(this);
33:   } //Commit point
34: }
```

Fig. 2. Example 1: Focus variables and rollback atomicity

Consider two normally-terminating (i.e., without executing abort()) concurrent executions of send for Msg objects msg1 and msg2. Consider the interleaving of actions by two threads (Figure 3) where an increment that msg2.send() being run by thread T2 performs on Msg.KBytesSentThisSec occurs between two updates to the same static field by msg1.send() running on thread T1. Here, the increment of the static field Msg.KBytesSentThisSec is split into three actions (read-modify-write) to emphasize the read-write data dependencies between consecutive increments to this field. These dependencies are important when considering which re-orderings are allowed by different non-interference criteria.

```
T1                                          T2
--                                          --
send 1000 Bytes of msg1
tmp1 = Msg.KBytesSentThisSec
tmp1 = tmp1 + 1
Msg.KBytesSentThisSec = tmp1
                                            send 1000 Bytes of msg2
                                            tmp2 = Msg.KBytesSentThisSec
                                            tmp2 = tmp2 + 1
                                            Msg.KBytesSentThisSec = tmp2
        send 1000 Bytes of msg1
        tmp1 = Msg.KBytesSentThisSec
        tmp1 = tmp1 + 1
        Msg.KBytesSentThisSec = tmp1
```

Fig. 3. A possible interleaving of actions in Example 1

Conflict serializability does not allow the reads and writes to Msg.KBytes-SentThisSec by msg1.send() and msg2.send() to be re-ordered in order to obtain a witness serial execution. Likewise, view serializability does not allow such a re-ordering either, as it requires that the value of Msg.KBytesSentThisSec seen by each read (results of which are written to local variables tmp1 and tmp2) to be the same in the concurrent and serial executions. Therefore, these two criteria declare such an execution unserializable.

Consider an interleaving of actions from threads in which a message is not sent during a period because MAX_RATE is exceeded. For such an execution, at the end of the one-second period, the value of Msg.KBytesSentThisSec does not match the value of Msg.KBytesSentThisSec that would have been obtained at the end of any serial execution consisting of only the successful executions of send. Thus, such an execution would constitute a commit atomicity violation [4] as well.

However, this execution is consistent with the designer's intentions and is atomic in a certain sense. If only accesses to the shared variables toSendQueue, contents and Msg.sent are considered, these concurrent executions can be serialized in the order that msg1 and msg2 are removed from toSendQueue. Declaring toSendQueue, contents and Msg.sent as the set of our focus variables while designating the rest of the shared variables as peripheral variables, rollback atomicity provides us a way of expressing the requirement that toSendQueue, contents and sent be updated atomically by each execution of send while Msg.KBytesSentThisSec only have a consistent value that allows these executions to complete normally.

2.2   Limitations of Other Non-interference Criteria

Formalizations of atomicity in the literature differ mainly in the notion of equivalence of serial and concurrent executions they use. This section presents a series

```
T1                          T2
--                          --
                            atomic {
        atomic {              acq(Lock_Z, Lock_Y)
                              read Z
                              write Z
                              rel(Lock_Z)

          acq(Lock_Z)
          read Z
          write Z
          acq(Lock_X)
          read X
          rel(Lock_Z)
          rel(Lock_X)

                              acq(Lock_X)
                              read X
                              rel(Lock_X)
                              write Y
                              rel(Lock_Y)
                            } // end atomic
        } // end atomic
```

Fig. 4. Demonstrating restrictiveness of reduction. The vertical axis represents time.

of scenarios where previous non-interference criteria are too restrictive or permissive in the context of runtime verification.

Reduction and its variants ([2,12]) are defined based on actions that are left-, right- and both-movers and actions that are non-movers. They require that it be possible to obtain σ^{ser} from σ^{conc} by swapping actions that commute. Reduction-based definitions have the advantage that it is possible to develop type and effect systems based on them that guarantee atomicity statically. Furthermore, at runtime, it is possible to efficiently check sufficient conditions for atomicity formulated based on whether the accesses within an atomic block adhere to a certain pattern. However, reduction by itself is too restrictive. For instance, acquiring and releasing a lock are right and left movers only. As a result, it is not even possible to re-order the two independent reads. Consider the execution fragment in Figure 4 and suppose that the atomic block in T2 must be serialized first because of the reads and writes to Z (e.g. because of a conditional statement in the original program). Intuitively, since the ordering of two lock-protected reads of X can be changed while preserving all thread-local and global assertions at any point in the execution it should be possible to commute all actions in T2 so they occur before all actions of T1 but reduction does not allow this.

Conflict serializability requires that σ^{ser} consist of the same accesses as in σ^{conc} and that the order of accesses to each variable remain the same. One can formulate a necessary and sufficient check for conflict serializability of an execution based on whether the graph of ordering dependencies between atomic blocks in the execution is acyclic [12]. While it can be checked efficiently, and

```
        T1                         T2
        --                         --
        atomic {
            write X
                                   atomic {
                                       read Y
                                       write X
                                   } // end atomic
            read Y
            write X
        } // end atomic
```

Fig. 5. Example demonstrating restrictiveness of conflict serializability

is more permissive than reduction (e.g. it allows the two lock-protected reads in Figure 4 to be commuted) conflict serializability is still often regarded as too restrictive. For instance, in the execution in Figure 5, the first write to X by T1 cannot be commuted after the accesses by T2although no read in this execution sees the first write to X by T1.

Given that multi-processing and multi-threading is becoming more commonplace, one would like to define a notion of atomicity that is as relaxed as possible while still enabling the programmer to reason in a sequential manner about atomic blocks. View serializability is a more relaxed notion for atomicity. It requires that σ^{ser} consist of the same accesses as in σ^{conc}, that the final write to each variable in both executions be the same, and that the write seen by each read be the same in both executions. But there are scenarios in which view serializability is more permissive than desired, and other scenarios in which it

```
            T1                 T2
            ------             ------
  1:        atomic {
  2:            X = 1          atomic {
  3:                               X = 2
  4:                               Y = 1
  5:                           }// end atomic
  6: ------------------------------------------> read X, Y reveals error
  7:            Y = 2          atomic {
  8:        } // end atomic        Z = 0
  9: ------------------------------------------> Rollback atomicity fails here
 10:        atomic {
 11:            X = 0
 12:                               Y = 0
 13:                           } // end atomic
 14:        } // end atomic
```

Fig. 6. Demonstrating added observability provided by rollback atomicity

is too restrictive. As explained in Section 2.1, in the example in Figure 2 view serializability is unnecessarily restrictive.

To see where view serializability is too permissive, consider the example σ^{conc} of a concurrent execution (Figure 6). At step 6 in the execution, the first atomic block in thread T2 has completed its execution but the values of X and Y are not consistent with any serial execution. This is undesirable because, in another execution, actions by another thread could have been interleaved at this point and these actions could have observed these inconsistent values of X and Y. View serializability and commit atomicity (discussed in more detail below) are not able to detect this error. Because there are no reads in this execution, the view serializability requirement amounts to the final writes to each variable in a serial execution σ^{ser} being the same as the ones (X = 0, Y = 0) in Figure 6.

This example illustrates the fact that view serializability of a single execution may not provide enough observation points along the execution to reveal bugs. Requiring that all executions of a concurrent program be view serializable does not suffer from this observability limitation, but, for a single execution, view serializability may miss some obvious errors.

Purity[3] can be seen as a way of relaxing the requirements of reduction by (i) disregarding accesses by normally-terminating pure blocks and, in essence, allowing them to commute with all other accesses, (ii) allowing one to reason about the atomicity of a more abstract version of the program in which reads within normally-terminating pure blocks can return non-deterministic values, and (iii) disregarding accesses to "unstable variables" such as performance counters which do not factor into the correctness requirement for the program and which may have races on them. If purity is used, the programmer, while performing sequential reasoning within an atomic block, must argue the correctness of a more abstract program where pure reads and accesses to unstable variables may return non-deterministic values. In the example in Figure 2, although it is not required for correctness for updates to Msg.KBSentThisSec to be atomic with the rest of the shared variables, the program will not work as intended for completely arbitrary values of Msg.KBSentThisSec. Therefore, making Msg.KBSentThisSec an unstable variable and marking the atomic block in Figure 2 will not give the desired semantics. The requirements on Msg.KBSentThisSec are more stringent than those on unstable variables.

Harris et al. [5] propose abstract nested transactions (ANT) as a mechanism to recover at runtime from a subset of benign conflicts between atomic blocks. ANT's still implement serializability but provide a mechanism for trying more than one witness serialization σ^{ser}. Furthermore, for the ANT recovery mechanism to be valid, the user is required to access each shared variable either only within or only outside an ANT. Therefore, even when ANT's are used, the example in Figure 2 would create a conflict that the runtime system cannot recover from.

In commit atomicity[4], the final state of a concurrent execution is required to match that of an execution in which atomic blocks are run one at a time, in the order of the occurrence of their commit points in the concurrent execution.

Commit atomicity comes closest to the definition of atomicity proposed in this paper, however, it is too restrictive since it requires that the entire program states match at the end of the execution (which would include Msg.KBytesSentThisSec in the example in Figure 2.). Also, commit atomicity requires that a commit point (a program location) for each atomic block be determined and marked explicitly by the programmer. Rollback atomicity does not have this requirement.

All atomicity criteria discussed in this paper, including rollback atomicity, require the existence of a single σ^{ser} in which all the actions of *every* atomic block in the concurrent execution σ^{conc} occur consecutively. This has the important benefit that the programmer can reason about his program (or at least a well-defined subset of variables) as if each atomic block is executed sequentially and by considering thread interleavings only at the atomic block level. Causal atomicity, introduced in [1], is different in that, for a given concurrent execution σ^{conc}, it is not necessary to find a single execution σ^{ser}. Instead, to show causal atomicity for a given σ^{conc}, it suffices to produce a separate witness execution $\sigma_{\mathbf{A}}^{conc}$ for each atomic block $\mathbf{A}$. We believe this makes causal atomicity too relaxed a non-interference criterion and difficult to use as a programming abstraction.

In the next section, rollback atomicity is formulated as a special case of view refinement [13]. This formulation makes clear that rollback atomicity, in a way similar to linearizability [6] and commit-atomicity [4], does not require the serial execution to be obtained by commuting actions of the concurrent execution.

3   Rollback Atomicity

3.1   Preliminaries

We focus on well-synchronized Java programs whose executions are free of race conditions and thus sequentially consistent. In our model of programs and executions, *Tid* represents the set of thread identifiers and *Addr* represents the set of object identifiers. Objects created during executions of a Java program have a unique identifier from the set *Addr*. Each object has a finite collection of fields. *Field* represents the set of all fields. A *variable* is a pair (o, f) consisting of an object o and a field f. V denotes the set of variables. Each thread executes a sequence of actions. An execution of a program is a linearly-ordered finite sequence of actions obtained by interleaving the sequences of actions from each thread. Actions $read(o, f)$ and $write(o, f)$ represent a read of and a write to the field f of an object o respectively.

We suppose that the programmer has annotated certain code blocks as *atomic*. We make the assumption of *strong atomicity*, where each action executed outside an atomic block is interpreted to be an atomic block consisting of a single action. We partition the set of variables V into the sets of *focus* and *peripheral* variables: $F \cup P$. In our implementation described in Section 5 this is accomplished by annotating field definitions of a class with the comments @Focus or @Peripheral. All variables (o, f) where f is a field marked @Focus are in the set F. The rest of the variables are peripheral variables, i.e., in P.

Consider a concurrent execution σ^{conc} of a program with a set of atomic code blocks $AtBlk$. We give every execution of an atomic block that occurs in σ^{conc} a unique identifier from the set XId. Rollback atomicity of σ^{conc} requires the existence of a serial execution corresponding to σ^{conc} and satisfying certain conditions. In order to make these conditions precise, we make use of the commit order and the rollback function, explained below.

The *commit order* on XId is a total order defined as follows: $\alpha \leq_{cmt} \beta$ iff $\alpha = \beta$ or the atomic block execution with the identifier α occurs before β in σ^{ser}. The commit order is uniquely determined by σ^{ser}. We omit a reference to σ^{ser} while referring to the commit order in order to keep the notation simple when the serial execution σ^{ser} is clear from the context. If $\alpha \leq_{cmt} \beta$, we informally say that α *commits before* β and β *commits after* α.

The *rollback function RlBk* is defined for certain states along a concurrent execution – those reached right after an atomic block with identifier α performs its last write to a focus variable. Roughly speaking, $RlBk$ has the effect of undoing actions by other atomic blocks that overlap with atomic block α in the concurrent execution but come after α in the commit order. $RlBk$ is formally defined as follows. Let σ_α^{conc} be the state in σ^{conc} right after the atomic block execution with identifier α has performed the last write access to a variable in F. We denote with $\mathbf{s}_\alpha^{conc} = proj(\sigma_\alpha^{conc}, F)$ be the projection of the state σ_α^{conc} onto the focus variables. Let σ^{ser} be the serial execution on which $\leq_{cmt}$ is defined. Then, for every focus variable (o, d), $RlBk(\mathbf{s}_\alpha^{conc}, \sigma^{conc}, \sigma^{ser}, F)((o, d))$ is the value of the last write in σ^{conc} by an atomic block β such that $\beta \leq_{cmt} \alpha$ or the initial value of (o, d) if no such α exists. Note that if α has performed the last write to (o, d) before $\mathbf{s}$, then $RlBk(\mathbf{s}_\alpha^{conc}, \sigma^{conc}, \sigma^{ser}, F)((o, d))$ simply returns this value. Rollback atomicity makes use of the rollback function to formulate a refinement check associated with each atomic block and to ensure that the writes to each focus variable (o, d) occur in σ^{conc} occur in the commit order.

3.2   Rollback Atomicity Definition

We say that a concurrent execution σ^{conc} is *rollback atomic* iff there exists an execution σ^{ser} of the program that satisfies the following conditions:

(i) For each thread t, the projection of the two executions onto t, $proj(\sigma^{ser}, t)$ and $proj(\sigma^{conc}, t)$, consist of the same sequence of atomic blocks. We can therefore use the same identifier from XId to refer to corresponding occurrences of an atomic block execution by the same thread in σ^{ser} and σ^{conc}.

(ii) Let σ_α^{ser} denote the state of σ^{ser} right after the block with identifier α has completed executing. Let $\mathbf{s}_\alpha^{ser} = proj(\sigma_\alpha^{ser}, F)$ be the projection of the state σ_α^{ser} onto the focus variables and let $\mathbf{s}_\alpha^{conc}$ be as defined above. It must be the case that for each α, $RlBk(\mathbf{s}_\alpha^{conc}, \sigma^{conc}, \sigma^{ser}, F)((o, d)) = \mathbf{s}_\alpha^{ser}((o, d))$.

Rollback atomicity is a special case of view refinement and can be seen as a variant of linearizability [6] where part of the data structure state is projected away. Similarly to other non-interference criteria, rollback atomicity only requires the existence of some serial execution σ^{ser} or, equivalently, a commit order. The next section describes how we use the dependencies between actions to infer a commit order heuristically.

4   Checking Rollback Atomicity

We check runtime atomicity of executions by performing a view refinement check as described in [13]. The abstraction function that realizes the rollback atomicity check is *RlBk* as described above. The view refinement check requires that the order of atomic blocks in σ^{ser} be explicitly provided by the user. In order to allow more flexibility in the choice of this order, we attempt to infer it from causality relationships in the execution. We construct two graphs representing causality dependencies between accesses in order to infer this order: $\mathbf{CG}_F$ and $\mathbf{CG}_{F \cup P}$. The rules for constructing the two graphs are the same and explained below. The former graph is constructed only using accesses to F variables while the latter takes into account accesses to all shared variables.

A *causality graph* of an execution σ^{conc} is a directed graph $G = (V, E)$ where V contains a unique vertex for each atomic block in the execution σ^{conc} and a unique vertex for each individual read and write action occurring in σ^{conc}. E consists of the following edges:

(i) For each read action r and the write that it sees, $W(r)$ (see [9] for a formal definition), E contains an edge $(W(r), r)$ from the node representing $W(r)$ to the node representing r. If $W(r)$ (alternatively, r) is part of atomic block with identifier α then the edge starts (alternatively, ends) at the node representing the atomic block α instead. The case when both $W(r)$ and r are in the same atomic block is handled in (iii) below.

(ii) For each read action r and the next write action w to the same variable after r in the concurrent execution σ^{conc}, E contains an edge (r, w) from the node representing r to the node representing w. If r (or w) is part of an atomic block α, the edge starts (or ends) at the node representing atomic block α. The case when both $W(r)$ and r are in the same atomic block is handled below.

(iii) If an atomic block contains a write w to a variable (o, d) and subsequent reads $r_1, r_2, ..., r_k$ of (o, d) with no write to (o, d) in the atomic block between w and $r_1, ..., r_k$, E contains the edges $(w, r_1), (w, r_2), ...,(w, r_k)$.

(iv) For each pair of nodes α and β representing actions or atomic blocks ordered by program order, E contains an edge from α to β.

We incrementally update $\mathbf{CG}_F$ and $\mathbf{CG}_{F \cup P}$ as each access in the execution σ^{conc} is processed in order. We search for cycles in each graph after adding an edge that starts/ends at a node representing an atomic block [11]. At each such point, there are three possibilities:

(i) Neither $\mathbf{CG}_F$ nor $\mathbf{CG}_{F \cup P}$ have a cycle containing an atomic block. In this case, we obtain a commit order of atomic blocks by applying the algorithm in [11] to $\mathbf{CG}_{F \cup P}$. In this case the entire execution up to this point is conflict-serializable and it is not necessary to perform a rollback atomicity check.

(ii) $\mathbf{CG}_{F \cup P}$ has a cycle containing an atomic block but $\mathbf{CG}_F$ does not. In this case, we obtain a commit order by linearizing $\mathbf{CG}_F$ only.

(iii) $\mathbf{CG}_F$ and $\mathbf{CG}_{F \cup P}$ both have cycles. In this case, we take as the commit order the order of the last focus variable writes by atomic blocks.

When the refinement check fails, this means we were not able to obtain a serialized execution satisfying the requirements of rollback atomicity using the commit orders provided by (i)-(iii) above. In this case, the implementation could truly have undesired behavior, or it could be the case that we were not able to find the right commit order. If the latter is the case, however, the commit order conflicts with some causality dependencies between atomic blocks created by reads and writes to focus variables. In this case, the programmer can aid our atomicity check by explicitly providing commit point annotations which may produce a commit order that conflicts with the dependencies captured in the causality graphs above. The programmer may also want to revise the partition of variables into focus and peripheral variables.

If there is a read action r to which there is more than one causality edge from write actions in $\mathbf{CG}_F$, a warning is declared. This warning corresponds to a case where a read in an atomic block should have seen a write within the same atomic block, but, instead, has seen another write from another atomic block. While this does not necessarily correspond to a rollback atomicity violation (e.g. the two writes may have written the same value), we point this case out to the programmer as it is probably unintended. Programmers declare blocks atomic in order to be able to perform sequential reasoning. The sequential reasoning is limited to focus variables in the case of rollback atomicity. The scenario described corresponds to a case where this sequential assumption is broken.

5 The Implementation

The runtime algorithm for checking rollback atomicity described in the previous section was implemented using the infrastructure built for the VYRD tool [13] which makes use of Java Pathfinder [7]. The block diagram depicting the refinement checking approach is reproduced in Figure 7. While the program runs and produces σ^{conc}, VYRD tracks the atomic blocks and accesses to the shared variables by these blocks throughout the execution. The beginning and the end of the atomic blocks are annotated by the method calls `Vyrd.beginAtomicBlock()` and `Vyrd.endAtomicBlock()`.

VYRD writes all the events during an execution (including instruction execution, object/thread creation and destruction) into a log file. In offline mode, after the execution completes, VYRD replays the execution using the log and detects the accesses to the focus variables and peripheral variables. The configuration file for VYRD includes the annotations for the focus variables.

Our current implementation only constructs the graph $\mathbf{CG}_F$ and computes a commit order corresponding to the order of the last writes to focus variables by

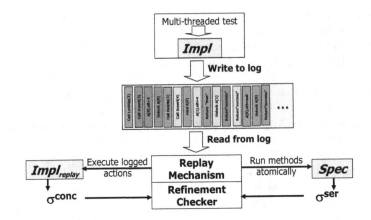

Fig. 7. Checking refinement using VYRD

atomic blocks. For atomic blocks that access no focus variables, their place in the commit order is chosen simply based on their order of occurrence in σ^{conc}. In addition, VYRD allows programmers to explicitly annotate commit points of atomic blocks by calling the special method Vyrd.commit() in the code. Using either method, VYRD is able to identify the commit point of the atomic block and perform the refinement check while replaying the execution from the log file. During the replay of the concurrent execution, on a separate instance of the program being verified, atomic blocks in the corresponding sequential execution are executed in the commit order. s_{α}^{ser} is computed on this separate copy.

VYRD provides a modular mechanism by which a separate software module observes log entries, computes a commit order and drives the execution of atomic blocks in σ^{ser}. Algorithms for incremental construction of and cycle detection for $\mathbf{CG}_F$ and $\mathbf{CG}_{F \cup P}$ will be a part of this external module that feeds the inferred commit order to VYRD. We have not implemented this feature yet.

Using the implementation outlined above, we were able to compute a commit order and verify rollback atomicity for the motivating example in Figure 2 for 10 concurrent threads and message lengths of 50.

6   Conclusion

We proposed rollback atomicity, a new notion of atomicity that we believe is a useful and natural non-interference criterion. We presented a runtime algorithm for checking rollback atomicity and reported on a preliminary implementation. Future work includes integrating cycle detection and the refinement checking implementation, trying other heuristics for inferring the commit order, and relaxing the strong atomicity assumption in the rollback atomicity definition in order to allow less stringent requirements on code blocks not marked atomic.

References

1. Farzan, A., Madhusudan, P.: Causal Atomicity. In: Ball, T., Jones, R.B. (eds.) CAV 2006. LNCS, vol. 4144, pp. 315–328. Springer, Heidelberg (2006)
2. Flanagan, C., Freund, S.N.: Atomizer: A Dynamic Atomicity Checker for Multi-threaded Programs. In: Proc. 31st ACM Symposium on Principles of Programming Languages, pp. 256–267 (2004)
3. Flanagan, C., Freund, S., Qadeer, S.: Exploiting Purity for Atomicity. In: Proc. the Intl. Symposium on Software Testing and Analysis (ISSTA 2004), ACM Press, New York (2004)
4. Flanagan, C.: Verifying Commit-Atomicity Using Model Checking. In: Graf, S., Mounier, L. (eds.) Model Checking Software. LNCS, vol. 2989, pp. 252–266. Springer, Heidelberg (2004)
5. Harris, T., Stipic, S.: Abstract Nested Transactions. In: The 2nd ACM SIGPLAN Workshop on Transactional Computing, TRANSACT 2007, available at http://www.cs.rochester.edu/meetings/TRANSACT07/papers/harris.pdf
6. Herlihy, M.P., Wing, J.M.: Linearizability: A Correctness Condition for Concurrent Objects. ACM Trans. on Programming Languages and Systems 12(3), 463–492 (1990)
7. Visser, W., Havelund, K., Brat, G., Park, S., Lerda, F.: Model Checking Programs. Automated Software Engineering Journal 10(2) (April 2003)
8. Larus, J.R., Rajwar, R.: Transactional Memory. Morgan & Claypool (2006)
9. Manson, J., Pugh, W., Adve, S.: The Java Memory Model. In: Proc. POPL 2005. Principles of Programming Languages, pp. 378–391. ACM Press, New York (2005)
10. Papadimitriou, C.: The Serializability of Concurrent Database Updates. Journal of the ACM 26(4), 631–653 (1979)
11. Pearce, D.J., Kelly, P.H., Hankin, C.: Online Cycle Detection and Difference Propagation: Applications to Pointer Analysis. Software Quality Control 12(4), 311–337 (2004)
12. Wang, L., Stoller, S.D.: Accurate and Efficient Runtime Detection of Atomicity Errors in Concurrent Programs. In: PPoPP 2006: Proc. of the 11th ACM SIGPLAN Symposium on Principles and Practice of Parallel Programming, pp. 137–146 (2006)
13. Elmas, T., Tasiran, S., Qadeer, S.: Vyrd: Verifying Concurrent Programs by Runtime Refinement-Violation detection. In: PLDI 2005: Proc. 2005 ACM SIGPLAN Conf. on Programming Language Design and Implementation, pp. 27–37 (2005)

Runtime Checking for Program Verification

Karen Zee[1], Viktor Kuncak[2], Michael Taylor[3], and Martin Rinard[1]

[1] MIT Computer Science and Artificial Intelligence Laboratory; Cambridge, USA
[2] École Polytechnique Fédérale de Lausanne; Lausanne, Switzerland
[3] University of California, San Diego; La Jolla, USA
{kkz,rinard}@csail.mit.edu, mbtaylor@ucsd.edu, viktor.kuncak@epfl.ch

Abstract. The process of verifying that a program conforms to its specification is often hampered by errors in both the program and the specification. A runtime checker that can evaluate formal specifications can be useful for quickly identifying such errors. This paper describes our preliminary experience with incorporating run-time checking into the Jahob verification system and discusses some lessons we learned in this process. One of the challenges in building a runtime checker for a program verification system is that the language of invariants and assertions is designed for simplicity of semantics and tractability of proofs, and not for run-time checking. Some of the more challenging constructs include existential and universal quantification, set comprehension, specification variables, and formulas that refer to past program states. In this paper, we describe how we handle these constructs in our runtime checker, and describe directions for future work.

1 Introduction

This paper explores the use of a run-time checker in a program verification system Jahob [29]. Our program verification system can prove that the specified program properties hold in all program executions. The system attempts to prove properties using loop invariant inference algorithms [42], decision procedures [30], and theorem provers [8]. As in many other static analysis systems [3, 14] this process has the property that if a correctness proof is found, then the desired property of the program holds in all executions. However, if a proof is not found, this could be either because the property does not hold (there is an error in specification or code), or because the example triggered a limitation of the static verification system (for example, imprecision of loop invariant inference, or limitation of the theorem proving engines). In contrast, run-time checking [11, 12, 13] compiles specifications into executable code and executes the specifications while the program is running. Although run-time checking alone cannot guarantee the absence of errors, it can identify concrete executions when errors do appear. Run-time checking is therefore complementary to static verification. Run-time checking is especially useful when developing the code and specifications, when the specifications and code are likely to contain errors due to developer's errors in formalizing the desired properties.

O. Sokolsky and S. Tasiran (Eds.): RV 2007, LNCS 4839, pp. 202–213, 2007.

Combining static and run-time checking. Given the complementary nature of these techniques, recent verification systems for expressive properties such as Spec# [3] and JML tools [14, 33] include both a static verifier and a run-time checker that can operated on same annotated source code. However, these systems use different semantics and apply different restrictions on specifications in these two cases. The reason is that the limitations of these two checking technologies are different: some specification constructs are easy to execute but difficult to check statically (e.g., recursive or looping deterministic code or complex arithmetic computations), whereas others can be checked statically but are difficult or impossible to execute (e.g., quantification or comprehensions over unbounded number of objects, specifications that involve mathematical quantities not representable at run time). In practice, however, most properties we encountered are executable if stated in an appropriate way. Note that the same specification would be written differently depending on whether it is meant to be executed or verified statically: compare for example 1) specifications of linked structures in systems such as Jahob [29], which use treeness annotations, mathematical sets, relations, and transitive closure operators with 2) manually written Java methods in systems for constraint solving over imperative predicates [9], which use deterministic worklist algorithms with loops to check the shape of the data structure.

Executing declarative specifications. The goal to perform both static and run-time checking can serve as the guidance in designing the specification language. We believe that specification languages, even if their goal is to be executable, should remain declarative in the spirit. In this paper we therefore start with Jahob's language, which was designed for static analysis in mind, and explore techniques necessary to verify Jahob's specifications at run-time. To assess some of these techniques we built an interpreter that executes both the abstract syntax trees of the analyzed program and the specifications in program annotations. The primary use of the run-time checker is debugging specifications and the program. In addition to verification, this research can also be viewed as contributing to the long-standing problem of executing expressive declarative languages.

Contributions. This paper outlines the challenges in executing specification language designed for static verification, describes the current state of our run-time checker for Jahob, and presents future directions. Our checker can execute specifications that involve quantifiers, set comprehensions, transitive closure, integer and object expressions, sets, and relations. Unlike the run-time checkers that we know of, it can evaluate certain expressions that denote infinite sets, as well as formulas that refer to old values of fields of an unbounded number of objects. Among the main future directions are the development of techniques for compilation, parallelization, and incremental evaluation of run-time checks, and the use of constraint solvers for modular run-time checking.

```
1   class Node { public /*: claimedby DLL */ Node next, prev; }
2   class DLL {
3      private static Node root;
4      /*: public static specvar content :: "obj set";
5          vardefs "content == {x. (root,x) ∈ {(u,v). next u = v}^* ∧ x ≠ null}";
6          invariant backbone: "tree[next]";
7          invariant rootFirst: "root = null ∨ (∀ n. n..next ≠ root)";
8          invariant noNextOutside: "∀ x y. x ≠ null ∧ y ≠ null ∧ x..next = y
9                          → y : content";
10         invariant prevDef: "∀ x y. prev x = y →
11                         (x ≠ null ∧ (∃ z. next z = x) → next y = x) ∧
12                         (((∀ z. next z ≠ x) ∨ x = null) → y = null)";
13     */
14     public static void addLast(Node n)
15     /*: requires "n ∉ content ∧ n ≠ null"
16         modifies content
17         ensures "content = old content ∪ {n}" */
18     {
19         if (root == null) {
20             root = n;
21             n.next = null; n.prev = null;
22             return;
23         }
24         Node r = root;
25         while (r.next != null) {
26             r = r.next;
27         }
28         r.next = n;
29         n.prev = r;
30     }
31     public static void testDriver()
32     /*: requires "content = {}" */
33     {
34         Node n1 = new Node();
35         addLast(n1);
36         Node n2 = new Node();
37         addLast(n2);
38     }
39 }
```

Fig. 1. Doubly-linked list with one operation specified in Jahob

2 Jahob Verification System

Jahob [29] is a program verification system for a subset of Java. The initial focus of Jahob is data structure verification [8, 29, 30, 31, 32, 42, 43] for which a simple memory-safe imperative subset of Java [29, Section 3.1] is sufficient.

Figure 1 shows a fragment of a doubly-linked list implementation in Jahob, with the addLast operation that inserts a given node at the end of the list. Developers write Jahob specifications in the source code as special comments that start with the ":" sign. Developers can therefore compile and run programs using standard Java interpreters and runtimes. Jahob specifications contain formulas in higher-order logic (HOL), expressed in the syntax of the Isabelle interactive theorem prover [35]. The specifications represent a class field f as total function f mapping all objects to values, with the convention that $f$null $=$ null and also $fx =$ null when $x.f$ is not well-typed in Java. Jahob specifications include declarations and definitions of specification variables (such as content in Figure 1), data structure invariants (such as *backbone, rootFirst, noNextOutside*, and *prevDef*), and procedure contracts consisting of preconditions ("requires" clauses), postconditions ("ensures" clauses) and frame conditions ("modifies" clauses). The contract for addLast specifies that the procedure 1) requires its parameter n to be outside the list content, 2) modifies the list content, and 3) inserts n into the list (and does not insert or delete any other elements). Specification variables such as content are abstract fields defined by the programmer for the purpose of specification and may contain a definition given after the vardefs keyword, which specifies an abstraction function. The content variable has the type of a set of object identities and is given by a set comprehension that first constructs a binary relation between objects and their next successors, then computes its transitive closure using the higher-order * operator on relations, and finally uses it to find all elements reachable from root.

Given the class invariants in Figure 1, Jahob invokes its inference engine Bohne [42, 43], which succeeds in automatically computing a loop invariant, proving that the postcondition of addLast holds, and proving that there are no run-time errors during procedure execution. In this case Bohne uses the MONA decision procedure for monadic second-order logic of trees [27], but in other cases it uses resolution-based provers [38], satisfiability-modulo theory provers [4], new decision procedures [30], or combinations of these approaches. In general, a successful verification means that the desired property holds, but a failed verification can also occur either due to an error in program or specification or due to a limitation of Jahob's static analysis techniques.

3 Debugging Annotated Code Using Run-Time Checking

For a successful verification of such detailed properties as in the example in Figure 1, the developer must come up with appropriate class invariants. A run-time checker can help in this process. For example, when we were writing this example, we initially wrote the following *prevDef0* version of *prevDef* invariant:

1 **invariant** prevDef0: "∀ x y. prev x = y → (x ≠ null → next y = x)"

This formula is reasonably-looking at first sight. Moreover, modular static verification quickly succeeds in proving that if addLast satisfies the invariants initially, it preserves the invariants and establishes the postconditions. Unfortunately, the *prevDef* invariant is false whenever there is a non-null object whose prev field points to null, so, even if true in the very first initial state, it is not preserved by allocation operations outside the DLL class.

Executing our run-time checker on the testDriver procedure in Figure 1 immediately detects that the prevDef0 invariant is violated when the execution enters addLast. As another illustration, suppose that we write a correct invariant prevDef but we omit in Figure 1 line 29 containing the assignment n.prev=r. Running the run-time checker on the same testDriver procedure identifies the invariant violation at the exit of addLast procedure. Compared to constraint solving techniques that could potentially detect such situation the advantage of run-time checking is that it directly confirms that a specific program fragment violates an invariant, it is applicable to constraints for which no decision procedures exist, and it can handle code execution with any number of loop iterations.

4   The Scope of Our Run-Time Checker

Our run-time checker verifies that program states occurring in a given execution satisfy the desired safety properties. These safety properties refer either to a specific program state (for example, the program point at which the assertion is written), or to a relationship between the current program state and a past state identified by a program point (such as program state at a procedure entry). As a result, if we assumed that each program state itself is finite, such run-time checking problem would reduce to the problem of evaluating a formula in a given finite model. This problem has been studied from the viewpoint of finite model theory [16, 22] where it was related to computational complexity classes, in relational databases [20, 36, 37] where the database takes place of program state, in model checking [7, 25], with techniques based on BDDs, and in constraint solving [23, 41]. While these ideas are relevant for our work, there are several challenges that arise when considering run-time checking based on our specification language: quantification over infinite or large domains, representation of specification variables that denote infinite sets, and computation of values that relate to previous program states. Although we cannot hope to support all these constructs in their most general form, we have identified their uses in the examples we encountered so far and we describe how we support these uses in our run-time checker.

5   Quantifiers and Set Comprehensions

Quantifiers and set comprehensions are a great source of expressive power for a specification language. They are essential for stating that a group of objects in a data structure satisfies the desired properties, for example, being non-null or initialized. The advantages of using quantifiers as opposed to using imperative constructs such as loops to express the desired properties is that quantifiers enjoy a number of well-understood mathematical properties, which makes them appropriate for manual and automated proofs. On the other hand, quantifiers are one of the main sources of difficulty in run-time checking.

Restriction to first-order quantifiers. Jahob's specifications are written in higher-order logic, which admits quantification over sets of objects. This allows expressing properties like minimum spanning tree or graph isomorphism. Most of our data structure specification examples, however, we do not encounter higher-order quantification (even though there are 120 classes that contain first-order quantification). One of the reasons is that higher-order quantification is difficult to reason about statically, so our examples avoid it. Our run-time checker therefore currently supports only first-order quantifiers. The quantified variables are either of integer or of object type. We note that the run-time checker does support some simple uses of higher-order functions, which it eliminates by beta-reduction.

Bounding integer quantifiers. Integers in Jahob denote unbounded mathematical integers. We encounter quantification over integers, for example, when reasoning about indices of arrays. Such quantifiers and set comprehensions are usually bounded, as in the form $\forall x.0 \leq x \wedge x < n \rightarrow \ldots$ or $\{v.\exists i.\ 0 \leq i \wedge i < n \wedge v = a.[i]\}$. We support such examples by syntactically identifying within the quantifier body the expressions that enforce bounds on integers. We use these bounds to reduce quantifiers to finite iteration over a range of integers.

Bounding object quantifiers. Our interpreter implicitly assumes that object quantifiers range only over allocated objects. While this is a very natural assumption, note that this in fact departs from the static analysis semantics of quantifiers in Jahob as well as systems such as ESC/Java [18] and Spec# [3]. The reason is that object allocation produces fresh objects with respect to all currently allocated objects, and the set of allocated objects changes with each allocation. A typical approach to soundly model allocation is to introduce a set of currently allocated objects, denoted `Object.alloc` in Jahob, and keep the domain of interpretation fixed. A statement such as `x = new Node()` is then represented by

```
1   assume x ∉ Object.alloc;
2   Object.alloc := Object.alloc ∪ {x};
```

The change of the set of allocated objects ensures that allocated objects are fresh, which is a crucial piece of aliasing information necessary to verify code that uses linked structures. With this technique, it is possible to use standard verification condition generation techniques to correctly represent state changes. On the other hand, in this model all objects that will ever be used exist at all program points, even before they are allocated. To execute an arbitrary quantification of objects at run-time, it is necessary to combine run-time evaluation of formula over allocated objects with symbolic techniques that determine the truth value for all objects that are not allocated. The last step is possible in many cases because objects that are not allocated are all isomorphic: they have no incoming and no outgoing fields.

Propagating variable dependencies in multiple quantified statements. Even bounded domains, however, may be large, and we would like to avoid considering all objects in the heap if at all possible. Consider the following formula:

$$\forall x.\forall y.\ x \in \texttt{Object.alloc} \wedge y \in \texttt{Object.alloc} \wedge \texttt{next}\, x = y \longrightarrow P(x,y)$$

In a naive implementation, the run-time checker would iterate over the set of all allocated objects for both of the universal quantifiers, an $O(n^2)$ operation. But in the above formula, the quantified variable y is introduced for the purposes of naming and can be easily evaluated without enumerating all elements of the heap. The runtime checker handles these cases by doing a simple syntactic check in the body of quantified formula to determine if the bound variable is defined by an equality. If it finds an appropriate definition, the run-time checker evaluates the body of the formula without having to enumerate a large number of objects. For example, when computing a set comprehension over all allocated objects, we could straightforwardly compute the elements of the set by evaluating the body of the formula for each element in the domain. But since this is very inefficient, the runtime checker first searches through the body of the formula to determine if the bound variable is defined by an equality. This is often the case, for example, when the set comprehension is expressed in terms of the reachable objects from some root using reflexive transitive closure. In this case, we can compute the elements of the set without having to enumerate all objects within the domain.

6   Specification Variables

Specification variables are useful for representing the abstract view of the state of a class. The developers can use specification variables to specify the behavior of abstract data types without exposing implementation details. Jahob supports two types of specification variables: derived specification variables and ghost variables. These are sometimes referred to as model fields and ghost fields, respectively, as in JML [33].

Ghost variables. A ghost variable is updated by the developer by assigning it values given by HOL formulas using special specification assignment statements in the code. Our run-time checker treats ghost variables similarly to ordinary Java variables. The difference is that, in addition to standard program types such as booleans, integers, and objects, these variables can also have types of tuples and sets of elements and tuples.

When a ghost variable is updated, the right-hand side of the assignment statement consists of a formula that the runtime checker evaluates to produce the new value of the ghost variable. It then stores the resulting value in the same way as it would for the assignment of a normal program variable. This formula is a standard Jahob formula and may contain quantifiers, set comprehensions, set operations, and other constructs not typically available in Java assignment statements.

The run-time checker supports certain forms of infinite sets. For example, the checker can evaluation the following code:

```
1  //: private ghost specvar X :: "int set";
2  int y = 0;
3  //: X := {z. z > 0};
4  //: assert y ∉ X;
5  y = y + 1;
6  //: assert y ∈ X;
```

where the ghost variable X is assigned the value of an unbounded set. The runtime checker handles such cases by deferring the evaluation of X until it reaches the assert statements. It then applies formula simplifications that eliminate the set comprehension. This is a particular case of a more general approach where some elements of theorem proving could be applied at run-time [2].

Derived variables. A derived specification variable (such as content in Figure 1) is given by a formula that defines it in terms of the concrete state of the program. When the runtime checker evaluates a formula that refers to a standard specification variable, it evaluates the formula that defines the specification variable in the context of the current program state.

7   The old Construct

In Jahob, an old expression refers to the value of the enclosed expression as evaluated on entry to the current procedure and is very useful to express state changes that procedures perform. One simple but inefficient method of providing the checker access to past program state would be to snapshot the heap before each procedure invocation. Unfortunately, this approach is unlikely to be practical because the memory overhead would be a product of the size of the heap and the depth of the call stack. Instead, our run-time checker obtains access to the pre-state by means of a recovery cache (also known as a recursive cache) [21] that keeps track of the original values of modified heap locations. There are several features of this solution. First, it takes advantage of the fact that we need only know the state of the heap on procedure entry, and not the state of any intermediate heaps between procedure entry and the assertion or invariant to be evaluated. Also, where the state of a variable is unchanged, the old value resides in the heap, so that reads do not incur a performance penalty excepting reads of old values. Finally, one of the ideas underlying this solution is that we expect the amount of memory required to keep track of the initial writes to be small relative to the size of the heap. While there is a trade-off between memory and performance—there is now a performance penalty for each write—the overhead is greatest for initial writes, and less for subsequent writes to the same location.

8   Further Related Work

Run-time assertion checking has a long history [13]. Among the closest systems for run-time checking in the context of static verification system are tools based on the Java Modeling Language (JML) and the Spec# system [3]. The JML compiler, jmlc [12] compiles JML-annotated Java programs into bytecode that also includes instructions for checking JML invariants, pre- and post-conditions, and assertions. Other assertion tools for JML include Jass [5] and jmle [28]. One of the goals in the design of JML was to produce a specification language that was Java-like, to make it easier for software engineers to write JML specifications. It also makes JML specifications easier to execute. Jahob, on the other hand, was designed as a static verification system and uses an expressive logic as its specification language. The advantage of this design is that the semantics of the specifications is clear, and the verification conditions generated by the system can easily be traced back to the relevant portions of the specification, which is very helpful in the proof process. One example of this difference in philosophy appears in the treatment of old expressions. In JML, an old expression may not contain a variable that is bound by a quantifier outside of that expression. This restriction ensures that the body of the old expression can be fully evaluated at the program point to which the old expression refers, but prevents writing certain natural specifications such as $\forall i.0 \leq i \wedge i < a.\texttt{length} \rightarrow a[i] = (\text{old } a[i])$.

We are not aware of any techniques used to execute such specifications as in Jahob in the context of programming language run-time checking systems. Techniques for checking constraints on databases [6, 19, 20, 24, 36, 37] contain relevant techniques, but use simpler specification specification languages and are optimized for particular classes of checks.

While run-time assertion checking systems concern themselves with checking properties of the heap, event-based systems [1, 34, 40] are concerned with checking properties of the trace. Quantification is implicit over all events that adhere to the pattern described by the specification. The matching of an event binds the free variables in the specification to specific objects in the heap. Since explicit quantifiers are generally not available in the specification language of event-based systems, the properties encoded can only refer to a statically-determined number of objects in the heap for each event instance, though the number of event instances matched is unbounded.

9   Conclusions and Future Work

We have described a simple run-time checker for a subset of an expressive higher-order logic assertions in the Jahob verification system. Our run-time checker can execute specifications that involve quantifiers, set comprehensions, transitive closure, integer and object expressions, sets, and relations. It can evaluate certain expressions that denote infinite sets, as well as formulas that refer to old values of fields of an unbounded number of objects. We have found the run-time checker useful for debugging specifications and code. The run-time checker is currently built as an interpreter and in our examples it exhibits slowdown of several orders of magnitude compared to compiled Java code without run-time checks, and is meant for debugging and analysis purposes as opposed to the instrumentation of large programs. Among the main directions for future work are compilation of run-time checks [10, 15] to enable checking of the assertions that were not proved statically [17], memoization and incremental evaluation of checks [39], and combination with a constraint solver to enable modular run-time checking [26].

References

1. Allan, C., Avgustinov, P., Christensen, A.S., Hendren, L., Kuzins, S., Lhotak, O., de Moor, O., Sereni, D., Sittampalam, G., Tibble, J.: Adding trace matching with free variables to AspectJ. In: Proc. 20th Annual ACM Conference on Object-Oriented Programming, Systems, Languages, and Applications, pp. 345–364 (2005)
2. Arkoudas, K., Rinard, M.: Deductive runtime certification. In: RV 2004. Proceedings of the 2004 Workshop on Runtime Verification, Barcelona, Spain (April 2004)
3. Barnett, M., Leino, K.R.M., Schulte, W.: The Spec# programming system: An overview. In: CASSIS: Int. Workshop on Construction and Analysis of Safe, Secure and Interoperable Smart devices (2004)
4. Barrett, C., Berezin, S.: CVC Lite: A new implementation of the cooperating validity checker. In: Alur, R., Peled, D.A. (eds.) CAV 2004. LNCS, vol. 3114, pp. 515–518. Springer, Heidelberg (2004)
5. Bartetzko, D., Fischer, C., Möller, M., Wehrheim, H.: Jass–Java with assertions. In: RV 2001. ENTCS, vol. 55, pp. 103–117 (2001)
6. Bernstein, P.A., Blaustein, B.T.: Fast methods for testing quantified relational calculus assertions. In: Proceedings of the 1982 ACM SIGMOD international conference on Management of data, pp. 39–50. ACM Press, New York (1982)
7. Beyer, D., Noack, A., Lewerentz, C.: Efficient relational calculation for software analysis. IEEE Trans. Software Eng. 31(2), 137–149 (2005)
8. Bouillaguet, C., Kuncak, V., Wies, T., Zee, K., Rinard, M.: Using first-order theorem provers in a data structure verification system. In: Cook, B., Podelski, A. (eds.) VMCAI 2007. LNCS, vol. 4349, Springer, Heidelberg (2007)
9. Boyapati, C., Khurshid, S., Marinov, D.: Korat: Automated testing based on Java predicates. In: Proc. International Symposium on Software Testing and Analysis, pp. 123–133 (July 2002)
10. Chen, F., d'Amorim, M., Rosu, G.: Checking and correcting behaviors of java programs at runtime with java-mop. Electr. Notes Theor. Comput. Sci. 144(4), 3–20 (2006)
11. Chen, F., Roşu, G.: MOP: An Efficient and Generic Runtime Verification Framework. In: OOPSLA 2007. Object-Oriented Programming, Systems, Languages and Applications (2007)
12. Cheon, Y.: A Runtime Assertion Checker for the Java Modeling Language. PhD thesis, Iowa State University, April (2003)
13. Clarke, L.A., Rosenblum, D.S.: A historical perspective on runtime assertion checking in software development. SIGSOFT Softw. Eng. Notes 31(3), 25–37 (2006)
14. Cok, D.R., Kiniry, J.R.: Esc/java2: Uniting ESC/Java and JML. In: CASSIS: Construction and Analysis of Safe, Secure and Interoperable Smart devices (2004)
15. Demsky, B., Cadar, C., Roy, D., Rinard, M.C.: Efficient specification-assisted error localization. In: Second International Workshop on Dynamic Analysis (2004)
16. Ebbinghaus, H.D., Flum, J.: Finite Model Theory. Springer, Heidelberg (1995)
17. Flanagan, C.: Hybrid type checking. In: POPL, pp. 245–256 (2006)
18. Flanagan, C., Leino, K.R.M., Lilibridge, M., Nelson, G., Saxe, J.B., Stata, R.: Extended Static Checking for Java. In: ACM Conf. Programming Language Design and Implementation (PLDI) (2002)
19. Griffin, T., Libkin, L., Trickey, H.: An improved algorithm for incremental recomputation of active relational expressions. IEEE Transactions on Knowledge and Data Engineering 9(3), 508–511 (1997)

20. Henschen, L.J., McCune, W., Naqvi, S.A.: Compiling constraint-checking programs from first-order formulas. In: Gallaire, H., Nicolas, J.-M., Minker, J. (eds.) Advances in Data Base Theory, Proceedings of the Workshop on Logical Data Bases, 2nd edn, pp. 145–169 (1984). ISBN 0-306-41636-0.

21. Horning, J.J., Lauer, H.C., Melliar-Smith, P.M., Randell, B.: A program structure for error detection and recovery. In: Gelenbe, E., Kaiser, C. (eds.) Operating Systems. LNCS, vol. 16, pp. 171–187. Springer, Heidelberg (1974)

22. Immerman, N.: Descriptive Complexity. Springer, Heidelberg (1998)

23. Jackson, D.: Software Abstractions: Logic, Language, & Analysis. MIT Press, Cambridge (2006)

24. Jagadish, H.V., Qian, X.: Integrity maintenance in object-oriented databases. In: Proceedings of the 18th Conference on Very Large Databases, Los Altos CA, Vancouver, Morgan Kaufmann pubs, San Francisco (1992)

25. Burch, J.R., Clarke, E.M., McMillan, K.L., Dill, D.L., Hwang, L.J.: Symbolic Model Checking: 10^{20} States and Beyond. In: Proceedings of the Fifth Annual IEEE Symposium on Logic in Computer Science, pp. 1–33. IEEE Computer Society Press, Washington (1990)

26. Khurshid, S., Marinov, D.: TestEra: Specification-based testing of java programs using SAT. Autom. Softw. Eng. 11(4), 403–434 (2004)

27. Klarlund, N., Møller, A., Schwartzbach, M.I.: MONA implementation secrets. In: Wilhelm, R. (ed.) Proc. 5th International Conference on Implementation and Application of Automata. LNCS, Springer, Heidelberg (2000)

28. Krause, B., Wahls, T.: jmle: A tool for executing JML specifications via constraint programming. In: Brim, L., Haverkort, B., Leucker, M., van de Pol, J. (eds.) FMICS 2006 and PDMC 2006. LNCS, vol. 4346, pp. 293–296. Springer, Heidelberg (2007)

29. Kuncak, V.: Modular Data Structure Verification. PhD thesis, EECS Department, Massachusetts Institute of Technology (February 2007)

30. Kuncak, V., Nguyen, H.H., Rinard, M.: Deciding Boolean Algebra with Presburger Arithmetic. In: J. of Automated Reasoning (2006), http://dx.doi.org/10.1007/s10817-006-9042-1.

31. Kuncak, V., Rinard, M.: An overview of the Jahob analysis system: Project goals and current status. In: NSF Next Generation Software Workshop (2006)

32. Kuncak, V., Rinard, M.: Towards efficient satisfiability checking for boolean algebra with presburger arithmetic. In: Conference on Automateded Deduction (CADE-21) (2007)

33. Leavens, G.T., Poll, E., Clifton, C., Cheon, Y., Ruby, C., Cok, D., Müller, P., Kiniry, J., Chalin, P.: JML Reference Manual. February (2007)

34. Martin, M., Livshits, B., Lam, M.S.: Finding application errors and security flaws using PQL: a Program Query Language. In: Proc. 20th Annual ACM Conference on Object-Oriented Programming, Systems, Languages, and Applications (2005)

35. Nipkow, T., Paulson, L.C., Wenzel, M.: Isabelle/HOL: A Proof Assistant for Higher-Order Logic. In: Isabelle/HOL. LNCS, vol. 2283, Springer, Heidelberg (2002)

36. Paige, R.: Applications of finite differencing to database integrity control and query/transaction optimization. In: Gallaire, H., Nicolas, J.-M., Minker, J. (eds.) Advances in Data Base Theory, Proceedings of the Workshop on Logical Data Bases, 2nd edn, pp. 171–209 (1984). ISBN 0-306-41636-0.

37. Qian, X., Wiederhold, G.: Knowledge-based integrity constraint validation. In: Chu, W.W., Gardarin, G., Ohsuga, S., Kambayashi, Y. (eds.) VLDB 1986 Twelfth International Conference on Very Large Data Bases, August 25-28, 1986, Kyoto, Japan, Proceedings, pp. 3–12. Morgan Kaufmann, San Francisco (1986)

38. Schulz, S.: E – A Brainiac Theorem Prover. Journal of AI Communications 15(2/3), 111–126 (2002)
39. Shankar, A., Bodik, R.: Ditto: Automatic incrementalization of data structure invariant checks. In: PLDI (2007)
40. Stolz, V., Bodden, E.: Temporal assertions using AspectJ (2005)
41. Torlak, E., Jackson, D.: Kodkod: A relational model finder. In: Grumberg, O., Huth, M. (eds.) TACAS 2007. LNCS, vol. 4424, Springer, Heidelberg (2007)
42. Wies, T., Kuncak, V., Lam, P., Podelski, A., Rinard, M.: Field constraint analysis. In: Proc. Int. Conf. Verification, Model Checking, and Abstract Interpratation (2006)
43. Wies, T., Kuncak, V., Zee, K., Podelski, A., Rinard, M.: Verifying complex properties using symbolic shape analysis. In: Workshop on Heap Abstraction and Verification (collocated with ETAPS) (2007)

Author Index

Lecture Notes in Computer Science

Sublibrary 2: Programming and Software Engineering

For information about Vols. 1– 4218
please contact your bookseller or Springer